KT-480-991

DISPOSED OF BY LIBRARY HOUSE OF LORDS

A Good School for Every Child

Sir Cyril Taylor has been at the heart of English education for over two decades, serving as an adviser to ten successive UK education secretaries and four prime ministers, both Conservative and Labour, including Margaret Thatcher and Tony Blair.

His passion for education has led directly to real school improvement, from the creation of city technology colleges to specialist schools and academies, which together now constitute over nine in ten secondary schools in England. The Specialist Schools and Academies Trust, the body he founded, is now a leading force in school improvement worldwide.

A Good School for Every Child draws on that wealth of experience. While offering an insider's look at some of the key challenges in education, it is also an invaluable guide for parents and teachers interested in how our schools work today. There is a particular focus on how to raise standards in low attaining schools, improving levels of literacy and numeracy, and teaching children the skills they need for the twenty-first century.

This book is also a clarion call to our political leaders about the challenges that still remain: the education of children in care, the failure to stretch able youngsters and the problems of recruiting enough good science teachers.

Education is more open today than ever before, with league tables and inspection reports. Yet for many outsiders, it can seem a world clouded by its own language and rituals. Sir Cyril Taylor opens the door to that world, through stories of inspirational head teachers and successful schools. By doing so he offers a vision that is both instructive and inspirational, one that shows how schools working with parents and the wider community can raise the standards of achievement for all their pupils.

DISPOSED OF
BY LIBRARY
HOUSE OF LORDS

A Good School for Every Child

With a foreword by Lord Baker and David Blunkett MP

Sir Cyril Taylor

Routledge
Taylor & Francis Group

LONDON AND NEW YORK

First published 2009
by Routledge
2 Park Square, Milton Park, Abingdon, Oxon OX14 4RN

Simultaneously published in the USA and Canada
by Routledge
270 Madison Avenue, New York, NY 10016

Routledge is an imprint of the Taylor & Francis Group, an informa business

© 2009 Cyril Taylor except foreword © 2009 Kenneth Baker and David Blunkett.

Typeset in Bembo by
Taylor & Francis Books
Printed and bound in Great Britain by
TJ International Ltd, Padstow, Cornwall

All rights reserved. No part of this book may be reprinted or reproduced or utilised in any
form or by any electronic, mechanical, or other means, now known or hereafter invented,
including photocopying and recording, or in any information storage or retrieval system,
without permission in writing from the publishers.

British Library Cataloguing in Publication Data
A catalogue record for this book is available from the British Library

Library of Congress Cataloging in Publication Data
    Taylor, Cyril, Sir.
    A good school for every child / Cyril Taylor ; with a foreword by Kenneth Baker and
David Blunkett.
        p. cm.
    Includes bibliographical references.
    ISBN 978-0-415-48252-3 (hardback) – ISBN 978-0-415-48253-0 (pbk.) – ISBN 978-0-
203-87848-4 (ebook) 1. Education–Great Britain. 2. School improvement programs–Great
Britain. I. Title.
    LA632.T37 2009
    370.941–dc22
                2008046973

ISBN10: 0-415-48253-4 (pbk)
ISBN10: 0-415-48252-6 (hbk)
ISBN10: 0-203-87848-5 (ebk)

ISBN13: 978-0-415-48253-0 (pbk)
ISBN13: 978-0-415-48252-3 (hbk)
ISBN13: 978-0-203-87848-4 (ebk)

This book is dedicated to the memory of Garry Weston, the Chairman of Associated British Foods and the Garfield Weston Foundation, which sponsored 500 English specialist schools and academies with over 30 million pounds of support.

Contents

Illustrations

Tables

Figures

Photographs (between pages 108 and 109)

About Sir Cyril Taylor GBE

Sir Cyril Taylor was born in Yorkshire, England in 1935 and educated at St Marylebone Grammar School, London and Roundhay School, Leeds. Awarded a National Service commission at age eighteen with the King's African Rifles, he served as a platoon commander in the Mau Mau emergency campaign in Kenya 1954–56. He then took an honours degree in history at Trinity Hall, Cambridge in 1959 and was awarded the Charles Bell Scholarship by the London Chamber of Commerce to study for the MBA at Harvard Business School. He is married with one daughter.

After attending Harvard Business School, he worked in brand management for Procter & Gamble at their headquarters in Cincinnati, Ohio. In 1964 he founded the American Institute for Foreign Study (AIFS), the Anglo-American international educational company of which he is still chairman. Group companies include the College Division, Camp America, Au Pair in America, the American Council for International Studies (ACIS) and the Summer Institute for the Gifted. AIFS has offices in the USA, UK, Germany, Poland, South Africa and Australia, as well as twenty-five offices in universities throughout the world.

In 1970, AIFS established Richmond, the American International University in London. Richmond is a unique, non-profit university with 1,000 full-time students from 100 countries accredited by both the American and British education authorities. Overall, AIFS organises programmes for 50,000 students each year with annual tuition income of $200 million, and celebrated the enrolment of its one millionth student in 2001.

From 1987 to 2007, Sir Cyril served as chairman of the Specialist Schools and Academies Trust (SSAT) and as adviser to ten successive secretaries of state for education on specialist schools and academies, serving in a voluntary unpaid capacity. In 2005, the SSAT was made the lead body to support the 400 city academies to be established on the sites of underperforming schools in socially disadvantaged areas. The specialist schools initiative (technology, arts, sports and languages colleges; business and enterprise; science; engineering; mathematics and computing; humanities and music) has established 3,104 specialist secondary schools and academies, educating to an increasingly high standard 3 million children; this is 90 per cent of all English secondary schools. Specialist schools have helped to improve the proportion of English 15-year-olds achieving five good grades in the English General Certificate of Secondary Education by more than a third over the past ten years. Specialist schools emphasise their chosen specialist subjects, as well as teaching the national curriculum. Over 600 private sector sponsors have contributed more than £300 million to the initiative.

Sir Cyril served on the Greater London Council from 1977 until 1986 and was elected deputy leader of the Conservative group from 1983. He was awarded a knighthood in

1989 in recognition of his services to education, and in 2003 was appointed a Knight Grand Cross of the Most Excellent Order of the British Empire (GBE). He was High Sheriff of Greater London from 1996 to 1997. He has published a number of books and pamphlets including most recently, in collaboration with Conor Ryan, *Excellence in Education: The Making of Great Schools*, published by Granada Learning in November 2004, with a revised edition in November 2005.

Although an active member of the Conservative Party until 1997, Sir Cyril resigned from the party when he was appointed David Blunkett's adviser on specialist schools in 1997 and has had no political affiliations since that date. In addition to education, Sir Cyril has specialist knowledge of local government, public transport, foreign affairs and business.

January 2009

Disclaimer

This book is written in a purely personal capacity and does not represent the views of the Specialist Schools and Academies Trust of which Sir Cyril Taylor is a trustee, or any other organisation with which he is associated.

Foreword by Lord Baker and the Right Honourable David Blunkett MP

Twenty years of education reforms have changed the landscape of schools in England. What was once a secret garden has been opened up through greater accountability to parents and taxpayers. The information provided by school inspections has ensured that hundreds of 'failing' schools have been turned around. Despite the current fashion for bemoaning their impact – and recent problems with their administration – the data provided by school tests and the challenge provided by clear targets have helped to raise teachers' expectations for their pupils.

Those whose children always had a chance of a decent education also had the knowledge to compare school to school. They could make their choice knowing the culture and ethos of schools as well as the headline results. It was easy to see that those who lacked such knowledge also lacked the means to make a choice; they remained trapped economically, socially and educationally. Ministers in both Labour and Conservative governments have rightly maintained their support for a more open education system, despite constant pressures to return to an era of concealment.

At the heart of this revolution has been Cyril Taylor. He has worked with successive administrations and many secretaries of state; his development of city technology colleges and the introduction of specialist schools for a Conservative government have been followed by him overseeing their rapid expansion and the introduction of city academies with Labour in power. Sometimes Cyril drove us mad, but always did so for the cause of improved standards, seeking to increase access to those standards and spread best practice.

The principles of specialism – where a focus on a strong subject helps to lift overall standards – were developed through his leadership. A host of invaluable sponsors has been introduced to the education world through his persuasive powers. The extent to which specialism has led schools to join together, sharing expertise and forming federations and new trusts, is a testament to the collaborative, rather than competitive nature of what has been achieved.

This is why we are so pleased to introduce his latest book. We have both benefited from Cyril's advice as secretaries of state, and we have both been on the receiving end of his gift for new ideas, as well as the occasional controversies generated by his impatience for change. Building the Specialist Schools and Academies Trust from its early days as a support mechanism for city technology colleges to its current role as an organisation embracing nearly 5,000 schools across the world was remarkable, and the Trust which he chaired until recently is now internationally recognised as being at the cutting edge of school reform and curriculum development.

This book is a fascinating and informative compendium of educational insights and ideas. Naturally, some chapters provide an invaluable reminder of why CTCs, specialist schools and academies have made their mark, and continue to do so. A chapter on the importance of strong independent head teachers is balanced by the importance of schools being at the heart of their communities, drawing on Henry Morris's vision for village schools in rural Cambridgeshire. The crucial importance of good English as the key to accessing the wider curriculum is stressed, with a recognition of the importance of phonics from an early stage. There are ideas about how to lift the horizons of children in care, who still languish in the league tables despite many efforts to improve their lot; there are experiments in boarding education underway, which spread more rapidly as a more cost-effective alternative to existing care provision. There are forward-looking chapters on the importance of science, vocational education and information technology. And there is a heartfelt plea for a greater emphasis on gifted and talented pupils in our schools, whose needs were neglected for far too long in a system that underemphasised the importance of diversity.

Cyril did not allow himself to be pigeonholed politically, and so he does not fit into any of the prevailing stereotypes or orthodoxies in the education debate. His outspoken criticism of 'failing' teachers has not prevented him from distinguishing between head teachers of low-performing schools who are succeeding against the odds, and those who are more clearly letting down their pupils. His recognition of the importance of nurturing the talents of more able pupils is accompanied by a chapter on school admissions advocating a greater use of systems, such as banding or random allocation, that would create a more balanced school intake. Support for faith schools is tempered by a proposal for multi-faith schools in areas of the greatest ethnic tensions.

This book is not only a testimony to the thoughts and achievements of someone at the heart of two decades of education reform in England. It is also a practical set of propositions for change; just as specialist schools use data to drive change and improvement. In a debate too often driven by sentiment, Cyril does not shy away from using facts and statistics which can lead to new insights. This book will also interest parents wishing to know how today's schools system operates.

Education is now seen as one of the most important political issues for any government. While we may disagree about some of the solutions, there is an important consensus on many of the fundamentals. And one thing on which we can both agree is the importance of having strong and active reformers within the system to help deliver change. Cyril's own personal commitment to educational reform – and his enthusiasm for its possibilities – has been unwavering in all the years that we have known him.

Lord Baker of Dorking
Secretary of State for Education from 1986 to 1989.

The Right Honourable David Blunkett MP
Secretary of State for Education and Employment from 1997 to 2001.

Introduction

Benjamin Franklin, in a letter to George Washington, the first president of the United States, said that 'the noblest question in the world is, "What good can I do in it?"' I passionately believe that there is no better way to do good in the world than to ensure that every child, whatever their social circumstances, can attend a good school. This book seeks to show how this great and important goal can be achieved. It seeks to identify the best practices in many countries throughout the world which have achieved excellence in their schools so that other schools in other countries can replicate these measures themselves.

It is hoped the book will be of interest to head teachers and principals of schools throughout the world who wish to improve their leadership skills; to teachers seeking ways to improve their teaching skills; to parents seeking advice on how to choose a good school for their children; to officials and political leaders in both central and local government responsible for the funding and oversight of schools; and finally to business leaders and philanthropists who wish to support state-funded schools.

Some readers may find one or more of my recommendations controversial. For example, I recommend that every 11 year-old entering secondary school be given a reading test to determine if they need help to learn how to read. I hope this particular recommendation will receive support, because as David Blunkett said, 'If a child can't read, he or she can't learn.' I can assure readers that all the recommendations in the book are based on their successful use in existing schools, and not on the figments of my imagination.

It should also be explained that when the text refers to English schools rather than British schools, this is because there are different school systems in Scotland, Ulster and Wales.

Where possible, any data or information quoted shows the source of the information. The case studies in Chapters 1, 4, 6, 10, 11, and 13, written by Christine Walter, use data provided to her by the schools being described.

Any statistical data used, unless otherwise specified, is official data provided by governments throughout the world as well as the Organisation for Economic Co-operation and Development (OECD).

I hope readers will enjoy the book and, more importantly, that its recommendations will help create more good schools.

Cyril Taylor

Acknowledgements

This book could not have been written without the dedicated support, advice and wisdom of the following people (listed alphabetically):

Hannelore Fuller, for her extraordinary skills in deciphering and typing my hand-written manuscript as well as working with the publishers to satisfy their requirements.

Professor David Jesson of York University, who contributed substantially to Chapters 3, 4 and 13 and wrote Appendix 3 (The Jesson Value-Added Analysis of School Performance).

Conor Ryan, who reviewed the book in its entirety and checked for errors of fact or omissions.

Christine Walter, who wrote the case studies of best practices in Chapters 1, 4, 6, 10, 11 and 13.

Jane Ware, who provided most of the statistical data on English schools used in the book.

Abbreviations

ACAS	Advisory, Conciliation and Arbitration Service
AQA	Assessment and Qualifications Alliance
AR	Accelerated Reading
Bac	Baccalaureate
BSF	Building Schools for the Future
BTEC	Business and Technician Education Council
BWP	Brooke Weston Partnership
CACHE	Leading Qualifications for Working in Children's Services
CEDEFOP	European Centre for the Development of Vocational Training
CEO	Chief Executive Officer
CLG	Communities and Local Government
CTC	City Technology College
CVA	Contextual Value Added
DCSF	Department for Children, Schools and Families
EBSD	Emotional, Behavioural and Social Difficulties
ECDL	European Computer Driving Licence
EMA	Education Maintenance Allowance
FE	Further Education
FSM	Free School Meals
GCSE	General Certificate of Secondary Education
GNVQ	General National Vocational Qualification
HBS	Harvard Business School
HSBC	Hong Kong and Shanghai Banking Corporation
IB	International Baccalaureate
ICT	Information and Communications Technology
IDC	International Data Corporation
JVA	Jesson Value Added
Ks	Key stage
LA	Local Authority
LRC	Learning Resource Centre
LSC	Learning and Skills Council
NAEP	National Assessment of Education Progress
NAGTY	National Association for Gifted and Talented Youth
NCSL	National College of School Leadership
NEET	Not in Education, Employment or Training

NFER	National Foundation for Educational Research
NQT	Newly Qualified Teacher
NUT	National Union of Teachers
NVQ	National Vocational Qualification
NVRT	Non-Verbal Reasoning Test
OECD	Organisation for Economic Co-operation and Development
OFA	Office of Fair Access
OfSTED	Office for Standards in Education
PFI	Private Finance Initiative
PfS	Partnerships for Schools
PGCE	Postgraduate Certificate in Education
PSAT	Preliminary Scholastic Aptitude Test
QCA	Qualifications and Curriculum Authority
RATL	Raising Achievement Transforming Learning
RIPA	Regulation of Investigatory Powers Act
SEU	Special Education Unit
SEN	Special Educational Needs
SIG	Summer Institute for the Gifted
SSAT	Specialist Schools and Academies Trust
STEM	Science, Technology, Engineering and Mathematics
TDA	Training and Development Agency
TUPE	Transfer of Undertaking (Protection of Employment)
UC	University of California
UCLA	University of California–Los Angeles

Chapter 1

What makes a good school?

Enormous progress has been made in raising standards in English schools in the twenty years since the passing of the great Education Reform Act of 1988, which introduced the national curriculum and national measures of accountability. Since 1997, the proportion of our 15 year-olds gaining at least five good grades at GCSE has increased by more than a third. The hard working head teachers of our 25,000 primary and secondary schools, together with their 435,000 dedicated teachers, deserve praise for their hard work in achieving this improvement. One of the reasons for this success has, of course, been additional funding. Since 1997 the core per pupil funding has risen by more than 50 per cent. We now have 36,000 more teachers and 110,000 teaching assistants in our schools, compared to ten years ago.

However, much more needs to be done to ensure that every English child, whatever his or her social background, can attend a good school, and that excellence in education is combined with equity of provision. The purpose of this book is to help achieve this great goal by highlighting the best practices in good schools, and by recommending ways to improve our low-attaining schools by the replication of best practice elsewhere. But it also seeks to address what may possibly be an even greater challenge: turning our coasting schools into high-performing schools. This chapter is also intended to serve as a guide to parents when evaluating schools for their children in which to enrol and to gain admission for their children to the schools of their choice.

As I argued in an earlier book[1] which I wrote with Conor Ryan, we must first agree on our definition of greatness before we can determine what makes a great school. Success in examination results is clearly one indicator, but is not the only one. The *Oxford English Dictionary* defines education as *the giving of intellectual, moral and social instruction*. Perhaps G. K. Chesterton put it more attractively when he wrote 'Education is simply the soul of a society as it passes from one generation to another.' Or, we could put if more simply: good schools produce good citizens. Certainly, good schools should also teach good values. Schools cannot be value-free zones.

Sometimes the debate about education creates false dichotomies. Some argue that education is about the acquisition of knowledge for its own sake. Certainly there is much to be said for broadening the mind and awakening creative impulses. But it would be naïve to suggest that education is not also an economic imperative. The needs of a highly competitive global economy require all our young people to be challenged to

---

[1] Cyril Taylor and Conor Ryan, *Excellence in Education: The Making of Great Schools*, London: David Fulton, 2005.

perform to the maximum of their potential. Sir Digby Jones, currently a UK trade minister, said when he was director general of the Confederation of British Industry, that 80 per cent of the jobs in the UK economy would soon require five or more GCSEs, including maths and English, or their vocational equivalent.[2] An equally persuasive case was made by Lord Leitch in his seminal 2006 report on skills.[3] The prime minister, the Rt Hon. Gordon Brown MP, said in a speech in June 2008 to the Specialist Schools and Academies Trust that:

> today, here in Britain we have six million unskilled workers. By 2020, as a result of the changes in the global economy, we will need only half a million. Today we have nine million skilled workers. By 2020 we will need fourteen million.

Yet more than half of our young people finish compulsory education at age 16 without achieving the required 5+ A★–C grades at GCSE including maths and English (though some will reach this standard by the age of 19 at further education colleges). There will soon be little work for those with few skills.

If these are the purposes of education and schools, which institutions are most likely to provide this happy combination to their students? One way of looking at it would be to say that good schools are also happy schools, where a high proportion of dedicated teachers are committed to their success and remain in post for a considerable time. As a result, they enable every student, whatever their background, to achieve their full potential, and prepare them for the challenges they will face in later life.

There are many ways in which we can identify a good school:

A good school will have an outstanding head teacher, supported by a good governing body and a good management team. Excellent leadership is a crucial ingredient for a successful school.

A good school will, of course, have good OfSTED inspection reports – these are the reports prepared on English schools by official Government Inspectors. These can be obtained from the website www.ofsted.gov.uk.

Just as important is the ability to attract and retain good teachers. When Sir William Atkinson, one of England's outstanding head teachers, took over the leadership of the low-attaining Phoenix High School in Hammersmith, over half of the teachers were either temporary or substitute teachers. See Chapter 6 for the story of how he improved this school. One of his first priorities was to attract and retain an outstanding group of dedicated teachers. If a school has a high turnover of its staff or a high vacancy level in staff – more than 10 per cent every year – that should be of concern to a prospective parent.

Good schools in England, will, of course, perform well in public examinations; these are the Key stage examinations at age 7 (Key stage 1), age 11 (Key stage 2), and at age 15 or 16 the General Certificate of Secondary Education (GCSE) examinations in particular subjects, and the Advanced Level examinations or International Baccalaureate at age 17 or 18.

However, as we shall see later, although the absolute performance level in these tests and examinations is important, it is the comparison of the intake of ability into a

[2] 'Firms Will Take Some Convincing', *Independent*, 18 February 2004.
[3] Sandy Leitch, 'Prosperity for All in the Global Economy – World Class Skills', London: HMSO, 2006.

particular school with its performance in public examinations which is the crucial indicator of a good school. Professor David Jesson's value added approach to evaluating performance is a far better and fairer way to judge a school than its raw figures alone.

This is particularly important when it comes to judging whether low attainment is always a sign of failure. When the English Secretary of State for Children, Schools and Families, Ed Balls, declared in the summer of 2008 that he wished to see every secondary school in England achieving a minimum of 30 per cent five good GCSEs including English and Maths by 2011, sadly the 638 schools that failed to meet that target in 2007 were branded as failures by some.[4] Yet, as is explained in Chapter 6, it is wrong to describe all the 638 English schools which failed to achieve five good grades at GCSE including maths and English in 2007 as failing. Less than half of these schools, taking into account their intake of ability and recent improvements, are genuinely low-attaining schools. The goal of every school achieving the national minimum target of at least 30 per cent of their 15 year-olds obtaining 5+ A*–C grades at GCSE is, of course, to be applauded.

Another crucial indicator of a good school is the proportion of its students who stay on in full-time education or training beyond the age of 16, when compulsory education ends in England. Only half of English secondary schools have sixth forms, taking 16–19 year-olds, but even for the schools which currently have no post-16 provision, an important criterion of their success is how many of their 16 year-olds they help to transfer to a school with post-16 provision, sixth form college or further education college to continue in full-time education. Sadly, only 80 per cent of English 16 and 17 year-olds are in full-time education compared to about 95 per cent in France and Germany.[5] A recent report said that 189,000 young people in England aged between 16 and 18 were not in education, employment or training – these are commonly known as NEETs.[6]

For schools with provision for 11–18 year-olds, another crucial indicator of success is the proportion of their school leavers who gain entry to university. At the current time, only 46 per cent of English secondary school pupils enter university. Clearly we need to increase this proportion.

For both primary and secondary schools, a key statistic is the proportion of their pupils who attend regularly and on time. Lord Harris of Peckham, a leading sponsor of both English specialist schools and academies, asks his head teachers to supply regular reports on attendance. Moreover, he wants to know how many of the children actually turn up each day – he is sceptical about non-attendance figures which do not include children with so-called authorised absence in their attendance data. Nearly all the Harris-backed schools achieve a 95 per cent attendance figure, reflecting the proportion of children actually attending each day. English government data now include figures for both authorised and unauthorised absence. Many schools are now using modern computer-based methods of tracking attendance through the use by pupils of smart cards to clock in when they arrive in the morning and even to monitor attendance at each class.

Another key measure of a successful school is that it has few or no permanently excluded children. Discipline is, of course, a particular challenge for low-performing schools in socially disadvantaged areas. However, successful academies, such as the

---

[4] See, for example, 'Brown threatens "failing" schools', *BBC News Online*, 31 October 2007.
[5] PISA data prepared by the OECD. www.pisa.oecd.org
[6] Source: Department for Schools, Children and Families SFR 21/2006.

Knight's Academy in Lewisham and the Harris Peckham Academy have managed to reduce drastically the number of their permanently excluded children by creating an ethos of good discipline, respect for high standards, including the celebration of success, and generally good behaviour.

A good school will have an extended day,[7] opening its doors at 7.30 a.m. in the morning, serving breakfast to those children needing morning nourishment, and will often remain open until 6.00 p.m. in the evening. After formal classes end at 3 or 4 p.m., it will arrange an extensive programme of extra-curricular activities including sports, music, drama activities, special instruction in foreign languages or information computer technology or even voluntary work. As the Olympic gold medallist Lord Coe said to me, 'competitive sport can be a crucial way to improve the behaviour of difficult children'.

Good schools will be very popular with parents, usually having many more applications than places. Chapter 2 recommends a new and fairer system of admissions for oversubscribed schools; but clearly where a school has few, or no first choice applications, this should be a danger sign to prospective parents.

Good schools will also have balanced budgets with good financial management.

Parents will ask: 'how will we be able to learn if a school meets the above criteria for excellence?' Each school should have a website; the best will give details of the above criteria. Examination and national test results can easily be obtained from the UK Department of Children, Schools and Families' own website at www.dcsf.gov/uk. The BBC news website also gives details of school examination performance in its education section, at http://news.bbc.co.uk/education. OfSTED (the Office for Standards in Education – www.ofsted.gov.uk) publishes its inspection reports for all schools, which are currently inspected every three years. If you are applying for a secondary school for your child, the Specialist Schools and Academies Trust also publishes an annual guide to school performance of specialist schools (www.ssatrust.org.uk). Over 90 per cent of all English secondary schools are now specialist schools, including 133 academies.

Just as importantly, parents should always visit a prospective school and, if possible, talk to existing parents and indeed pupils. A guide to the admissions process is contained in Chapter 2.

The identification of best practice is, of course, crucial in helping all our schools to achieve the above criteria of success. Much of this book will focus on examples of best practice which have been identified in recent years.

I have always found two important research studies to be excellent sources of good practice. The first is 'Seven Habits of Highly Effective Schools: Best Practice in Specialist Schools' by James Tooley and Andy Howes,[8] and 'High Performing Schools: What Makes the Difference?' written by a team of researchers led by Peter Rudd, from the National Foundation for Educational Research.[9]

From these two studies, together with other sources of best practice, including research for *Excellence in Education*,[10] we identified as described at the start of this chapter, a number of common characteristics in high-performing schools.

---

[7] See also Chapter 10.

[8] London: Technology Colleges Trust, 1999. The trust is now the Specialist Schools and Academies Trust.

[9] Specialist Schools and Academies Trust, London, 2002.

[10] Taylor and Ryan, *Excellence in Education*.

In summary, these are:

- A good leadership team of the head teacher, heads of department and governing body;
- Their ability to attract and retain good teachers;
- A focus on the basics such as literacy and numeracy;
- The setting of targets for each student in every year group and use of data to monitor progress;
- Discipline and order including strict attendance requirements;
- Curriculum innovation, which may include vocational awards and/or the International Baccalaureate;
- Extensive use of information communications technology including wireless-linked laptops and interactive whiteboards;
- A longer school day and non-traditional term dates;
- A focus on individual learning to create an ethos of achievement, so that every child realises his or her optimum potential;
- Seeking the support of parents and using older students as mentors.

Great schools, including independent schools, also teach their students, some of whom come from privileged backgrounds, to care for others who are less advantaged, through participation in voluntary work. It would be interesting to learn how many of our 25,000 head teachers of primary and secondary schools would rate their own school as achieving all of the above.

Let us consider some of these factors in greater detail.

The need for competent, inspirational leadership

A good school's most important requirement is to have an inspiring, highly respected leader. It is also vital that he or she is backed up by a strong team of deputies and department heads, and that they in turn are supported by a good governing body. A mythology has grown up around the notion of the 'hero head', who battles to succeed against everybody else in the school, but those who are most likely to succeed will have the backing of others in the school's leadership team, as well as the school governors. Good leadership can be driven by an inspiring individual, but that alone is not enough; it also requires teamwork.

Governors have a crucial role in supporting the head teacher and ensuring targets are met

More attention needs to be paid to the importance of good governing bodies, especially for schools in socially disadvantaged areas. The School Governors' One Stop Shop[11] funded by the government to identify good prospective governors, has done much to help improve governing bodies, but much more needs to be done.

Low-attaining schools usually have both weak governing bodies and head teachers. The two go together. Similarly, the head teachers of high-performing schools will have

[11] www.sgoss.org.uk

the support of dedicated, committed and able governors. A supportive and competent local education authority is also important.

Perhaps we need to develop a new and more user-friendly manual for school governors. The Association of Governing Boards of Universities and Colleges in the USA gives trustees and governors the following advice on the role of a governing body:

1 To select the principal or head teacher and heads of departments;
2 To monitor the principal's progress in achieving goals agreed by governors;
3 To determine the mission of the institution;
4 To approve financial budgets including capital expenditure;
5 To ensure financial solvency;
6 To defend the autonomy and independence of the institution;
7 To enhance the public standing of the institution including helping with fundraising;
8 To serve as a court of final appeal.

The above summarises the key duties of a school governor. However, the English school governor has many other statutory functions such as admissions (including appeals), exclusions, and health and safety. The extent to which they can carry out all their legal duties is varied, and there are real difficulties in recruiting enough good governors in many schools. A clear and consistent definition of the school governor's role is clearly important. Current guidance is voluminous.

Schools must be able to attract and retain good teachers

If good leadership is essential, the ability to attract and retain good teachers, especially in key shortage subjects such as mathematics, science and modern languages, is no less important. An unacceptable proportion of teaching, especially in many state schools facing challenging circumstances, is done by teachers without specialist degrees. Moreover, because of vacancies, supply or substitute teachers teach a significant amount of lessons. One way of solving the problem, which was pioneered by some of the country's most successful specialist schools, is by employing teaching assistants and other administrative staff to relieve qualified teachers of administrative burdens. Another way is to reduce the turnover of teachers. Sadly, 40 per cent of newly qualified teachers leave the profession within five years of becoming a teacher.[12]

Training your own teachers is an excellent way to ensure good teaching, and more schemes should be developed like the South London Teacher Training scheme, a genuine partnership between ten very varied schools, independent and state, with the Open University as validator of the PGCE. This equips potential secondary school teachers to survive and thrive in any school within the age range 11–19, providing them with the necessary confidence, understanding and competence.

Almost a third of new teachers are now trained in schools under the Graduate Training Programme.[13] Under this scheme, the trainee teachers who have typically spent time in other jobs first work as teaching assistants, being paid an unqualified or qualified teacher's salary depending on responsibility and experience, with the school receiving a grant

[12] Source: Training and Development Agency. www.tda.gov.uk/
[13] See www.tda.gov.uk/Recruit/thetrainingprocess/typesofcourse/employmentbased/gtp.aspx

two days a week out of school on a Young Apprenticeship programme. Over 120 students are off-site at some point during the school week. The flexibility and choice within the consortium continues post-16 when over fifty A levels and vocational courses are available across the collaborative.

ContinU

Dr Kershaw also strongly believes in collaboration and cooperation with neighbouring schools, and has led the initiative to set up a trust of local schools and partners.

The consortium, ContinU, is made up of seven Worcestershire high schools, two special schools, an FE college and other training providers. It will achieve trust status on 1 September 2008. By working together the institutions offer a hugely expanded curriculum and the partners plan to deliver the new diploma entitlement by 2013. It has increased post-16 staying on rates and reduced the numbers of non-viable post-16 courses. Dr Kershaw states that collaboration is hard and compromises have to be made, but it is certainly worth it. The school has always worked towards finding a suitable course for every child – a 70 per cent success rate at GCSE means a 30 per cent failure rate and that is not acceptable – and the chances of doing this are now vastly improved.

A further benefit is that when children have a poor record in one of the schools, often in terms of behaviour, there can be a system of 'managed moves', giving them a chance in another school in the consortium rather than resorting to exclusion.

Are there any downsides to the collaboration? Dr Kershaw concedes that travel between sites is a potential issue, although travel times within the consortium are manageable at a maximum of around 35–40 minutes. If a student is going to another site for a full day they may go under their own steam; if they are going for half a day the school minibus is used.

What about quality assurance with Haybridge's students being taught in other institutions? Dr Kershaw again concedes the concern. It is vital that a student's experience off-site is at least as good as at their home base. Heads have to be honest with each other and this puts everyone on their mettle. However, a consortium approach also provides support for head teachers and senior staff. Where there are weaknesses, joint training can be planned. Professional development can be undertaken jointly. He believes very strongly that the concept of 'stronger' and 'weaker' members is over-simplistic. All schools have their strengths. For example Haybridge works particularly closely with Baxter College, which faces many challenges in a relatively deprived area. Haybridge gains from its great strengths, innovation and energy. The staff of the two schools train together and both benefit enormously from the collaboration.

The collaborative approach is central to Dr Kershaw's approach to education. His next career move is to become the DCSF 14–19 Adviser for the West Midlands. He will have the opportunity to roll out what he believes to have been an excellent development for both his own school and the other schools in ContinU, and to ensure that more pupils across the region have access to courses at which they can succeed.

Suggested further reading

Conor Ryan and Cyril Taylor, *Excellence in Education: The Making of Good Schools*, London: David Fulton, 2005.

Chapter 2

How to choose a good school for your child

Getting their child into a good local school can be a major challenge for many parents, particularly in urban areas. This chapter is intended to help parents understand the admissions procedures as well as how to choose a good school for their child.

The first question to answer is 'To which schools should your child apply?'

Chapter 1 of this book discussed the characteristics of good schools. We indentified the key common characteristics as:

- A good leadership team of the head teacher, heads of department and governing body;
- Their ability to attract and retain good teachers;
- A focus on the basics such as literacy and numeracy;
- The setting of individual learning targets for each student in every year group and use of data to monitor progress and the achievement of good examination results;
- Good discipline and order;
- Curriculum innovation, which may include vocational awards and/or the International Baccalaureate;
- Extensive use of information communications technology, including wireless linked laptops for every child and interactive whiteboards;
- A longer school day with an extensive programme of after-school education;
- A focus on individual learning to create an ethos of achievement, so that every child realises his or her optimum potential;
- The involvement of parents and the use of older students to act as mentors for younger children.

In addition to the above criteria for excellence, there are other statistical measures which can help a parent in the choice of a school. These include:

- Turnover of staff – if a school has a high turnover of staff, it is often an indication that all is not well with the school;
- The proportion of pupils who stay on in full-time education at age 16;
- The proportion of pupils who gain entry to university;
- The percentage of pupils who attend regularly;
- The number of permanently excluded pupils;
- Whether a school has more applications than its number of places;
- The record of the school in public examinations such as GCSEs and A levels;
- Whether or not the school has had good OfSTED inspection reports.

Most of the previous information about schools in your area will be available either from the local authority or from the school's website and brochure. OfSTED reports can be obtained from www.ofsted.gov.uk.

For parents interested in applying to private schools there are two valuable sources of information: the *Good Schools Guide* published annually, which gives details of 1,000 independent schools for children aged 5–18; and the website of the Independent Schools Council, www.isc.co.uk.

Parents are strongly advised to make a short list of at least three, and as many as six, good schools and to visit each of the schools, if possible talking to parents of children already enrolled. Before doing so, parents should obtain a copy of their local education authority's admissions guide. The following are important basic facts.

First, all maintained schools must follow the Schools Admissions Code, published in 2007 by the Department of Education and Skills. Copies can be obtained online from www.dcsf.gov.uk/sacode.

Second, 70 per cent of all schools are community or voluntary controlled schools in which the local authority is responsible for admissions. Applications to these schools are made directly to the local authority.

Most of the remaining third are either voluntary aided or foundation schools, who determine their own admissions through an approved admissions procedure after consulting with neighbouring schools and the local authority in the local admissions forum. There are also a growing number of academies which must have a clear admissions policy agreed with the DCSF in accordance with the School Admissions Code.

Third, most local authorities now organise admissions for all the maintained schools in their area, but applications to academies and voluntary aided and foundation schools usually require parents to apply directly to their schools.

Fourth, for community, voluntary aided and foundation schools, priority is usually given to those children who live closest to the school to which they apply, or in a defined catchment area. Preference is also given to applying children in care, children with special needs, and siblings.

The existing procedure results in some schools, especially those which are high-performing, becoming oversubscribed. There is criticism of this procedure, because for very popular schools, using proximity as the principal admission criteria means that admission to a particular school can be linked to the value of neighbouring houses and the size of a mortgage. The wealthy thus gain access to good schools, leaving the socially disadvantaged to enrol in underperforming schools. There are at least 300 such low-attaining secondary schools with over 300,000 children in them.

However, to be fair, most parents do, in fact, gain entrance to a school of their choice, or at least to one of those – between three and six, depending on the area – for which they express a preference. One measure of this is in the number of appeals – parents dissatisfied about an admissions decision may appeal to an independent panel. Some 1.5 million children either start primary or secondary school, or change school, each year. 56,610 cases were heard by a panel in 2006/7, of which 19,450 were decided in the parents' favour, suggesting that only around 1.3 per cent of admissions were not, though this figure excludes those who thought an appeal not worth it or opted for a private school instead.[1]

[1] DCSF Statistical First Release 11/2008.

The basic assumption of the admissions code is that admissions, where possible, should be determined locally after due consultation with all those concerned. The legislation requires that all notifications of places are made at the same time, so that some parents do not sit on several offers while others have none.

Local authorities must follow the School Admissions Code in determining which children are awarded places at oversubscribed schools. Priority can be given to those of a particular faith, siblings, those living within a catchment area or nearest to the school. Schools can also use a lottery – a better word is random allocation – to determine which children should be admitted if they are oversubscribed. In addition, children in care and those with special needs *must* be given priority.

Regrettably, some parents have resorted to cheating in order to get their child into a good school. Michael Harvey, writing in *The Times*[2] identified the following examples of illegal techniques used by some parents:

- Renting an address within their preferred school's catchment area to act as a document drop even though they do not live there;
- Saying your child lives with a relative within the catchment area;
- Renting a hotel room within the catchment area when the application form is filled out;
- Claiming sibling links to a 'new' partner's/cohabitee's children already at the over-subscribed school;
- Pretending to have a faith which they do not generally possess when applying to a faith school, most of which are oversubscribed.

Parents inclined to try one or more of these tricks may face tough sanctions. Local authorities are increasingly using investigative powers to screen school applications. Poole Borough Council in Dorset reportedly used the Regulation of Investigatory Powers Act (RIPA) to spy on parents it suspected of breaking the rules.[3] The sanctions for cheating are serious.

Clearly every child in the country should be able to attend a good local school. The government's recently announced initiative to require all low-attaining secondary schools to achieve an average of 30 per cent 5+ A*–C grades including maths and English at GCSE by 2011 is a welcome step.

While the admissions code works reasonably well, and will work even better as the number of low-attaining schools is reduced through either conversion to an academy or being linked with a high-performing school in a trust, there are many people, including head teachers of both academies and specialist schools, who believe that a better approach to oversubscribed schools would be to use fair banding – where schools allocate a fixed proportion of places to pupils of different abilities to achieve a comprehensive intake – and/or random allocation of places to achieve a similar result. This could work best with an inner catchment area for local children and outer catchment areas to give access to a wider range of families.

With the help of officials at the Department for Children, Schools and Families, the author recommended such a system to head teachers of specialist schools in the autumn of 2007. The recommended system would work as outlined in the following section.

---

[2] Michael Harvey, 'Parents Who Cheat at School: Reportage', *The Times*, 30 April 2008, pp. 10–11.
[3] Fay Schlesinger, 'Council Uses Criminal Law to Spy on School Place Applicants', *Guardian*, 11 April 2008.

Basic requirements

The School Admissions Code requires all schools to have admission arrangements that are clear, fair and objective, which comply with equal opportunities and admissions legislation, the code's mandatory requirements and any coordinated admission scheme operating in their local authority.

Many specialist schools are oversubscribed. A key part of admission arrangements is the oversubscription criteria, which are used to decide which children should have priority for admission if there are more applicants than places available. Admission authorities have significant discretion and flexibility to choose oversubscription criteria that comply with the new code, taking account of local circumstances. However, they must exercise this discretion reasonably. The oversubscription criteria must be clear, objective, easily understood, based on known facts, and procedurally fair and equitable. Admission authorities must not make subjective decisions or use subjective criteria, or ask for personal information about parents. They must make clear the order in which the criteria will be applied, and how tie-break decisions will be made.

There are also some specific requirements:

(a) Children in public care – 'looked-after children' – must be given the highest priority in school admissions. Faith schools must give first priority to all looked-after children, whether of the faith or not, but they are allowed to give first priority to looked-after children of their faith above other children of their faith, and where they give any element of priority to children not of their faith above other children not of their faith.
(b) Children with a statement of special educational needs that names the school must be admitted to that school.
(c) The School Admissions Code[4] (paragraph 2.13) prohibits the use of specific oversubscription criteria that unfairly disadvantage one child compared to another.

The code also provides guidelines on the use of fair and commonly used criteria including sibling links, distance from the school, ease of access by public transport, medical or social grounds, catchment areas and transfer from named feeder primary schools. Schools designated as having a religious character may give priority to children who are members of, or who practise their faith or denomination. In doing this, they should have regard to any guidance provided by their religious authority, as far as this is consistent with the code.

The law allows a school with a specialism in one or more subjects to give priority to a proportion of children who can demonstrate an aptitude in certain subjects. See later under 'Selection' for eligible aptitude tests. Below is further guidance to respond to three particular questions specialist schools have asked the Specialist Schools and Academies Trust in the past:

- In what circumstances can a school's admission arrangements include aptitude or ability selection?
- In what circumstances can they include banding?
- Catchment areas.

---

[4] The *School Admissions Code*, published by the Department for Children, Schools and Families, came into effect on 17 January 2008.

Selection

Designated grammar schools (of which there are 164 in England) can continue to select all their pupils by high academic ability, unless either the governing body decides that they should adopt non-selective admission arrangements or parents in their area request a ballot and vote for change.

Schools that selected for a proportion of places by ability or aptitude, or used banding, in the school year 1997–98 and whose selective admission arrangements have remained unchanged since then, may continue to do so unless there is an objection to the Schools Adjudicator, who decides that the arrangements should be modified. Giving priority for places by ability or aptitude in partially selective schools is an oversubscription criterion and admission authorities must not leave places unfilled if there are not enough children to fill the proportion of selective places. In this case, places must be filled by children who meet the school's other published oversubscription criteria.

The School Standards and Framework Act 1998 allows a school with a specialism in one or more prescribed subjects to give priority to up to 10 per cent of children who can demonstrate an aptitude in the relevant subject. This flexibility is not restricted to schools in the specialist schools programme, but does require that the school has a particular expertise or facility.

Tests for aptitude must be related to one of the following prescribed subjects:

- Modern foreign languages, or any such language;
- The performing arts, or any one or more of the performing arts;
- The visual arts, or any one or more of the visual arts;
- Physical education or sport, or one or more sports;
- Design and technology and ICT. Schools already selecting in design and technology and ICT before the 2008 school year may continue to do so, but no further selection in these subjects can be introduced in respect of subsequent years.

Admission authorities determine how aptitude is assessed. They must ensure that tests do not assess any aspect of general academic ability or aptitude for any subject other than the subject in question, and are free from any form of discrimination. The School Admissions Code gives further guidance on what the law permits, as do recent decisions by the Chief Schools Adjudicator.

Use of fair banding

Either separately – or, preferably, within a group of schools working together – fair banding is an approach that can be used by oversubscribed schools to achieve a wide ability range intake. The School Admissions Code[5] sets out the only forms of banding that can be legally introduced. Banding may now operate over two or more schools, providing this has been agreed through the statutory consultation process by the governing bodies of all the schools involved. Admission authorities may now adopt admission arrangements that band applicants to produce an intake that is representative of:

---

[5] The legal basis for this part of the code is section 101 of the School Standards and Framework Act 1998, as amended by section 54 of the Education and Inspections Act 2006.

(a)   The range of ability of applicants for the school (or group of schools banding jointly);
(b)   The range of ability of children in the local area; or
(c)   The national ability range.

Banding can only be used when a school is oversubscribed; it cannot be used to keep places open if, for example, some bands are oversubscribed and some are not. Banding is not a way to select children by high academic ability or aptitude for a particular subject. Admission authorities proposing to use banding to allocate places must set out in their published admission arrangements how this will work and what other oversubscription criteria will be used within each band.

Under banding, all applicants are asked to sit a test of ability. It is for admission authorities themselves to decide which tests to use, ensuring they give an accurate picture of children's abilities. The most commonly used tests are the National Foundation for Educational Research (NFER) non-verbal reasoning tests or the QCA Year 5 tests. Admission authorities also have discretion to decide how many bands to use and what proportion of children to place in each band, so long as they ensure that no level of ability is substantially under- or over-represented.

Once tested, all applicants to a school (or group of schools) are placed into ability bands based on their performance in the test. Once children have been allocated to bands, the admission authority must not apply another test of ability or give priority within bands according to performance in the test (see paragraph 2.77 of the code). The admission authority can use a range of criteria to decide which children from within each band should be offered a place – commonly used criteria include distance, siblings, feeder primary schools, etc.

For example, if a school were to have three ability bands it could decide to place the top 25 per cent ranked pupils in the top band, the next 50 per cent ranked pupils in the middle band and the bottom 25 per cent ranked pupils in the bottom band. Alternatively it might place pupils in five bands of 20 per cent, i.e. the top 20 per cent of ranked pupils in the top band, the next 20 per cent in the next band, and so on. Whatever number of bands is chosen, the proportion of applicants placed in each band must be mirrored by the proportion of applicants offered places from each band. In other words if a school places the top 25 per cent of applicants in the top band, the middle 50 per cent in the next band, and the bottom 25 per cent in the bottom band, then it must offer 25 per cent of its places to pupils from the top band, 50 per cent of its places to pupils from the middle band, and the final 25 per cent of its places to pupils from the bottom band. Where places become vacant within a particular band and all applicants from that band have already been allocated a place, they should be evenly filled by children falling into the next nearest bands from above and below in turn.

Giving some priority to non-local children with inner and outer catchment areas

Some English specialist secondary and academy schools simply wish to serve their local neighbourhood. But, as the choice of specialist schools increases, others believe that a balance should be struck between the needs of children living in the immediate vicinity of the school, and those who live further afield but still within a reasonable distance and whose parents wish to enrol their child in a specialist school whose subject appeals to their child.

Having a catchment area or areas does not mean that children from outside the catchment area cannot apply to a school. Parents have a right to express a preference for their child to attend any school, regardless of where they live, and to have their application considered. However, where an oversubscribed school uses catchment areas, it can give priority in its admissions to those children who live within the particular area or areas.

One way to improve choice for parents among different specialist schools in a particular area is to set more than one catchment area. For example, an admission authority may use inner and outer catchment areas: the inner being set at a distance to facilitate the admission of children living in the immediate vicinity (e.g. within 2 miles of the school); and the outer covering children over a wider area but still within a reasonable travelling time of the school (e.g. between 2 and 5 miles from the school). The school could then give priority for a specified proportion of places to applicants from the inner catchment area, and the remaining places allocated to applicants from the outer area. Catchment areas can be applied before or after other oversubscription criteria.

Local circumstances will vary and whilst admission authorities are responsible for drawing up their own catchment areas, they should ensure that these reflect the diversity of the community served by the school and should monitor the effect that their arrangements have. Catchment areas should not be set so that a child is given priority simply because they live in the local authority area where the school is situated (R. v. Greenwich London Borough Council, ex parte John Ball Primary School (1989)).

Random allocation

Schools using this system which are oversubscribed in either or both their inner and outer catchment areas – they have more applications than places – may use random allocation to determine who is offered a place.

This is the system used by Harris City Academy Crystal Palace, whose admissions procedure is outlined with their permission in Appendix 2.

Harris City Academy Crystal Palace was opened in 1990 as one of the original city technology colleges. It took over the former Sylvan School, which was a very low-attaining school with no first choice applicants and only 9 per cent of its pupils gaining 5+ A★–C grades at GCSE. It was sponsored by the Philip and Pauline Harris Trust. In 2008, 93 per cent of its 15 year-olds achieved 5+ A★–C grades, and 80 per cent of its pupils achieved 5+ A★–C grades including maths and English. In September 2008 it converted to academy status with its outstanding head teacher, Daniel Moynihan, becoming chief executive of the federation of eight Harris academies in South London. It is now hugely oversubscribed.

The huge advantage of the Harris Academy procedure is that despite the school receiving ten times as many applications as it has places, there are few appeals from disappointed parents because the system is so fair and transparent. The system also ensures that the school admits a wide range of ability. The Haberdasher Academies in Lewisham and many other schools use a similar approach.

The author strongly recommends that groups of specialist secondary schools adopt this procedure, working together to allow a wide choice of different specialisms to children living in a particular area.

Chapter 3

Why we need to empower our head teachers

In the first chapter, we recognised an outstanding head teacher as the first and most important characteristic of a good school. But do we have sufficient outstanding head teachers to meet our needs for better leadership in our schools?

Around 1000 out of 20,000 schools in England do not have a permanent head teacher. Steve Munby, the head of the National College of School Leadership (NCSL), told his annual conference in 2008 that more than half of our current head teachers are likely to have retired by 2012.[1] Clearly, if we are to attract the most able potential head teachers into applying for a headship, we need to make the position more appealing.

Salary is one incentive. Some city academies in London are now offering their head teachers a salary of over £120,000, and salaries for head teachers in England have risen relatively rapidly in recent years. We will also have to provide better training to prospective head teachers. The Specialist Schools and Academies Trust (www.ssatrust.org) is running a very successful programme for aspirant young head teachers, and the NCSL does excellent work. However, the best way to persuade more able heads of department and leading teachers to consider becoming a head teacher is to give them much greater freedom to take the decisions necessary to improve their schools. Government and local authorities should provide the broad framework of the school's curriculum and fair accountability, but they should avoid micro-managing maintained schools.

In his excellent book on the subject, Jeffrey Fox recommends a ten-part guide to good leadership.[2] I accept that our American colleagues use language differently from ourselves, but head teachers in all countries might find his formula for success of interest.

The Great Boss Simple Success Formula

- Only hire top-notch, excellent people;
- Put the right people in the right job; weed out the wrong people;
- Tell the people what needs to be done;
- Tell the people why it is needed;
- Leave the job up to the people you have chosen to do it;
- Train the people;
- Listen to the people;

---

[1] BBC News Online, 19 June 2008.
[2] Jeffrey J. Fox, *How to Become a Great Boss: The Rules for Getting and Keeping the Best Employees*, New York: Hyperion, 2002, pp. 4–5.

- Remove frustration and barriers that fetter the people;
- Inspect progress;
- Say 'thank you' publicly and privately.

A major issue in our schools is to remove ineffective staff. Despite several recent attempts to simplify the process, many head teachers tell me that the procedures to move on ineffective teachers or staff in English schools are absurdly complicated, time consuming and frustrating. Head teachers have told me that it can take as long as 18 months of frustrating activity to terminate the employment of a poor teacher.

Jim Collins, author of a best-selling American treatise on management, said that good leaders usually start their careers as a chief executive by 'getting the right people on the bus, the wrong people off the bus, and the right people in the right seats'.[3]

While the great majority of teachers and teaching assistants and staff in our schools do their jobs admirably well, OfSTED has said that while 11 per cent of teaching and learning in schools is outstanding, 3 per cent is 'inadequate'.[4] An extrapolation of that figure to the 441,000 total number of teachers employed in state-funded schools would suggest a figure of 13,230 inadequate teachers. As reported in *The Times*,[5] Keith Bartley, chief executive of the General Teaching Council of England, estimates that there are as many as 24,000 incompetent teachers working in state schools, but only forty-six teachers have been judged incompetent since 2001, as procedures for proving teachers are not up to the job are so onerous. A concentration of too many of these ineffective teachers in our most challenging low-attaining schools makes it difficult to improve them, although programmes like Teach First are starting to change the balance in those schools.

Good discipline is another essential criterion of a good school. But yet again, we do not give our head teachers sufficient powers to enforce good discipline. There are about 8,700 badly behaved children who are permanently excluded from our schools each year.[6] This is a very small proportion of the 7.5 million children in state schools. But the procedure to exclude a seriously misbehaving child, including appeals by parents to an independent panel, are long and tiresome; this can lead to children who belong in a special educational school for children with emotional, behavioural and social difficulties (EBSD) being kept in a mainstream school, causing disruption to the other pupils.

Other powers which should be given to head teachers include the following:

- The ability to pay outstanding teachers, particularly in shortage subjects such as physics, maths and chemistry, a greater salary than the norm. (At present, they may receive 'golden hellos' when they start teaching, but are on the same salary scale as their colleagues.) The teaching unions, with their fixation on one-size-fits-all, may be horrified by this idea, but it is time we recognised that if we are to attract more science and maths graduates into teaching, we must pay them more.

[3] Jim Collins, *Good to Great: Why Some Companies Make the Leap … and Others Don't*, New York: HarperCollins, 2001, p. 13.
[4] *The Annual Report of Her Majesty's Chief Inspector 2006/07*, London: Ofsted, 2007.
[5] John O'Leary, 'Incompetent Teachers: Problems Should Be Dealt With, Not Passed On', *The Times*, 2 May 2008.
[6] DCSF Statistical First Release 14/2008.

- The ability to make changes to admissions arrangements to ensure they are both fair and efficient. Chapter 2 recommends a radical new approach to admissions, using fair banding, inner and outer catchment areas and random selection if a school is over-subscribed. Current admissions arrangements are unnecessarily complex and the appeal procedures for parents denied a place can lead to head teachers having to devote substantial amounts of time in hearings.

- More flexibility between capital and recurrent spending in their budgets. There is an artificial distinction in state schools budgets between so-called recurrent operating expenditures for teachers' salaries and basic running costs such as cleaning, and capital expenditure. The highly complex Building Schools for the Future programme promises that every secondary school will be refurbished or even rebuilt by 2020, but its procedures have been so complicated that its budget has been underspent by 1 billion pounds in 2007 (and far more in previous years). Head teachers and their governing bodies should be given much greater authority and more capital funding through their dedicated capital grant to handle significant improvements and maintenance.[7] It is unacceptable that state-funded schools do not have to meet the same strict health and safety standards, such as fire alarms equipped with sprinklers or the removal of asbestos, which independent schools must meet.

- Providing their governing bodies agree, head teachers should have the right to vie expenditure between their operating and capital budgets. An even bolder step would be for schools to introduce an annual depreciation cost of their buildings and equipment into their budgets, and to receive the necessary funding to replace out-of-date equipment, especially IT, and to make the necessary infrastructure expenditure.

- Giving the chief executive of a school the necessary powers to take the hard decisions necessary to raise standards is a crucial requirement. One of the reasons for the success of the Specialist Schools initiative, as described in Chapter 10, is that head teachers have the responsibility for submitting the initial application for specialist school status, including the setting of their own targets for improvement, both overall and in the specialist subject.

- Reducing central initiatives by introducing greater continuity at the centre. Another issue of concern to head teachers is the constant stream of new initiatives which come from the Education Department. For example, in July 2008, the Department for Children, Schools and Families issued thirty new statutory instruments, including twelve orders with revisions of the national curriculum.[8] Head teachers are not given the time to implement a new policy change before yet another one requires their attention. This problem affects most UK government departments, and reflects the constant turnover of both ministers and officials. Between 1986 and 2008 I worked with eleven secretaries of state (that is an average term of office of only 18 months), with even greater changes at the minister of state and under secretary level, although there are outstanding long-serving exceptions such as Lord Adonis, to whom we are all indebted. We were all sorry to lose him when he was promoted to be minister of state at the Department of Transport in October 2008. With the exception of those few education secretaries – such as Kenneth Baker, Gillian Shephard and David Blunkett – who

---

[7] Secondary schools typically receive around £120,000 a year in direct capital funding to enable them to do basic maintenance; they may accumulate the money over several years for larger projects.

[8] Source: Department for Children, Schools and Families.

remained in post for several years, and were thus able to accomplish a great deal, our education secretaries do not remain in a post long enough to achieve their goals. In the last seven years there have been six different secretaries of state. The same is true for our most able and senior officials, with some outstanding exceptions, who frequently change positions after only one or two years in post. This is because the only way many good officials can gain promotion and a higher salary, is to apply for another job, frequently in another department. In the private sector, if you want to keep an able employee in the same job, you offer them financial incentives. Why can't the government do this too?

The following list details the eleven education secretaries who served between 1986 and 2008:

1   *Kenneth Baker*, May 1986–July 1989 (3 years, 2 months)
2   *John MacGregor*, Aug. 1989–Oct. 1990 (15 months)
3   *Kenneth Clarke*, Nov. 1990–April 1992 (17 months)
4   *John Patten*, May 1992–Sept. 1994 (2 years, 4 months)
5   *Gillian Shepherd*, Sept. 1994–May 1997 (2 years, 8 months)
6   *David Blunkett*, May 1997–June 2001 (4 years 1 month)
7   *Estelle Morris*, May 2001–October 2002 (17 months)
8   *Charles Clarke*, October 2002–December 2004 (2 years, 2 months)
9   *Ruth Kelly*, December 2004–May 2006 (17 months)
10 *Alan Johnson*, May 2006–June 2007 (13 months)
11 *Ed Balls*, June 2007–present.

The author served as adviser on city technology colleges, specialist schools and academies to all the above except Ed Balls.

Greater empowerment of our head teachers will require more accountability to their governing bodies, pupils and parents and to the taxpayers' elected representatives, the local education authority and the DCSF. However, we need accountability which is fair and transparent, as well as consistent. The current system of examination league tables, which compares the performance of schools on a raw score basis, and the confusing new contextual value added tables, are not by themselves good measures of accountability.

A much better measure would combine the accountability measure of the raw scores of the percentage of pupils gaining five good GCSE grades including maths and English with Professor David Jesson's approach to value added. He calculates the average point count for 11 year-olds entering each English school at Key State 2 tests in maths, science and English. This averages about 27 points for the 600,000 11 year-olds taking this test. With this average Ks2 point count, a school should achieve 48 per cent of its pupils obtaining five good GCSEs including English and maths. But if a school's intake of ability has an average of only 25 points, its forecasted GCSE score will fall to just 20 per cent. Conversely, if a school's average intake of ability averages 30 points, 80 per cent of its pupils should achieve five good GCSEs, not 48 per cent.

His accountability measure, which compares the intake of ability of the year 7 pupils entering a secondary school at age 11 with both the predicted outcomes of those gaining five good GCSE grades, with their actual results, is highly regarded by specialist school head teachers (see Figures 3.1 and 3.2).

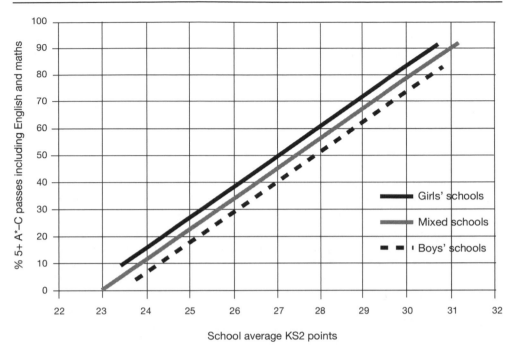

Figure 3.1 Predicted GCSE scores including English and maths for non-selective schools

Figure 3.1 shows that girls' schools perform better, on average, than mixed or boys' schools with similar Key stage 2 point scores. The size of this 'gender difference' may even be slightly larger than it is on the traditional measure, reflecting girls' strength in English. Nationally 68 per cent of girls achieve an A*–C grade in GCSE English whereas only 53 per cent of boys do so. There is no significant gender difference in performance in maths – around 55 per cent of all pupils achieve A*–C passes.

The appeal of this accountability measure is that it is so easy to understand and to calculate. This is not the case with the government's preferred Contextual Value Added calculation. The SSAT report[9] shows that the two approaches provide broadly similar indicators on the performance of a particular school:

- Around 90 per cent of schools assessed as having 'average' CVA measures have JVA measures relatively close to zero;
- A similar proportion of schools with 'above average' CVA measures have positive JVA results;
- The great majority of schools with 'below average' CVA measures have negative JVA results.

But the statistical procedures used are very different. England is the first nation in the world to apply such a system to its national education system, and CVA represents one

[9] *Data Driven School Transformation 2007*, analysis by Professor David Jesson and David Crossley, London: SSAT, 2008 (ISBN 978-1-906524-04-3).

of the most sophisticated performance models, one of great interest to statisticians across the world, though Jesson and his co-author David Crossley say there are concerns about its year-on-year comparability. However, JVA takes a simpler, almost visual approach which, though less informative on some aspects of performance, provides observable results which are easy to understand.

Should we make allowances for disadvantage?

There is, moreover, one major important philosophical difference between the two approaches. CVA uses a range of factors representing aspects of pupils' socio-economic 'disadvantage'. This has been the subject of considerable debate. For example, if pupils with a particular characteristic generally 'do less well' than otherwise similar pupils, should expectations be lowered for these pupils? Some believe this to be 'essential'; others feel that it 'reduces challenge' and can be used to justify under-performance.

JVA and CVA take opposing views on this question, and this explains some of the differences between the two evaluations. There is no clear 'right' or 'wrong' answer here, but interpretations of performance need to recognise the reasons behind different results. It is the author's view that in some cases, the Contextual Value Added system, by overemphasising certain socio-economic factors such as free school meals, can be used to justify the poor examination results of a school, particularly as the use of average Key stage 2 scores in maths, English and science to predict performance at GCSE already takes some of these social deprivation factors into account.

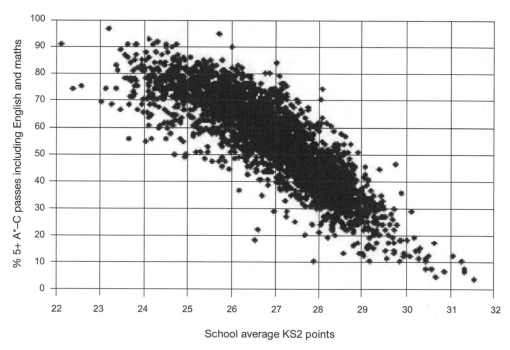

Figure 3.2 Proportion of five good GCSE passes including English and maths for non-selective schools

The complexity of CVA versus the simplicity of JVA

One major criticism of CVA is that it is both difficult to understand and difficult to interpret. The Association of School and College Leaders[10] is one of several organisations to argue that OfSTED inspectors are over-reliant on its findings. JVA, for all its lack of statistical complexity, provides clear messages for schools in their search for improvement. Also, by offering an analysis that includes English and maths achievement, it is arguably more sophisticated in some important respects.

Where CVA and JVA provide different interpretations of schools' performance there is, therefore, no suggestion that one is 'right' and the other 'wrong'. But where this contrast does occur, as in any scientific research, the situation warrants deeper investigation.

It is our hope that as schools become more familiar with the variety of ways of assessing and evaluating their performance, they will become more aware of the potential of the data to exemplify excellence and identify poor performance.

Following up 'matters of concern'

A further difference between CVA and JVA is in the provision of supplementary information to help schools to identify matters of concern. CVA provides charts which identify the performance of different groups of pupils, for example: girls and boys; those eligible for free school meals and those not; different ethnic groups; or distinct subject area evaluations.

These CVA charts are complemented by the CVA median value for each group – and an indication as to whether the performance is 'OK', 'better' or 'worse' than expected.

By contrast, the JVA approach relies on an explicit grouping of pupils by their Key stage 2 point scores when they entered secondary schools and a comparison of their achievement with the expected achievement of similar pupils nationally.

Appendix 2 is a detailed explanation of the Jesson Valued English and Maths measure. The SSAT website, www.ssatrust.org.uk, gives details of the Jesson Value Added score of every English secondary school.

Tests and exam scores are not the only way in which heads should be judged. We saw in Chapter 1 how several other statistical measures could be used in a fair system of accountability for schools. Other measures could include:

(a) Turnover of staff – if a school has a high turnover of staff, that is often an indication that all is not well with the school;
(b) The proportion of pupils who stay on in full-time education at age 16;
(c) The proportion of pupils who gain entry to university;
(d) The percentage of pupils who attend regularly;
(e) The number of permanently excluded pupils;
(f) Whether a school has more applications than its number of places;
(g) whether a school operates within a balanced budget, matching expenditure with income;
(h) Whether a school has a good OfSTED inspection report.

[10] www.ascl.org.uk/MainWebSite/Homepage

Greater empowerment of our head teachers, together with a fairer system of account-ability, is surely one of the most effective ways to raise standards in our schools as well as to attract more able new head teachers.

Suggested further reading

Data Driven School Transformation 2007. Analysis by Professor David Jesson and David Crossley, London: Specialist Schools and Academies Trust, 2008.

Chapter 4

Why we must improve standards of literacy

Even though much good work has gone into improving literacy levels in our schools in recent years, there is still a serious problem that needs to be addressed. Her majesty's chief inspector of schools, Christine Gilbert, has reported that improvement in literacy standards in schools have stalled.[1]

Nineteen per cent of English 11 year-old children do not master the literacy skills needed to achieve level 4 at Key stage 2 – 107,000 children.[2] Even worse, half of these 11 year-olds do not achieve level 3 and have the equivalent reading age of 7 year-olds. There is insufficient improvement by age 14 when 27 per cent of 14 year-olds do not reach the standard expected in English.[3] Furthermore, only 66 per cent of 14 year-old boys achieve the target level 5. That means nearly 200,000 14 year-old boys do not have the required reading and writing skills. In the 2005 National Reading Campaign survey, 20 per cent of the children taking part reported their mother did not teach them to read and 25 per cent of children reported that their father had never spent time reading to them. Booktrust[4] reports that currently only 33 per cent of parents of primary school children read to their children, compared to 43 per cent two years ago.[5]

An estimated 5 million adults are functionally illiterate in the United Kingdom. This is an appalling statistic, bearing in mind the modern definition of literacy is the ability to read and write at a level adequate for communication, or at a level that lets one understand and communicate ideas in a literate society, so as to take part in that society.

These worrying statistics are of even greater concern because literacy is so important to general learning; reading is the key to learning. It has been estimated that 75 per cent of academic success is predicted by reading ability. Virtually the entire school curriculum requires children to read if they are to learn successfully. Practical subjects are no exception. Success in science and maths tests also depends on one's ability to read. If you can't read the maths problem you can't solve it. Children must know how to read in order to be able to read to learn.

Not being able to read leads to boredom at school, truancy, and sometimes worse things, especially for boys. In 1996 and 1997, I had the honour of serving as high sheriff of Greater London. I spent most of my term of office working with young offenders,

[1] BBC News Online, 19 May 2008.
[2] DCSF Statistical First Release SFR 19/2008.
[3] DCSF Statistical First Release SFR 20/2008.
[4] www.booktrust.org.uk/Home
[5] See 'Parents Too Busy or Tired to Read', by Stephen Adams, *Daily Telegraph*, 18 September 2008.

including visiting young offenders' prisons such as Feltham. I learned, as the 1996 Audit Office study 'Misspent Youth'[6] showed, that most young offenders have poor literacy skills. Each young offender can cost the taxpayer over £2 million over a twenty-year period, because of the very high re-offending rates.

Independent research confirms what common sense suggests. Students who score in the top 5 per cent on standardised reading tests read 144 times more than students who score in the bottom 5 per cent. A 2002 study by the OECD[7] (Organisation for Economic Co-operation and Development) of 174,000 students in thirty-two countries showed time spent reading books is the single best predictor of academic achievement, more highly correlated to success than even socio-economic status or ethnicity. One of the reasons for high performance of Finnish schools in the PISA comparison is the high proportion of Finnish parents who read to their children.

I remember arriving at Harvard Business School (HBS) in 1961 to study for a master's degree in business administration after completing a history degree at Trinity Hall, Cambridge. I thought I was a pretty good reader, but to my surprise, I scored poorly in the reading test that HBS then gave its students upon arrival. The test indicated I read slowly and research indicates that slow readers do not comprehend what they are reading as well as fast readers. So I took the Evelyn Wood Rapid Reading Course. This not only improved my grades at Harvard Business School, but has proved invaluable in my various careers – particularly in reading boring government policy papers!

Sir Jim Rose, the government's chief adviser on literacy, has recommended that synthetic phonics be used in primary schools to teach basic reading skills, a recommendation I strongly support.[8] But what if an 11 year-old entering secondary school is not able to read?

That is why I was so intrigued when four years ago I visited St Paul's Elementary school in a very poor area of Harlem in New York, which has exceptional reading test scores. The primary school children in the school I visited were reading two grade levels higher than similar children in other schools in Harlem.

It is an amazing school. All the children read books enthusiastically. An hour a day is set aside for supervised silent reading in school. Of course, it's one thing to set aside time for reading, it's another thing to get actual reading engagement. At this school the students were very engaged, and the reason they were so engaged was down to the teachers and a programme called the Accelerated Reader.[9] Students would read a book and as soon as they finished they would run to the computer to take the Accelerated Reader (AR) comprehension quiz.

Well, all the children insisted I take a quiz, too. So I skimmed a short children's book, called *Three Crocodiles and an Island*, took the AR test, and got only three out of five questions right. The children danced around shouting with great glee: 'He got two wrong!'

It was at this Harlem school that I was introduced to Terry Paul, the CEO and co-founder with his wife Judi, of Renaissance Learning, one of the most effective systems of recommended reading. A mutual friend, Bill Ruane, a very successful Wall Street

---

[6] Audit Commission, *Misspent Youth: Young People and Crime* (National Report), London: Audit Commission for Local Authorities and the National Health Service in England and Wales, 1996. ISBN 1-86240-007-5.

[7] www.oecd.org

[8] Jim Rose, *Independent Review of the Teaching of Early Reading, Final Report*, London: Department for Education and Skills, 2006, p. 2.

[9] For further information see www.renaissance-learning.co.uk/

businessman and philanthropist, also a friend of Bill Gates and Warren Buffet, introduced me to Terry. It was also Bill Ruane who had funded the purchase of Accelerated Reader and Star products at the school, along with all the computers and books and even paid for a full-time librarian. Subsequently, he founded the Carmel Hill Trust, whose director, Judy Parker, is a leading light in improving literacy levels in New York City schools and several other areas in the United States. Carmel Hill supports nearly 100 schools in the US with the Accelerated Reader programme.

Several things struck me during that school visit. First, it is clearly essential for students to read a lot of books to become good at reading. In a small way I could identify with those students in Harlem, particularly the English learners who were new immigrants. I grew up in the Congo in Africa, the son of missionaries. I did not speak a word of English until I came to England at the age of 6. Luckily for me I learned how to read quickly, taught by an inspirational teacher in Halifax. Then, once I learned how to read, I began to read books. I got hooked on books and read a lot. Book reading became a lifelong passion. I am who I am in large part because of the many books I have read.

The Rose Review[10] recommendations have been accepted by the Department for Children, Schools and Families in England. They are a major step forward, because it is essential that we teach children how to read phonetically, how to decode letters and sound words out. But as Rose says, teaching students how to read is just the first step in encouraging students to read a lot and to understand what they are reading. Acquiring word recognition skills through a good phonics programme should be a time-limited accomplishment with all 7 year-olds having achieved this. I agree with Rose that word recognition is an essential first step. Failure to learn to decode and encode print leaves children demotivated, floundering and in need of expensive catch-up programmes.

The second thing that struck me on that visit to Harlem was how important it is for students to have time at school to read books. I was lucky I had books at home. Indeed, I used to read under the bedclothes with a flashlight when my mother turned off the light. Those Harlem students didn't have books at home. I was lucky, too, in that I did not have the distractions that kids have today. Do you know that it is believed that in the typical home in England the TV is on for over 7 hours a day? Seven hours![11]

Let's face it. Many of the students who are behind in their reading are not going to read at home because there are often no books in their homes, and the TV is on for over 7 hours a day. To develop good readers, there must be time set aside during the school day for students to read books. And time at school for reading books is just as important in secondary schools as in primary schools.

The visit to the Harlem primary school was a revelation but I've learned over the years to maintain a sceptical attitude; also, as chairman of the Specialist Schools and Academies Trust my main interest was secondary schools. So I was keen to learn if these techniques would work in secondary schools.

In early 2005, I was holidaying with my daughter Kirsten in Miami, and Terry Paul arranged for me to visit Ammons Middle School, in a socially disadvantaged area of Miami. Ammons has around 1,100 students aged 11–13, 52 per cent of whom are Hispanic and 26 per cent black. Yet, under the outstanding leadership of Principal Irwin Adler, the Ammons Middle School has won numerous awards for test score improvement and

---

[10] Rose, *Independent Review of the Teaching of Early Reading, Final Report.*
[11] http://blogs.zdnet.com/ITFacts/?p = 14831

parental involvement. Eighty-six per cent of Ammons 8th grade students score at or above grade level because of the Accelerated Reader programme compared to 49 per cent for other 8th grade students in Florida.[12] They set aside a 45-minute teaching period every day when all students do nothing but read in their classroom. It was the most amazing thing; during reading time at 8.30 in the morning every single student reads a book. It was so quiet you could hear a pin drop.

But this revolution in teaching reading was not just occurring in the US. It had started to catch on in the UK as well. Kathy Heaps, then head teacher of John Kelly Girls Technology College in the London Borough of Brent, who was using the Accelerated Reader, told me she was seeing the same thing. Children had become hooked on books, library circulation had rocketed and much to the librarian's glee, so did the book budget. The library was busy, and to this day it still is. In fact, they have moved computers out of the library to fit more books in.

What I had seen at Ammons and from what Kathy Heaps told me, reinforced for me one of those common characteristics of high-performing schools described in Chapter 1. At both Ammons and John Kelly Girls, there was good leadership: both Irwin Adler and Kathy Heaps were very enthusiastic, and worked together with the teachers to set measurable goals. They used the test data from the Accelerated Reader and the Star Reading Test[13] to monitor progress. There was a focus on individual personalised reading and learning. Students chose their own books with the help of the teacher and the librarian. The teacher made sure the books were within the students' respective reading level as determined by the Star reading test, so every student was assured of success at their individual level.

As at Ammons, Kathy Heaps had invested in the books needed and had a full-time librarian. They started with only 3,000 books and they now have over 16,000 books in the John Kelly Girls school library. How many secondary schools in England have 16,000 books in their libraries? Only one third have a qualified librarian and a further third have a teacher with library skills, but one third have neither.

The charity Booktrust[14] recommends that school libraries should spend £10 a head for primary schools and £14 per head for secondary schools each year. This figure is based on fiction and non-fiction reading books and *does not* include materials such as set texts, textbooks or study guides. But, on average, secondary schools spend an average of £4.28 per head per year on the library, while the figure is £10.25 in primaries.[15] Many school libraries don't even allow children to take books out on loan.

Still, even with the John Kelly Girls School, Ammons and the Harlem examples, there remained the question: Would the Accelerated Reader and Star products work in other secondary schools in England? The only way the Specialist Schools and Academies Trust (SSAT) could support the use of Renaissance products would be if they had proven success in England's secondary schools. So, three years ago SSAT and Renaissance Learning entered into an agreement to pilot the programmes in English secondary schools. At the same time Terry Paul agreed to fully Anglicise their online comprehension tests. So far,

---

[12] Figures obtained during the visit to the school from the head teacher, Irwin Adler.

[13] For further information see www.renaissance-learning.co.uk/

[14] www.booktrust.org.uk/Home

[15] Research by the Institute for Public Finance for Booktrust (July 2007) available at www.booktrust.org.uk/show/feature/School-libraries-research

10,000 tests have been Anglicised, but there are a further 100,000 books for which the US test needs to be Anglicised. The Star products have even been adapted to provide equivalent Key stage test scores and reading age, and are aligned to the English National Curriculum with the reliability of their tests verified by NFER.[16]

The pilot went very well. Twelve schools and a total of 423 students completed the research study. The total implementation period was 6.5 months. Over that period the average pupil's reading age increased 40 per cent faster than expected. St Joseph's Roman Catholic Secondary in Newcastle did a particularly good job with their students nearly doubling the progress rate expected; one class showed 23 months reading age growth in 6.5 months. Each student spent about 15 minutes reading each day, on average, as they worked their way through three books a month, or 42,000 words. 'The Book in the Bag' became the mantra for pilot schools up and down the country.[17]

Obviously the fact that the pilot schools were only able to devote 15 minutes of reading per day shows that they have a way to go to get to the level of implementation I saw at Ammons and in Harlem. The increase in the number of schools using an extended school day should help to provide the necessary extra time for reading and thus not require reducing time given to other subjects. Still, even 15 minutes a day produced exceptional gains in reading in the pilot schools. I would expect that as the principal and teachers gain experience with the programme, we will see even higher gains in the second and third year. All the pilot schools have decided to renew their contract with Renaissance Learning and have extended it to include even more of their students, with a longer daily independent reading period.

I recently visited two London schools, both of which are using the Renaissance Learning techniques with great success: the William Burrough Primary School in Tower Hamlets and the Woolwich Polytechnic School in Greenwich (see the case studies of these two schools at the end of this chapter).

We need to take action on a wider scale to improve literacy in English schools. This is not an easy problem to solve, particularly with the growing numbers of children who do not speak English as their first language at home. But programmes like Accelerated Reading show the difference that schools can make. There are 70,000 schools using Accelerated Reading in the United States; approximately 5,000 are implementing the programme well enough to be getting exceptional results.[18] The question is, just what does it mean to implement AR well? What are the steps necessary to close the literacy gap?

In my view, a number of measures can help solve the literacy problems:

- First, we need to teach students how to read from an early age, using phonics, so they learn how to decode and sound out words.
- Second, we need to motivate students to read a lot of books. The amount of book reading students do directly translates into improved academic performance in all subjects. Thirty minutes of independent, supervised silent book reading practice per day at school strikes me as the minimum for secondary schools, perhaps up to 60 minutes for primary schools (perhaps linked to after-school clubs), and the pupils need to be tested on their comprehension. Many of the students we most want to help do not

[16] Source: Renaissance Learning, www.renaissance-learning.co.uk/
[17] Ibid.
[18] Ibid.

read at home. Many homes in socially disadvantaged areas have no books at home and the TV is on for over 7 hours a day. The Letterbox Club, run by the national charity Booktrust,[19] runs an excellent scheme to supply books to families to read to their children, especially to foster parents of children in care.

- Third, we need sufficient books in the school library to support 30 minutes of reading per day. I think this means at least ten books for every student – three times the current average – or an average 10,000 books per secondary school with a suitable range of books appropriate for the age range in the school. Many of the books should be multiple copies of the same book: you need more than one copy of each J. K. Rowling, Roald Dahl, Jacqueline Wilson and Malorie Blackman book. In some areas, the local authority is moving the public library into a local school. This is an important step which should be followed elsewhere, not least as it helps to share costs.

- Fourth, all secondary schools need a full-time qualified librarian, or at least a teacher with librarian skills, and the library needs to be at the heart of the learning experience. A study by Loughborough University in 2005 found a 14 per cent drop in professional library staff in the schools' library service from 2000–05, with 72 per cent of under-14s not actively using any public library service (45 per cent aren't even members).[20] A 2006 OfSTED report shows the strong correlation between well funded libraries and full-time librarians and achieving exceptional results.[21]

- Fifth, for students to be motivated and book reading to be effective, it must be personalised, individualised and accountable. Given the amount of reading practice necessary to build good readers, and the number of books students should be reading, the need to personalise, motivate, and monitor through testing is essential.

- The sixth and most important requirement is to have skilled and enthusiastic head teachers and teachers, who can use data to help them make decisions about how to interact with students. And it takes an enthusiastic head teacher who insists on fully funding the library, getting the teachers the training they need, and ensuring a minimum of 30 minutes of in-school reading time every day, to create the culture of reading which will greatly improve pupil literacy.

This approach works well, not only with poor readers, but good readers too. Everyone can benefit, as can be seen from our two case studies from the Renaissance Learning Accelerated Reading programme. The first is the Sir William Burrough Primary School in Tower Hamlets, London. Eighty-five per cent of the children in the school come from ethnic minorities and 60 per cent are eligible for free school meals. The second is the Woolwich Polytechnic School in Greenwich, London. Both schools have used Renaissance Learning techniques to dramatically improve their results.[22]

But there is one other thing we need to do to get it right on literacy. Every 11 year-old, when entering secondary school, should be given a recognised reading test in order to diagnose those in need of support. In addition to the Star reading tests, there are other valuable tests such as the London reading test and the Richmond reading tests.

---

[19] www.letterboxclub.org.uk/Home

[20] Claire Creaser and Sally Maynard, *A Survey of Library Services to Schools and Children in the UK 2005–6*, Loughborough: Loughborough University, 2006, available at www.lboro.ac.uk/departments/ls/lisu/pages/publications/sch-chil06.html#download

[21] OfSTED, 'Good School Libraries: Making a Difference to Learning', London: Ofsted, 2006.

[22] See the case study at the end of this chapter.

There is also concern among our schools that some 11 year-olds arrive in secondary school with the requisite level 4 in Key stage 2 English, but still have a reading problem, possibly because some schools spend too much time coaching to the Key stage 2 English test rather than teaching good reading skills. Clearly the Key stage tests need to be reviewed. This is not to argue against national tests as a measure of accountability for primary schools; rather it is to recognise that a diagnostic test at the start of secondary school could serve a very different purpose.

Children who are diagnosed as having a reading problem will need special coaching by teachers who are trained in synthetic phonetics teaching. If necessary, the normal timetable for these children should be suspended until they have learned to read. What is unacceptable is for the children to pass through secondary school and to leave school at 16 and still not be able to read properly. After all, how can Great Britain plc compete in the global market when so many of our workers have such poor reading skills?

Case study: Sir William Burrough Primary School, Tower Hamlets, London, by Christine Walter[23]

Despite its social deprivation, Sir William Burrough (SWB) School, in the London Borough of Tower Hamlets, gets remarkably good test scores and has been rated outstanding by the school inspectorate, OfSTED.

Eighty-five per cent of its pupils come from minority ethnic backgrounds and 80 per cent have home languages other than English. Twenty per cent are at the early stages of learning English. Sixty per cent of pupils are eligible for free school meals, and there is a high mobility rate of 20 per cent of pupils each year.

However, the school would never use these statistics as an excuse for poor achievement. On the contrary, there is an 'SWB Guarantee' that at least 85 per cent of 7 year-olds and 78 per cent of 11 year-olds will either exceed or be at national standards. This is borne out by results. OfSTED found that by the end of Year 2 pupils were achieving average standards in reading and by the end of Year 6 they ere above average. OfSTED concluded in 2008 that the school merited a grade 1, 'outstanding', report.

In 2007, 83 per cent of Year 6 pupils were at level 4 or above in English and 41 per cent achieved level 5 or above. The school is in the top 6 per cent of schools for adding value over a three-year average when compared to similar schools.

One of the ways the school ensures this outstanding performance is by what they call the 'core skills continuum'. This runs alongside an exciting thematic International Primary Curriculum, a thriving, creative arts enrichment programme and an absolute commitment to a 'you can do it' ethos. In reading this means that 'Jolly Phonics'[24] ensures robust reading competence while Accelerated Reader, which the school has been using for 8 years, keeps older children hooked on books.

Accelerated Reader has helped to motivate pupils to read more, increase their reading ability, and improve their performance in other subjects. It also provides the continuous constructive feedback that helps to motivate pupils, dramatically accelerate learning and improve test marks, while reducing teacher paperwork.

---

[23] Information for this case study was obtained from personal communication with Avril Newman, head teacher of Sir William Burrough School.
[24] www.jollylearning.co.uk/jp.htm

It increases library circulation and boosts reading levels by encouraging pupils to take the Accelerated Reader quiz on books they have read. They then get immediate feedback on how they have done and teachers get guidance via reports on each and every pupil's reading ability.

When the author visited the school in 2008, he was impressed by the enthusiasm of the pupils. At the concert they gave in his honour, all the pupils crammed into the school hall to sing, reading the words of the songs from a giant screen in the front of the hall.

Avril Newman, the head teacher, says:

> Accelerated Reader is a very simple idea, which has maximum effect in terms of helping pupils to be successful. The impact on the teacher's time and energy is minimal. Instead it adds to the teacher's own store of knowledge of the pupil's reading. It also motivates the pupil in a way that other reading systems just don't and gives them instant feedback, which again is very valuable to further their progress.

Case study: Woolwich Polytechnic, Greenwich, London, by Christine Walter[25]

Boys at Woolwich Polytechnic School, in the London Borough of Greenwich do much better than similar schools in GCSE English.

The school is an 11–16 school for boys, with a mixed sixth form, in a special arrangement with a neighbouring girls' school. It has around 1,400 pupils who come mainly from the Woolwich and Thamesmead areas. Most enter the school with low attainment at Ks2, as is usual for pupils with deprived inner-city backgrounds. Forty per cent of students have special educational needs and 35 per cent have a mother tongue other than English, resulting in students with over seventy different home languages being on roll at any one time. Many ethnic groups are represented in the school, with fewer than 50 per cent classed as White British. Nearly 30 per cent of students are eligible for free school meals. It is the largest boys' school in the country with this socio-economic profile.

The school has seen a period of rapid growth over the past few years and yet because of the excellence of learning and teaching, which is apparent throughout the school, it is experiencing improving exam results at both Ks3 and GCSE. According to Professor Jesson's SSAT research, the school has a positive value-added rating of 7 when you look at the percentage of pupils gaining five good GCSEs including English and maths. In particular, over the last three years, there have been outstanding improvements in Key stage 4 literacy and the school is now in the fourth percentile rank nationally. In 2007, 46 per cent of students gained an A★–C grade for GCSE English, and this year 54 per cent of pupils achieved 5+ A★–C grades in all subjects while 34 per cent achieved 5+ A★–C including English and maths.[26]

Many students possess poor literacy skills on entry. In early 2007, the school decided to address this problem by using Renaissance Learning's Accelerated Reader (AR) and STAR Reading programme. Initially, they ran the programme with the Year 8 cohort during the summer term, but expanded this to work with Years 7 and 8, and some in the

---

[25] Information for this case study obtained from personal communication with Byron Parker, head teacher of Woolwich Polytechnic School.
[26] Provisional self-reported results 2008 obtained from Woolwich Polytechnic.

Low Attainers Project in Year 9. Year 7 pupils have a reading lesson in the learning resource centre (LRC) – a combination of a library and IT research centre – once a week for lower sets and every fortnight for top sets. Year 8 pupils similarly have a lesson a week for lower sets and every other week for top sets. Using Accelerated Reader has allowed the school to ensure students are reading at their correct level and are able to develop their skills rapidly. 2007–8 being the first full year of using the programme, results are still improving all the time, but the mean reading age of students in Year 7 has already increased by an average of at least 6 months, bucking the national trend for pupils in this age group to remain at the same level or even regress in the first year of secondary school.

The initial reading test gives teachers a wealth of valuable information, such as national curriculum levels and estimated reading ages; this has been much appreciated by staff. A focus group of Year 9 students from the schools Low Achievers' Project is working successfully with students in Year 7 who struggle with reading. The project has had huge benefits in raising the self-esteem of all the boys involved, not just the younger boys, as well as improving their reading.

During the autumn term the LRC manager designed a high-profile display in the learning resources centre of the names of students who had achieved 100 per cent in book quizzes. The display also showed how many words each student had read during the term. This visual aid has been extremely popular with the boys and introduces a slight competitive element, to which they respond very well. Even pupils who have only basic reading skills can achieve 100 per cent on a quiz, as they are reading titles within their own ability. The learning support department is using the programme to work with the neediest pupils, and they have found that students are very keen on marrying reading with ICT.

Promoting reading has not been solely focused on fiction. Reading lists of non-fiction AR-quizzed books that tied in with topics studied by Year 7 pupils in all subjects were produced; this is to be built on in 2008–9 with the implementation of an alternative Year 7 curriculum. Boys typically prefer non-fiction, so by giving equal importance to factual books at their level, they are not turned off reading by story books.

As part of the school's focus on literacy during the National Year of Reading, a teacher or assistant was chosen from each school department to read books with AR quizzes and very visibly to take the quizzes in the LRC. There is even competition amongst these staff members to get their name on the 100 per cent board, all of which helps raise the profile of reading with the school's reluctant boy readers.

A whole school reading period has also been instigated, with the timetable adjusted so that every Wednesday for 20 minutes everyone in the school, from staff to students, stops and reads. This has been very popular with staff as it ensures a calm start to the lesson immediately after morning break. It has naturally also increased loans from the LRC, helping to ensure that the area is seen as at the heart of the school, whilst keeping reading at the forefront of everyone's minds.

Suggested further reading

Cyril Taylor, speech to the 1st Renaissance Learning Conference, Radisson Hotel, Stansted, 4 October 2007.
——'How We Can Stay Ahead in a Changing World', speech to the Xchanging Insurance Market Conference, Brighton, 8 November 2007.

Chapter 5

How to ensure that all English 16 and 17 year-olds remain in full-time education or training

The current low level of participation in either full-time education or training of English 16 and 17 year-olds is a major problem. It is the main reason why the UK government is so keen to increase the age at which young people finish full-time education or training from 16 to 18, and to introduce diplomas as an additional qualification with a stronger vocational element.

Seventy-nine per cent of English 16 year-olds are in full-time education, a proportion that falls to 67 per cent at age 17.[1] While it is true that this figure has recently improved and around 16 per cent of 17 year-olds are in work-based training, including apprenticeships, this still means that nearly 18 per cent of 674,000 English 17 year-olds are not in any education or training.

The recent decision to raise the age of compulsory education from 16 to 18 will require the provision of a very large number of additional places in schools, sixth form colleges and further education colleges, possibly as many as 200,000 additional places.

This is how participation in education and training of 17 year-olds breaks down by percentage of age group:[2]

Full-time education	66.5 per cent
Work-based learning	7.6 per cent
Employer-funded training	4.0 per cent
Other education and training	4.3 per cent
Not in any education or training	17.6 per cent
Total	100.00 per cent

By contrast, over 90 per cent of German and French 17 year-olds are in full-time education or training.

There are many causes of this failure to educate adequately such a large proportion of our young people. The first is historical. In my opinion, the Butler 1944 Education Act[3] was never properly implemented. While a third of the population were well educated in the selective grammar schools, many of the rest did not receive a good education in the secondary modern schools, and sadly there were never more than 200 technical schools established. By contrast, the English education mission which advised Germany on how

---

[1] DCSF Statistical First Notice SFR 13/2008
[2] Figures are rounded to one decimal point so may not add up to 100 per cent exactly.
[3] www.opsi.gov.uk/RevisedStatutes/Acts/ukpga/1944/cukpga_19440031_en_1

to establish a similar system in 1945, did a much better job of advising that country on how to provide high-quality vocational education in addition to the provision of schools for the academically gifted, as is explained later on in this chapter and in Chapter 15.

When the comprehensive schools were introduced in England in the 1960s and 1970s, to rectify the unfairness of the 11+ examination which decided who went to the grammar schools, the focus was on equity of provision rather than the provision of different types of courses required for children with different aptitudes. This 'one size fits all' mantra bedevilled English education until the introduction of specialist schools and academies provided a wider range of schools and more choice for parents. It is now important to build on this diversity to provide the high-status vocational courses necessary to persuade non-academically inclined 16 and 17 year-olds to stay in full-time education.

A second crucial cause is the fact that over half of English maintained secondary schools do not have post-16 provision.[4]

Every year, over 300,000 16 year-olds have to transfer to another school, sixth form college or further education college. Many go to very large further education colleges which are often unable to provide the pastoral support which students of this age group require. These are often the students who need most support, often to retake GCSEs. As a result, the drop-out rate of FE students is very high – over a fifth do not complete their courses successfully, a figure that rises to 40 per cent for apprenticeships, though these figures have been improving. Overall in 2007, only 317,000 students took either A-levels or other level 3 examinations out of a total age cohort of over 650,000 children.[5]

Another cause has been the mixed reputation of many vocational awards and indeed over-frequent changes to the awards themselves. For example, the city technology colleges introduced the BTEC diplomas into their schools, being the first schools to do so, and these proved very popular. Eventually these were replaced by the General National Vocational Qualifications in particular subjects, which were given the equivalency of four GCSE passes. Despite their popularity, GNVQs were phased out in 2007 and will now be replaced by the new National Diplomas which will be discussed later in this chapter.

These constant changes, with the requirement for teachers to learn new curricula, have not been helpful. Not surprisingly, none of the new vocational awards has achieved the high status of the 'gold standard' A-levels. It is also puzzling that proven awards, like the City & Guilds diplomas in technical skills such as carpentry, plumbing and electricity, and more recently the Oracle and Cisco IT diplomas, have not been incorporated into the new vocational awards. Both Cisco and head teachers have assured me that an 18 year-old acquiring the Cisco Certified Network Associate Diploma after taking the 280-hour Cisco Academy introductory course, can walk straight into a £25,000 p.a. IT position, such is the shortage of IT workers (see Table 9.1).

Yet another difficulty is that since 2007, the former Department of Education and Skills has been split into two different departments; the Department for Children, Schools and Families (DCFS) headed by a new secretary of state, Ed Balls, and the Department for Innovation, Universities and Skills (DIUS), whose new secretary of state is John Denham. The DCFS is responsible for schools and the DIUS is responsible for post-school education, including universities.

[4] Source: Department for Children, Schools and Families. www.dcsf.gov.uk/publications/further-educationdocs
[5] DCSF Press Release 2007/0065

These two separate departments with different secretaries of state and different civil servants cover the education of 16 and 17 year-olds. Whilst there is, of course, close cooperation between the two departments, there is clearly an issue of who is primarily responsible for the education of this age group. It is true that pre-18 education is the responsibility of the DCSF but it is unclear who is responsible for colleges which cater for all ages and for apprenticeships.

Before discussing the new diplomas, it will be helpful to describe the successful system used in Germany. The European Centre for the Development of Vocational Training (CEDEFOP) has recently published a fascinating study of vocational education and training in Germany by Ute Hippach-Schneider et al.[6] The data quoted in the next pages is taken from this report, with the permission of the publisher.

The paper quotes the coalition agreement on education between the three major German political parties, the CDU, CSU and SPD on 11 November 2005.

> The cohesion and social development of our society, our prosperity and the competitiveness of our industry depend more and more on the importance which is attached to education. Education is the decisive factor, not only for the future of our country, but also for the opportunities of each and every person.
>
> ('Working Together for Germany – with Courage and Compassion'[7])

As the paper states:

> Germany is one of the European countries in which learning on the job is a traditional component of the education system. All vocational training is aimed at imparting comprehensive professional competence in the occupation. Vocational training in Germany is guided not only by the requirements of the labour market, but also by the need for individuals to acquire skills, knowledge and competences that enable them successfully to prove themselves on the labour market. Training programmes are designed on the principle that they should be as broad as possible and as specific as necessary.

Under article 20, the Basic Law (CG) of the German Constitution,[8] the sixteen *Länder* or states which form the German Federal Republic, are responsible for education. Each *Land* is fundamentally responsible for education and culture. However, in order to ensure a minimum level of common factors, there is a standing conference of the *Länder* ministers of education. While the *Länder* are responsible for vocational training in schools, the federal government is responsible for in-company vocational training, including apprenticeships.

The German economy is strongly export-oriented. In 2005, exports were equivalent to 35 per cent of GDP, while imports only accounted for 28 per cent. Because of the skills of its workers, Germany is the world's largest exporting nation, ahead of the USA, China and Japan. In 2008, the *Economist* estimated that Germany achieved a trade surplus

---

[6] Ute Hippach-Schneider, Martina Krause and Christian Woll, 'Vocational Education and Training in Germany', Cedefop Panorama Series 138. Luxembourg: Office for Official Publications of the European Community, 2007. Copies in English can be accessed at www.cedefop.europa.eu

[7] Coalition Agreement between the CDU, CSU and SPD, 11 November 2005 published by the Press and Information Office of the Federal Government.

[8] Bundesministerium für Bildung und Forschung.

of \$285 billion. This compares to the trade surplus of China of \$253 billion and a deficit for Britain of \$187 billion and the United States of \$849 billion.[9] Germany's main exports include cars and car parts, machines, chemical and electrical products, and foods.

A high proportion of students in Germany achieve an upper secondary school level qualification. One reason for this is the long-standing institution of the dual system of vocational training in Germany.

Sixty per cent of German 16 and 17 year-olds achieve an upper secondary school qualification, compared to only 42 per cent in the UK. There is a very high participation level of employers in the provision of education. Overall, 25 per cent of all German employers are currently providing training, with 91 per cent of the largest employers participating.

The German educational system starts in kindergarten for 3–6 year-olds. Children then transfer to primary school, where they remain until age 10.

At age 10, pupils choose, with the advice of the parents and guidance from their teachers, to enter one of three different types of secondary school. Additionally, there are also comprehensive schools in almost all the *Länder*.[10] There is no equivalent to the 11+ entry examination for English grammar schools.

The three different main types of school are:

First, the *Gymnasien* or grammar school. This offers primarily academic courses for 10 to 18 year-olds. Approximately 33 per cent of German children attended a *Gymnasien* in 2005. Interestingly, at age 16, about a quarter of *Gymnasien* students transfer to a specialist grammar school (*Fachgymnasium*).[11]

Second, intermediate schools or *Realschulen*. Twenty-seven per cent of German 10 year-olds choose to enrol in a *Realschule*, which prepares pupils for vocational qualifications as well as teaching the basic skills in German, maths and science. Again, it is up to the children and their parents, with guidance from the teachers, whether they enrol in a *Realschule* or *Gymnasien*.[12]

Third, secondary general schools (*Hauptschulen*). These are similar to British comprehensive schools, which 24 per cent of German children attend. However, these have not proved to be as popular as the *Gymnasien* or *Realschulen*. In addition, there are also some comprehensive schools in almost all the *Länder*.

A particularly interesting aspect of the German school system is that for all three types of secondary school, there is an orientation stage for two years. If a pupil is not performing well or enjoying their school, there is a provision for them to change to a different type of school at age 12.

At age 16, students in *Realschulen* and *Hauptschulen* transfer to one of six vocational training options which form the dual system. These are:

- *Fachhochschulen*;
- Full-time vocational schools (*Berufsfachschulen*);
- Specialist schools for nurses, midwives, etc.;

[9] *Economist*, back page, 27 September 2008. www.economist.com
[10] Source: Hippach-Schneider et al., 'Vocational Education and Training in Germany', p. 22.
[11] Source: Grund–und Strukurdaten 2007/2008, Bundesministerium für Bildung und Forschung, p. 25
[12] Hippach-Schneider et al., 'Vocational Education and Training in Germany'. Copies in English can be accessed at www.cedefop.europa.eu.

- Vocational extension schools;
- Dual system (in-company training and part-time vocational studies);
- Foundation vocational year.

Figure 5.1 shows the basic structure of German education.

   The dual system is by far the largest provider of education at upper secondary level. Fifty-three per cent of the age cohort train for a particular occupation, such as engineering. After completing their training in the dual system, the majority of students take up

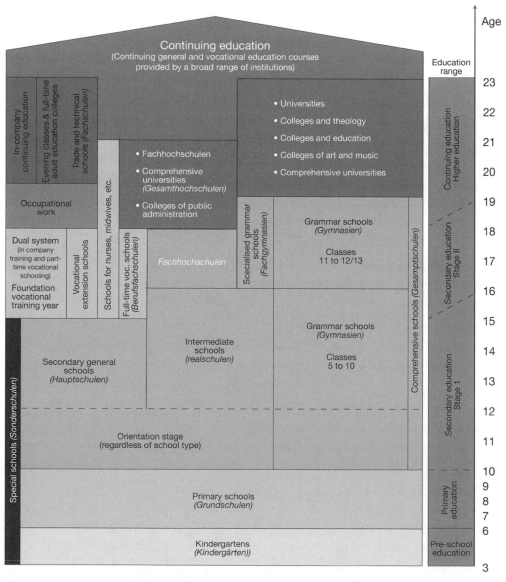

Figure 5.1 Typical structure of the education system in the Federal Republic of Germany

employment as a skilled worker, but are encouraged to take additional qualifications. Of the vocational schools, the full-time vocational schools have the highest number of students. These schools prepare students for an occupation or for vocational training in the dual system.

Figure 5.1 shows the crucial importance of dual training in Germany, with over half of the age cohort completing a course of vocational training in the dual system.

The system is described as dual because training takes place in two places of learning – companies and vocational schools. The entrepreneurs bear the costs of the in-company training, and pay the trainees remuneration which averages about one third of the starting pay for a trained skilled worker.

At age 18, German students can choose to continue their education in either one of the 117 universities or one of the 164 *Fachhochschulen*. Entitlement to study in *Fachhochschulen* is provided by a certification confirming the academic standard required for entry (*Fachhochschulreife*).

Another important part of the German vocational educational provision is the provision of continuing vocational education, including preparation for higher diplomas in subjects such as engineering or construction skills. As the chart above shows, there is a wide variety of continuing vocational educational training in Germany.

The new diploma initiative for England was announced initially in 2005 when the government decided not to accept the recommendation of Sir Mike Tomlinson for a single diploma covering academic and vocational subjects. It started in September 2008 with only 12,000 students and is intended to be a completely new type of school qualification for 14–19 year-olds which could in theory replace both the existing GCSE examinations at age 16, which currently English children are required to take, and the A-level examinations for 16 and 17 year-olds.

There are currently five diplomas on offer (Construction and the Built Environment; Creative and Media; Engineering; Information Technology and Society, Health and Development), and a further nine are being developed for September 2009 (Hair and Beauty; Hospitality; Business, Administration and Finance; Environmental and Land-based Studies; Manufacturing and Product Design; Public Services; Retail; Sport and Leisure; Travel and Tourism). Most of the planned diplomas are vocational, but they have latterly been expanded to include three academic subjects – Modern Languages, Humanities and Science. These additional diplomas, to be available from September 2011, will incorporate the best of the existing GCSE and A-level qualifications along with new content specially developed by groups of leading academics and employers.

The government's plan is for the diplomas to provide pupils with a broader education, more focused on the skills needed by business and industry, while still meeting the needs of higher education. As well as the specific subject of the diploma, pupils will develop maths, English and IT skills appropriate to each of the three levels of the diploma.[13] Each diploma will have pathways to accommodate a wide range of aspirations, so that they will appeal to young people preparing for the most demanding university courses, as well as those planning to enter the workforce directly from their diploma studies. It will be possible to move from the practical to the academic and vice versa, so they will also accommodate those who are unsure in which direction they wish to progress. They will combine an in-depth theoretical knowledge of the subject area with practical skills.

[13] Source: DCFS 14–19 website at www.dcsf.gov.uk/14–19/

In addition, pupils will develop a framework of skills to equip them for successful employment and lifelong learning, such as how to participate effectively and appropriately, how to think creatively, and how to manage their own independent learning.

The Sector Skills Councils are leading the design of the diplomas. In addition, Diploma Development Partnerships have been set up with representation from employers, higher education, schools, colleges, professional bodies and awarding bodies, to design the diplomas to ensure they meet the needs of all stakeholders. For example, the University of Cambridge has been closely involved with the development of the Diploma in Engineering and Dr Geoff Parks, director of admissions for the Cambridge colleges, welcomes it as a better preparation for the mathematical aspects of a university engineering course than the current maths A-levels. (N.B.: Marshalls in Cambridge is proposing to sponsor an engineering academy with the university's Department of Engineering with a view to supplying the local economy with technicians.)

The diploma in Business, Finance and Administration, starting in 2009, is being developed by the Financial Services Skills Council in conjunction with the Council for Administration and Skillsmart Retail Limited.

The diplomas have the following equivalence:[14]

Advanced diploma (top marks)	more than 3 A-levels
Progression diploma	2 A-levels
Higher level diploma	7 GCSE grades A★–C
Foundation level diploma	5 GCSE grades A★–C
	(source: DCSF)

Concurrent with the introduction of the new national diplomas, the British government announced in 2007 its plan to raise the age of compulsory education or training from the current 16 years to 18 years of age by 2015.

Reaction to the proposals has been mixed, especially the additional announcement in October 2007 of additional diplomas in languages, humanities and science. Richard Lambert, director general of the Confederation of British Industry, has criticised the additional diplomas in languages, humanities and science as an 'unnecessary distraction'.[15] The academic subjects are clearly a departure from the original announcement of fourteen work-based diplomas.

As the respected former BBC education editor Mike Baker said in his BBC Education Online statement of 2 July 2008, 'the fundamental issue was to clarify just what sort of award a diploma is meant to be'.[16] Are they primarily intended to introduce new high-status vocational awards as the Germans have, or are they intended to replace both GCSEs and A-levels?

As former government adviser Conor Ryan put it:

> The Government is in severe danger of losing the essence of diplomas in its confusion about their purpose. Diplomas were originally intended to provide robust vocational

---

[14] See: www.dcsf.gov.uk/14–19/index.cfm?go = site.home&sid = 3&pid = 224&lid = 456&ctype = Text&ptype = Single
[15] 'Bosses Cool on Academic Diplomas', BBC News Online, 23 June 2008.
[16] 'Should Employers Doubt Diplomas?' BBC News Online, 2 July 2008.

and applied qualifications in key economic sectors as a choice for students alongside GCSEs, A-levels, apprenticeships and the International Baccalaureate. Instead, they have been turned into a difficult hybrid which makes sense in some subjects, like IT and engineering, but not in others, especially those that may prove more attractive to the young people the Government wants to see staying in education or training until 18, where a more practical focus is essential.

In the autumn of 2007, the Secretary of State, Ed Balls started hinting that the Diplomas might replace all other examinations including the A-level by 2013, though he wisely insisted that students would decide. Diplomas in science, humanities and languages were added to the mix. Shortly afterwards – completely missing the point – the Government decided to abandon a modest funding for schools and colleges that wanted to prepare for the IB (which requires a mix of disciplines in 6 subjects, unlike Diplomas), although all the signs are that more schools are likely to adopt the IB regardless. But the Government failed to address the biggest problem with Diplomas; a lack of clarity about their purpose. The result is that only 12,000 students – only about a third of the Government's target – started diplomas in their first year in 2008. Colleges and employers remain anxious that the practical element so crucial to the new qualifications is being eroded by an obsession with promoting a generic brand rather than each Diploma on its specialist merit. So, it is good that the CBI – which is a firm supporter of the principle behind Diplomas as originally envisaged by Tony Blair has expressed its concerns. Any other supporters of Diplomas who want them to succeed should speak up now before it is too late to get them back on track.[17]

Quite reasonably, head teachers are being cautious in their support for the new diplomas. They would like to see how the first students taking the diplomas cope with the new awards. They are also asking the question of whether more schools will be allowed to add post-16 provision in order to avoid their pupils having to switch to another school or an FE college at age 16 in the middle of the new award.

Clearly, the original intention of new high-quality vocational diplomas is a worthy cause which should be supported, as we must increase the proportion of our 16 and 17 year-olds in full-time education or training. But as the German example shows, this does not require the abolition or sidelining of existing high-status academic awards such as the International Baccalaureate or A-levels, whose primary purpose is to serve as a university entrance qualification.

As well as allowing more existing schools to add post-16 provision to support the new diplomas and to encourage more students to remain in full-time education at age 16, a substantial number of the proposed new academies should be established as 14–19 academies, specialising in one or more of the diplomas. There are a number of exciting proposals to do this.

Clearly, most 14 year-olds will have already decided if they want to pursue an academic stream by taking A-levels and going to university or to choose instead vocational training. It is to be hoped that a number of sponsors will support the establishment of 14–19 academies specialising in such fully rounded skill areas as construction skills and engineering.

[17] Conor's Commentary blog, 23 June 2008, at www.conorfryan.blogspot.com

And, drawing upon the successful German experience, it is vitally important that the new diplomas increase the proportion of time in training provided by an employer and thus replicate the successful German dual system.

Suggested further reading

Ute Hippach-Schneider, Martina Krause and Christian Woll, 'Vocational Education and Training in Germany', CEDEFOP Panorama Series 138, Luxembourg: Office for Official Publications of the European Community, 2007. Copies in English can be accessed at www.cedefop.europa.eu

Chapter 6

How to improve low-attaining schools

In early June 2008, the Secretary of State for Children, Schools and Families, Ed Balls, announced that up to 270 of the poorest performing schools in England would be closed if they did not improve, and replaced either with an academy or be partnered with a high-performing school in a new trust.[1] At the same time, a list of 638 schools was published whose 15 year-olds in 2007 did not achieve at least 30 per cent 5+ A★–C grades at GCSE including maths and English.

The secretary of state said local authorities should lead the drive to improve low-attaining schools, but where they failed, he would step in and order the schools be closed by 2011 or within three years should they fail to take 'radical action'. Legally, the Schools Commissioner, currently Sir Bruce Liddington, acting on behalf of the secretary of state, has the right to institute proceedings to close a failing school. So far this authority has not been used by the government.

There are about 600,000 children aged 11–15 attending the 638 schools which in 2007 did not reach the 30 per cent target. This is about 20 per cent of the 3 million 11–15 year-olds attending state-funded English secondary schools – there are 600,000 children in each age cohort attending all state schools, with a further 50,000 attending independent schools.[2]

Social justice clearly demands that steps should be taken to improve genuinely low-attaining schools. All children in England, one of the most prosperous countries in the world, should be entitled to attend a good school. The author has been highlighting this issue in his own speeches and publications ever since he was first appointed a special adviser to Kenneth Baker (now Lord Baker of Dorking), who was the education secretary in 1987, a post he held with nine subsequent education secretaries until 2007. But as we saw in Chapter 1, it is not just raw examination results which make a good school. A detailed new analysis of the performance of each of the 638 schools which in 2007 did not reach the required 30 per cent 5+ A★–C passes at GCSE including maths and English was prepared for this book.[3] Using the Jesson Value Added approach, 81 of the 638 schools had a value added of at least 5 per cent. In other words, taking into account the intake of ability of these schools, at least 81 of them are getting results which are 5 per cent better than their intakes of ability would predict.

---

[1] Patrick Wintour and Polly Curtis, 'I Will Close up to 270 Failing Schools to Improve Standards, Says Minister', *Guardian*, 10 June 2008.
[2] Source: Department for Children, Schools and Families, www.dcsf.gov.uk/nationalchallenge
[3] See Appendices 3 and 4 for sample calculations using this approach for a number of schools.

For example, Grange School in Oldham, where 99 per cent of its pupils are from Asian-origin families, many of whom do not speak English at home, and 64 per cent of whom are eligible for free school meals, is on the list of 638 schools because only 20 per cent of its pupils achieved 5+ A*–C grades at GCSE including maths and English in 2007. This has already improved in 2008 to 26 per cent.

But this is a significant achievement given that the average Key stage 2 point score for the pupils entering the school in 2002 was only 23.8 compared to the national average of 27.0 points. This school's intake score, in similar schools, produces an outcome of just 9 per cent of the pupils achieving 5+ A*–C grades including maths and English. At Grange School, however, their pupils achieved 20 per cent – more than double what might have been 'expected', and representing a 'value-added' of 11 per cent. The school also achieved well on the 5+ A*–C (overall) measure – achieving 65 per cent in 2007 compared with similar schools' level of 32 per cent. (In 2008 the school increased its performance on both of these measures to 26 per cent on the first and 71 per cent on the second.)

Clearly, the Grange is not a failing school, though it may need to improve its English and maths performance even further.[4]

The Jesson review of the 638 schools also used another key criterion for a good school – the rate of improvement in GCSE results. Given that the national average improvement between 2004 and 2007 was 3.4 points,[5] it is reasonable to assume that if a school has improved its results by at least five percentage points including English and maths over the same period, it is making significant progress. By this token, 240 schools of the 638 are improving their results significantly and should not be regarded as failing. Appendices 3 and 4 show how the Jesson approach to reviewing the performance of the 638 schools works with both schools doing well and those that according to the approach are genuinely low-attaining.

The Manchester Academy, which has 51 per cent of its pupils eligible for free school meals, has improved its proportion of pupils gaining five good grades from only 6 per cent in 2004 to 21 per cent in 2007. On an individual English and maths basis, they do better still, with 40 per cent achieving at least a C in maths and 36 per cent doing so in English. But it is because the proportion of pupils achieving at least a C in both English and maths is only 21 per cent that the school is placed on the list of the 638 low-attaining schools. Again, the Manchester Academy is not a failing school.[6]

If we were to add the number of schools achieving a value added score of 5 per cent or better with those that have improved their proportion of pupils getting five good grades by more than five percentage points over three years, we get a total of 301 schools (some of which succeed in both categories). This would indicate that the real number of *genuinely* low-attaining schools in 2007 was 337, not 638. Moreover, provisional results for 2008 show that a total of 260 of the 638 at-risk schools, including sixteen academies, have now reached the 30 per cent threshold. However, there are nearly 100 schools which were not on the 2007 list[7] but whose performance in 2008 dropped them below the 30 per cent figure. Therefore the new figure of schools who did not achieve the threshold of 30 per cent in 2008 is likely to be 475, much lower than the 638 figure.

[4] Source: personal communication with Graeme Hollinshead, head teacher, Grange School.
[5] DCSF Statistical First Release 2008/01, 9 January 2008.
[6] Personal communication with the head teacher Mrs K. M. August.
[7] www.dcsf.gov.uk/performancetables/

It is my belief that the 301 schools on such a clear road to improvement should not be included on any list of failing schools And it is unfortunate that many newspapers and commentators described all the 638 schools as 'failing' rather than 'low-attaining', the more accurate description used by ministers and officials.

If a school is trying its best to improve, it is clearly discouraging to be labelled as failing. Nevertheless, even if we remove the 301 improving schools, we were still left in 2007 with 337 genuinely low-attaining schools responsible for the education of 350,000 children attending them. The 2008 results might well lower these figures even further.

Before considering measures to help these schools, we must first agree on the causes of this low attainment. I believe these can be broken down into five major factors:

The first and probably the most important reason is that their pupils had performed below par in primary school, as measured by the average Key stage 2 point score. The average ability of the intake at 11 was significantly below average. Indeed, 90 of the 638 schools are secondary moderns in local authorities which still have selective systems, including Kent and Lincolnshire.

The average Key stage 2 point score of the pupils attending the 638 low-attaining schools was only 25 points. Nationally, the 600,000 children entering comprehensive or modern schools in 2002 had an average score of 27 points.[8] Five years later, 46 per cent of these 600,000 pupils achieved five good GCSEs, including maths and English. The 638 schools only achieved 23 per cent, whereas the Jesson predicted achievement was 27 per cent. While they underperformed by four points, most of the performance differential with the national average reflected their lower ability intake.

The second reason is poverty: most of the pupils attending the 638 low-attaining schools come from socially disadvantaged families. Their average eligibility for free school meals in 2007 was 27 per cent compared to the national average of only 15 per cent.[9] Now, of course, there are many children who are eligible for free school meals who do well at school, but poverty has a statistical association with low achievement.

The third reason is the quality of their leadership. There are some outstanding head teachers whose schools appear on the list of 638 low-attaining schools – many of those who are engineering the improvements described above fall into this category – but, sadly, many of the lowest-attaining have weak head teachers and poor governing bodies, and are located in areas with poor local authorities.

Fourth, many of the 638 schools also have more than their share of children with emotional, behavioural and social difficulties (EBSD), who have often been excluded from other schools, as well as a high number of children in care. Nationally, there are only 60,000 children in care, an average of just under three pupils in each primary or secondary school. But some schools on the 638 list will have as many as twenty children in care as well as an unfairly large number of pupils excluded from other schools. All schools should be encouraged to take their fair share of difficult pupils through a top-up payment of around £5,000 per pupil for those given EBSD status. This would cost much less than sending such children to special residential referral units, where the costs can be over £100,000 per pupil per year.[10]

---

[8] Ibid.
[9] Ibid.
[10] Source: Department for Children, Schools and Families.

Fifth, many of the schools have been neglected over the years through poor maintenance and occupy run-down facilities.

All these factors, combined with a lack of popularity among aspirant families, as indicated by the limited number of first-choice applications they receive from prospective parents, make it difficult for a significant proportion of the 638 to reach the 30 per cent target. What can be done to help these schools to raise their standards?

It is not just about money. Their per capita funding is among the highest in the country and more funds are being made available to help. Nor can most of the 337 be turned around just by improvements in teaching the basics.

More radical action is needed. I support the view that most of these 337 schools should be closed, with as many as possible being converted to academy status.[11] For those limited number of schools where it is not possible to convert to academy status, they should be partnered by a high-performing school in a trust.

Trust schools are non-profit educational charities with a central board of trustees who have responsibility for the overall reference of their group of schools, including the appointment of a chief executive, the independent head teachers, approval and budgets of capital expenditure and the appointment of governing bodies for each school. They are similar to federations, which predated them.

The model requires the ability to set up a single trust to cover a number of schools, with each school naming its own head teacher and governors; the ability to appoint a chief executive of high calibre; the freedom to take the actions necessary to raise standards, including, if necessary, terminating the contracts of weak staff. Crucially, the trust structure is permanent, and accountable to the Department for Children, Schools and Families for results.

There are some case studies later in this chapter on the successful use of federations and partnerships, including a detailed description of how Brooke Weston CTC has joined with the former Corby Community College to form a federation of two academies. Another good example is the Ninestiles Federation in Birmingham, led by Sir Dexter Hutt.

The Ninestiles Federation began in February 2001 with Ninestiles School taking over responsibility for the improvement of Waverley School, another Birmingham school which faced being placed in Special Measures – or failed – by OfSTED inspectors. During two contracts over four and a half years, Waverley's proportion of pupils gaining five good GCSE grades (in any subject) improved from 16 per cent to 75 per cent. Waverley was the most improved school in Birmingham in 2003 and the third most improved nationally in 2005. By 2006, its proportion of pupils gaining five good GCSEs including English and maths had risen in two years from 15 to 27 per cent (though there was a dip in 2007).[12]

In September 2003, the International School in Birmingham and Community College, in East Birmingham, was also facing Special Measures, when it joined the Ninestiles Federation on a three year contract. Results at the end of the first year of federation increased from 9 per cent in 2003 to 34 per cent in 2004, making the school the most improved in Birmingham in 2004. In 2006, as the contract ended, the five-GCSE pass rate was 51 per cent; and the proportion including English and maths rose from 10 per cent to 24 per cent between 2004 and 2007. Central Technology College, in Gloucester,

---

[11] See Chapter 7 for an analysis of the success academies have had in raising standards in low-attaining schools.

[12] Personal communication with Sir Dexter Hutt, executive head of the Ninestiles Federation.

destined for closure in the summer of 2006 as it faced being failed by OfSTED, was reprieved when it joined the Ninestiles Federation.[13]

Ninestiles, as the lead school, has itself progressed during the federation, with the proportion of pupils gaining five good GCSEs, including English and maths, up from 31 per cent in 2003 to 49 per cent in 2007 (78 per cent get five good GCSEs in any subject). This is important, to reassure the lead school's own governors that their own progress is enhanced rather than impeded by helping partner schools.

Sir Dexter Hutt has this advice for head teachers considering setting up a new trust or federation made up of a high-performing school with low-performing partner school:[14]

- The trust must provide enhanced leadership capacity and enable schools to take the bold decisions which need to be taken.
- Trusts should also enable the resources of the lead school to be deployed to support the partner school – for this to be meaningful, the lead school has to build in additional capacity, so that teachers are available to work intensively with teachers in the partner school. This necessitates additional staffing in the lead schools and this has to be paid for.
- The executive head should not try to be the head of both schools – it is a complete nonsense to regard the head of the partner school as a 'site manager'. The head of the partner school has to have above average headship skills to lead and manage the rapid changes that are necessary for school improvement. In Dexter's case, as his federation expanded, he could not do justice to both the role of head of Ninestiles and meet federation commitments, so Ninestiles now has its own head teacher and Dexter has overall responsibility for the progress of all schools in the federation. One of his personal criteria for success is not to be regarded as 'head' of any of the schools. His 'co-construct' strategy with the head of each school and the federation is only justified if each school makes more rapid progress than would otherwise be the case.

Unfortunately, many find it hard to think past the traditional standalone role of the head that they are familiar with. This leads them to assume that the head within a federation of schools cannot be a proper head, but is more of a site manager, with the implicit assumption that the executive head must be a 'super head' and the 'real' head of all the schools within the federation.

Dexter believes that anyone who has tried this site manager model soon realises its limitations, but the notion is one that many find hard to lose. Perhaps we ought to pay more attention to the Royal Navy, where no one would question that each ship within a fleet has – and needs to have – its own captain. At the same time, the fleet is line-managed not by a 'super captain' but by an admiral. This does not diminish each captain, but it does result in an organisational structure that facilitates collaboration, and results in powerful progress. Its organisational structure underpinned Britain's naval success in the nineteenth century. Admiral Nelson may have been called the victor of the Battle of Trafalgar, but the captains of his ships deserve equal credit. Trust structure is the educational equivalent of the leadership of Nelson's fleet. Might it help us achieve educational success in the twenty-first century?

The trust structure doesn't just benefit school leaders, it benefits teachers, parents, students and the system as a whole.

---

[13] Ibid.
[14] Ibid.

This is apparent in the extraordinary achievement of the Haberdashers' Trust, set up in Lewisham, which in just two years transformed the previously failing Mallory School in Lewisham. Mallory became part of a joint academy with the highly successful Haberdashers' Aske's City Technology College in Hatcham, in September 2005, acquiring a new name in the process, The Haberdashers' Aske's Knights Academy.

The Haberdashers set up a new trust to supervise the two schools. The outstanding head teacher of the Haberdashers' CTC, Dr Elizabeth Sidwell, was appointed chief executive of the two schools with individual heads appointed to each school. The deputy head of the CTC became the head of the new Knights Academy. All the existing Mallory pupils transferred to Knights, as did most of the staff.

The Haberdashers' leadership made it a deliberate goal of its new partnership to replicate the successful Haberdasher focus on stretching pupils to the maximum of their potential in the new school. Funding was made available for all of the pupils to acquire the smart navy blue blazer, white shirts and ties of the Haberdashers' Hatcham School. When I visited the school in July 2006, I found that many characteristics of a good school had been achieved in a remarkably short time: order and discipline with a high level of attendance; the school opens at 7.30 a.m. with breakfast available, and stays open until 6 p.m.; there is a very good programme of extracurricular activities in the afternoon, including sports; there is a huge emphasis on acquiring literacy and numeracy skills.

And the results showed an equally rapid improvement. In just three years, the proportion of pupils gaining five good GCSE grades in any subject went from just 8 per cent in 2005, to 52 per cent in 2008. Including English and maths, there was an improvement from 14 per cent in 2006 to 19 per cent in 2008. Parents started to vote with their feet. In the last year of the previous school there were almost no first-choice preferences for the school – now the school is 50 per cent *oversubscribed*; parents are actively involved in the school where before there was little such involvement; the proportion of pupils with free school meals remains very high at 53 per cent; but only two pupils were excluded during the past year; attendance has improved from around 60 per cent to 95 per cent. This is a remarkable achievement which is being replicated by other similar trusts.[15]

This approach – high achiever helping a low attainer in a trust structure – could be particularly useful in selective areas, enabling partnerships between the 164 high-performing selective grammar schools with low-attaining local modern schools. There are already examples of such partnerships. The Ripon Grammar School[16] has partnered the former secondary modern Ripon College, which specialises in technology. Forty-four per cent of pupils at Ripon College achieved five good GCSEs including maths and English in 2007, giving the school a Jesson Value Added score of plus 13 per cent. The schools now even have a joint sixth form.[17]

Interestingly, the partnership was formed during the only ballot to be held on the future of a grammar school, where parents at feeder schools voted 2–1 against its closure. Perhaps either the present or a future government should promise to safeguard the future of all the grammar schools (by removing the possibility of a local ballot to change their admissions procedure) which enter into trusts with nearby low-attaining schools.

---

[15] Source: personal communication with the chief executive principal of the Haberdashers' Federation, Dr Elizabeth Sidwell.
[16] www.ripongrammar.co.uk/
[17] Personal communication with head teacher Barry Found.

Federations and partnerships

Partnerships between successful and less successful schools are clearly one way of addressing the issue of raising standards. Many of the original fifteen city technology colleges, most of which are now academies, have formed such partnerships to try to replicate their success in a lower-achieving school. These partnerships can take different forms.

Thomas Telford School has sponsored two academies in Walsall and Sandwell in partnership with its sponsor, the Mercers' Company. It has also sponsored the nearby Madeley Academy, with which it was formerly federated. These schools, all led by former vice principals at Telford, have adopted key elements of the 'Telford model', although they are not actually in a federation.

Emmanuel CTC has sponsored two academies, one in Middlesbrough and one in Doncaster, to form the Emmanuel Foundation. Dixons Academy in Bradford has a three-year improvement partnership with Wyke Manor School. John Cabot Academy in Bristol has a partnership with the Bristol Brunel Academy, formerly Speedwell School. David Carter, former principal at John Cabot CTC, is executive principal of the two schools with overall responsibility for both, although both schools also have their own principal. Other former CTCs with similar plans include the BRIT School, Bacons College and ADT College.

Examples of federations include the Haberdashers' Federation, described above, and Harris Federation.

In the case of the Harris, now eight academies in South London, all sponsored by Lord Harris of Peckham, have come together in a federation. The federation has a chief executive officer, Dr Dan Moynihan, former principal of the very successful Harris CTC, now the Harris Crystal Palace Academy. There are principals in each school and a local governing body for each. There is also a federation main board, chaired by Lord Harris, which sets central policies, provides some central services and rolls out the Harris 'brand' so successfully established at Harris CTC. I have the privilege of serving on the board of trustees of this federation. Its success in raising standards is quite extraordinary. Below in Table 6.1 are the GCSE results for the six Harris academies for the past three years – the results for 2008 are provisional.

There are many different models of partnership and federation, of which these are just a few examples. The next case study, written by Christine Walter, will look in more detail at one that started in September 2008.

Case study: Brooke Weston and the Corby Business Academy – siblings, not clones, by Christine Walter[18]

In September 2008 Brooke Weston CTC became an academy and Corby Business Academy opened, replacing Corby Community College. Both come under the umbrella of the Brooke Weston Partnership (BWP), led by Peter Simpson, former principal of Brooke Weston. Peter Simpson is aware of other federations and partnerships around the country and says he has learned from them, but BWP has its own individual approach.

---

[18] Statistics obtained from information published by OfSTED and the Department for Children, Schools and Families. Information obtained from conversations with Peter Simpson, executive head of the Brooke Weston Partnership. The case study has been approved by the head teacher.

Table 6.1 Provisional examination results

% pupils with	Bermondsey		Crystal Palace		Harris Girls'		Merton		Peckham		South Norwood	
	5+ IA★–C	5+ IA★–C Incl. En/ma	5+ IA★–C	5+ IA★–C Incl. En/ma	5+ IA★–C	5+ IA★–C Incl. En/ma	5+ IA★–C	5+ IA★–C Incl. En/ma	5+ IA★–C	5+ IA★–C Incl. En/ma	5+ IA★–C	5+ IA★–C Incl. En/ma
Result 2006	47	26	88	75	39	32	29	23	30	23	38	23
Result 2007	58	32	91	80	39	31	40	28	39	24	29	20
Result 2008	56	41	93	80.36	52	41	74	38	45	28.4	57	30

Brooke Weston Academy is sponsored by the Garfield Weston Foundation and the de Capell Brooke family. Both sponsors are key players in the partnership. Brooke Weston is one of the five highest-achieving state comprehensives in England. In 2007, 86 per cent of its pupils gained five good GCSEs, including English and maths, and all gained five good GCSEs in any subject, as has been the case for many years. Jesson Value Added gave the school a positive rating of +7 in 2007. OfSTED's 2006 inspection rated the school 'outstanding' on all measures. The report spoke of an 'outstandingly successful college' with 'outstanding leadership [by] the principal', a 'distinctive ethos', 'outstanding curriculum' and 'can do attitude'. The inspectors also praised the 'outstanding quality of the relationships between students themselves and with staff'.

Corby Community College, by contrast, has a more chequered history. It was formed in September 2000 under the Fresh Start initiative, whereby failing schools were closed and reopened with a new name and leadership, from two failing schools. Though it has seen some improvements in the past eight years, achievement has remained very low. In 2007, 19 per cent of students gained five good GCSEs in any subject and only 8 per cent including English and maths.[19]

The partnership certainly enjoyed a long planning period, with discussions starting back in 2002. But in September 2008, as the new academy opened, it did so with all the Corby Community College students and around 60 per cent of its staff. So, how will this partnership work?

Peter Simpson sees the schools as siblings rather than clones. Unlike some other federations he does not use the 'brand' analogy. He sees the two schools more as members of a family with individual identities, but shared values. He talks of a 'transfer of philosophy' and a 'transfer of operational matters'. The central philosophy being transferred from Brooke Weston to Corby is that 'the student [is] at the heart of everything'.[20]

Peter gives practical examples of how this is translated into action. Many children lack good role models at home so they need as much contact with staff as possible. Therefore, there is no staff room at Brooke Weston or Corby. He also rejects the concept of staff being 'on duty' and supervising children during breaks. Instead he goes for 'passive supervision' – adults are always present, there are no dark corners in which children can misbehave, so children should always feel safe and secure.

How are the principal and staff of the new Corby Business Academy going about raising standards? The new principal, Dr Andrew Campbell, who was formerly a vice principal at Brooke Weston, was already in post for a year before the new academy opened. This year of preparation time was crucial for appointing staff, developing policies, meeting students and overseeing the new building. He and Peter Simpson undertook a realistic assessment of each individual student's current level of attainment and potential. This was an important starting point – there is no room for over-optimistic illusions.

Under the new regime there are high levels of accountability. Performance management systems have been put in place and a clear message given to staff that they are going to be held accountable for performance. There are high expectations of staff and students. During the lead-in year the principal interviewed all the Year 10 pupils, the new school's Year 11s, to talk about expectations, and he will see them several times more during the first year of the new school. The students have a new school uniform

---

[19] Statistics from DCSF performance tables and verified by the head teacher, Peter Simpson.
[20] Quotations from an interview with head teacher Peter Simpson by Christine Walter.

with a smart blazer as part of a programme of raising esteem. This is starting to engender a feeling that things have changed and someone cares; but also that someone is watching and they expect great things.

How long will it take for this approach to feed through into results? Peter Simpson says that the Fischer Family Trust[21] data would indicate only modest results in this first year, with fewer than 30 per cent of pupils gaining five good GCSEs. However, Brooke Weston has had enormous success with lower-ability children. His official target for 2009 is for 33 per cent to achieve five good GCSEs and he hopes to meet the national target of 30 per cent including English and maths. Privately he hopes to do even better. In five years' time he hopes that at least 60 per cent of the students at Corby Business Academy will be gaining five good GCSEs including English and maths.

So, how will the partnership itself work? Each school will have its own principal, Campbell at Corby and Trish Stringer at Brooke Weston. Simpson, as the executive principal, sees himself as the 'glue', which holds it all together. He will take a lot of pressure off the principals by handling all the finance and information technology at partnership level. Other functions such as grounds maintenance will be added in due course and joint professional development activities will be developed. There will be two separate governing bodies under a single trust.

Is there the danger of a negative effect on the highly successful Brooke Weston School? Peter Simpson says that he and Stringer are very conscious of this and are determined to maintain the school's high standards. But they know that it is crucial that the new partnership does not become a drain on Brooke Weston and that the ex-CTC does not stall. It may be difficult to improve on its last OfSTED report, but the school still has improvement targets such as increasing the percentage of A* and A grades achieved at GCSE and these must be met. It also has its own challenges as an institution, such as a £4 million building programme and conversion to academy status, which involves new admission arrangements.

Peter Simpson is optimistic that Brooke Weston will not only continue to thrive, but will benefit from the partnership. He says that Brooke Weston's conversion to academy status was made easer because of the experience of developing Corby Business Academy, and while Corby has benefited from Brooke Weston's graphic design, IT and financial expertise, the 'thin client solution' developed by the IT people for Corby has been a benefit for Brooke Weston. So, the benefits go both ways. The greatest benefit of all is the combined strength of the two senior teams being available to each school, providing an unrivalled pool of expertise. The next stage will be for the partnership to move on to curriculum matters and look at things like joint music and drama productions.

The website of the Brooke Weston Partnership[22] summarises the benefits in the following way

For the students in the schools

- A principal more able to concentrate on the core business of teaching and learning with other activities managed centrally;
- Access to a range of 14–19 courses across the group of schools.

[21] Fischertrust.org
[22] www.brookeweston.org; by kind permission of Peter Simpson, executive head teacher of Brooke Weston Partnership.

For the principals

- Managed induction and mentoring of the new principal in any of the group's schools;
- Immediate reference to an experienced principal for advice, support and guidance;
- Empathetic support from other principals in the group;
- An experienced principal available to handle crises, relationships with the press and local politics;
- Some managerial functions being taken over by central or group services;
- Promotion possibilities within the group and elsewhere as this model becomes more widespread.

For the senior management teams

- The opportunity to work across a number of schools;
- The opportunity to be influential in the development of new schools;
- The opportunity to participate in the development of a new management model.

For the governors

- An executive principal who is able to act as an objective evaluator of a school's performance for governors;
- An executive principal who is able to act as an objective evaluator of the principal's performance;
- An executive principal who is an active promoter of the group's ethos acting to ensure that the climate in each school is in line with expectations;
- An executive principal who is an insurance in case of the illness or underperformance of the principal.

For each school

- Access to the expertise of staff in the whole group;
- Economies in the appointment of staff, especially non-teaching senior professionals who may be shared between the schools;
- Provision of shared services, e.g. catering, grounds maintenance, financial management, etc.;
- Increased opportunities for staff across the group of schools for training and for promotion;
- Opportunities for sharing expertise, e.g. in vocational education or data management;
- Increased opportunities for disaffected students to have a fresh start within the group.

For sponsors

- A person available to manage any proposed expansion of the family of schools;
- A single reference point for the group's performance;
- A person able to act so as to ensure that the sponsors' interests are represented at all times.

Peter Simpson is a strong believer in this approach. Brooke Weston is hoping to add further schools, both primary and secondary, to the partnership. It will be fascinating to watch their progress

Case study: Phoenix High School, by Christine Walter[23]

When William Atkinson (now Sir William Atkinson) joined Phoenix High School in the London Borough of Hammersmith and Fulham in 1995, he was already an experienced head teacher, having held two former headships. This experience was extremely fortunate as he took on a school named as one of the eight most challenging schools in England. He admits today that the size of the task proved to be greater than even he had initially imagined.

The pattern of social deprivation of the school's pupils, from the surrounding White City area, was complex, with fifty nationalities in the school, forty-seven languages spoken and 40 per cent of pupils speaking English as an additional language. Fifty-five per cent of pupils were eligible for free school meals and 60 per cent were on the SEN register. Prior attainment of pupils on entering Year 7 was extremely low and at GCSE only 5 per cent achieved five good GCSEs. The school was, not surprisingly, in Special Measures.

Today Sir William Atkinson reflects that the school was basically in turmoil. There was a 30–35 per cent turnover of pupils each year and a similar percentage turnover for staff. A significant number of staff were supply teachers or on short-term contracts. Staff morale was very low and many turned to their unions for support. The local community had lost faith in the school, with only forty pupils in Year 7 naming it as their first preference.

William Atkinson quickly realised that the task was much more complex than simply laying down the law and establishing discipline, important though that was. He had to tackle the causes of ill discipline, which were basically that the fundamentals of what makes up a properly functioning school were not in place. He had to move things on so that Phoenix High School looked like a proper school, with teachers who behaved like teachers, an environment fit for learning, parents with confidence in its ability to deliver and children with self-belief and a focus on learning.

He was appointed to start in the summer term of 1995. He was the fifth head in two years. The school looked like a war zone, so during the Easter holidays he arranged for the whole interior to be painted to cover the graffiti, for the broken windows to be replaced, for the damaged furniture to be removed and for the playground, a health and safety hazard, to be re-laid. This two-week programme may remind some readers of the opening scenes of *Hope and Glory*, a BBC series based on Phoenix High School. When pupils arrived at the beginning of the summer term they found not only a new head and a newly named school, but also a new environment.

The head also met with parents very quickly. Around 100 attended a meeting. He found many were cynical – he was, after all, the fifth new head in two years – but he quickly established their priorities. They were: a stable staff; homework; a safe environment; fewer disruptive pupils (Phoenix had been accepting many excluded pupils from other schools) and fair treatment for their children. When he met the parents again, 6 weeks

[23] Statistics obtained from information published by OfSTED and the Department for Children, Schools and Families. Information obtained from and conversations with Sir William Atkinson, head teacher of the Phoenix School. The case study has been approved by the head teacher.

later, 200 attended the meeting. This time there was at least some mild satisfaction that progress was being made and that Phoenix was now looking more like a normal school.

The main priority for William Atkinson, however, had to be the staffing situation. Without a good and stable team there could be no proper provision for the pupils. Of course there were some good individual teachers, but you need a whole team or a 'full crew' as the head puts it. He uses an Olympian analogy. He says if you had a rowing crew of five including Sir Steve Redgrave and Sir Matthew Pinsent, but the other three were himself, the author of this case study (Christine Walter) and Sir Cyril Taylor, we would not win the gold medal!

Recruiting and keeping good staff remained a huge priority and a huge difficulty for many years. It was not helped by the school's position in the league tables and the overall teacher shortages in the late 1990s. In 2000 an incentive payment of £2,800 was introduced for existing staff who stayed in post and for new staff who stayed for three years. Gradually the recruitment position improved and staff turnover was reduced.

Other strategies for staff included: a requirement to plan lessons; a requirement to hand in lesson proformas and a requirement to submit to lesson observations

These staff requirements led to a threatened walkout by the NUT, but using ACAS to mediate, William Atkinson pushed ahead with his plans. Building a strong and stable team of staff with a shared vision was crucial to moving Phoenix High School forward. It took time, but the head now says he has a 'committed' team.

Strategies for pupils included: a rewards system for good behaviour and results; a reporting system with incident sheets; highly visible staff, with walkie-talkies, around the school premises; peer counselling; pupils being asked to repeat a year following bad performance; and effective work with parents and carers.

Basically William Atkinson set about imposing a new culture of high expectation among both staff and pupils in the school. A new partnership was forged with parents; something he believes was helped by his own Afro-Caribbean origins. Social deprivation was no longer to be an excuse for academic failure. A more stable staff meant more staff development opportunities could be put in place. Teaching and learning improved and so more success came for the children. In time the dominant culture became one of young people succeeding academically, rather than one of 'kids having a laugh'.

The improvement process took time. Relative calm and order came first (although issues around challenging behaviour did not disappear), but academic results took longer. The school established what has been described as a 'forensic approach' to targets, with annual goals for pupils and regular progress reports. In 1997 the school came out of Special Measures, but continued for a while with 'serious weaknesses'. By 2003 OfSTED called it 'improving' and 25 per cent of pupils achieved five good GCSEs. In 2005 the school achieved specialist science college status.

The school has also benefited from a range of national initiatives and projects. In addition to specialist science status these include: thirty interactive whiteboards in class-rooms; the redevelopment of the learning resource centre; a completely refurbished and re-equipped staff room; a technology block; a new swimming pool and fitness centre, and refurbished dining facilities for students.

A crucial local initiative was the Phoenix High School Regeneration Project, which came on-stream in 2001. Based on the White City area, this gave the school additional resources which they could use to employ additional non-teaching staff. These included: a person to handle primary/secondary school transition issues; a social worker to work with parents; a speech and language therapist and a full-time school counsellor. The employment of these people meant that teachers could concentrate on teaching and learning, knowing that other adults were dealing with wider issues. The resources also enabled the school to introduce a range of extra-curricular activities and Saturday morning sessions.

Today, in 2008, the transformation in Phoenix High School is quite extraordinary. The social deprivation still exists. 60 per cent of pupils are eligible for free school meals, over 60 per cent have special educational needs, many of which are behavioural, emotional or social in nature, over 70 per cent come from single parent families and there is an annual mobility rate of 25–30 per cent. Levels of prior learning on joining the school are significantly below national averages. So, the profile is little changed from 1995 and the challenges remain.

Yet, in 2007, 67 per cent of pupils achieved five good GCSEs, 43 per cent if you include English and maths. Results in 2008 look to be slightly higher. This is broadly similar to national levels, something OfSTED in its January 2008 inspection, called 'outstanding progress' given the exceptionally low starting point in Year 7 and high numbers joining after the start of Year 7. Under the value added measures prepared by David Jesson for the SSAT, the school scores +22. In other words, the expected level of five good GCSEs including English and maths, given normal progress, would have been 21 per cent.

OfSTED also paid tribute to pupils' behaviour – 'Students behave very well in lessons and around the school.' The report observed that science college status had played a very significant part in the school's dramatic improvement, with a comprehensive curriculum in science and targets constantly being exceeded. Students told inspectors that success in science boosted their confidence and improved their overall motivation, and the inspectors agreed.

Overall the school received a grade 1, 'outstanding' rating. The inspectors commented that

> The school is exceptionally well lead by a charismatic, indefatigable head teacher who receives excellent support and challenge from a fully committed governing body. Students speak warmly of the head teacher's aspirational outlook and view him as a powerful motivating force. They are right to do so. He is very ably supported by a cohesive senior leadership team who consistently deliver the school's vision.

The report concluded that

> The Phoenix is a remarkable school; it continues to transform the life chances of both students and their families. It can do this because the school operates from a deeply rooted understanding, and heartfelt appreciation of, the challenging circumstances that many of the students come from.

This is a long way, indeed, from the Special Measures of 1995.

So, where does the school go from here? Provision for post-16 education is certainly on the agenda, with the head wanting to establish a sixth form. The target date is 2010. Phoenix is a lead school for the ICT diploma. However, it is the concern that every pupil maximise his or her potential within a culturally diverse community which is key. Sir William would also be the first to say that success in schools should not only be measured by league tables, which can distort success, but by what children achieve as individuals. Individual success is celebrated at Phoenix. Motivating the pupils to succeed through education and hard work is key. The school believes in working with the entire young person – this is more than an institution solely geared to examination success.

Suggested further reading

Cyril Taylor, 'Turning Round School Achievement', Speech to the Federation on School Leadership, *The Times*, 21 September 2006.

Department for Children, Schools and Families, *Promoting Excellence for All*, London: DCSF, June 2008.

Chris Davies and Cheryl Lim, *Helping Schools to Succeed*, London: Policy Exchange, 2008.

Department for Children, Schools and Families, *National Challenge – A Toolkit for Schools and Local Education Authorities*, London: DCSF, 2008.

Chapter 7

Are academies a good thing?

Located mainly in socially disadvantaged areas, 'academies' are new types of non fee-paying independent state schools which will transform the educational prospects of many of our most disadvantaged young people.

The purpose of the government's Academies Programme is to help raise standards and aspirations in schools in challenging circumstances. There were 130 academies open in September 2008. The initial target was for 200 academies to be open or in the pipeline by 2010. In November 2006, Prime Minister Tony Blair announced an expansion of the programme to a total of 400 academies, which will represent more than 13 per cent of all state-funded secondary schools in England. The target may be increased as a result of the government's focus on raising standards in low-attaining schools.[1]

What are academies?

Academies were launched in 2002 as a development of the original and highly successful City Technology Colleges (CTCs) initiative. CTCs had been first launched in 1987, and there are fifteen of these ground-breaking schools, each backed by generous sponsors. They are ranked among the best schools in the country, with an average of 90 per cent of their pupils gaining five good GCSEs in 2008 (in any subject) or 69 per cent including English and maths.[2] This compares to only 62 per cent for all non-selective secondary schools (5 A*–C in all subjects) and only 48 per cent for 5 A*–C including maths and English. Not only are academies modelled closely on the original CTCs; most of the CTCs have now been converted to academy status.

Academies are independent, all-ability state schools supported by sponsors, both financially and professionally. They admit children of all abilities, following the National Admissions Code, and provide free education without fees being charged to parents. They are also specialist schools forming part of the wider specialist schools movement.

Some academies occupy buildings which are either newly built or remodelled existing buildings. Others open initially in their existing buildings. Annual recurrent funding is paid directly by the DCSF at the same per capita rate as for other similar maintained schools in the area. This averages over £6,000 per pupil.[3]

---

[1] www.dcsf.gov.uk/schoolscommissioner/academies.shtml
[2] Provisional GCSE 2008 results as reported by the city technology colleges
[3] Source: Department for Children, Schools and Families. www.dcsf.gov.uk/foischeme/subPage.cfm? action = collections.displayCollection&i_collectionID = 190

While academies are required to teach a broad and balanced curriculum, including core national curriculum subjects, they have additional freedoms and flexibility to use innovative approaches to leadership, governance, organisation, staffing and the curriculum. Each academy adopts a specialism, such as business and enterprise or modern foreign languages. Like other specialist schools, they may admit up to 10 per cent of their intake on the basis of aptitude in particular subjects. Many place a special emphasis on vocational courses.

Some academies are new schools in areas that need more school places, but most have replaced existing weak or underperforming schools. The 400 academies will mostly be situated in inner-city urban areas. Many of these schools currently occupy run-down, ill-maintained buildings. The circumstances in which these young people receive their education give them a very poor message about the importance which society places on their educational achievement and life prospects. Staff working in these schools face enormous challenges, often made worse by having to accept a large number of children excluded from other schools because, being an unpopular choice for many parents, they have spare places. All too often a spiral of decline sets in for these challenged schools. Social justice requires that radical action be taken to transform these institutions.

It is also in our country's best economic interests to act without delay. Many of the children attending our underperforming schools leave full-time education at 16 without the skills necessary to obtain gainful employment. Many will spend their lives on welfare benefits at great cost to the taxpayer. Others will drift into crime or become teenage mothers. To compete in the global economy, our nation needs a highly skilled workforce which is equipped to add value to goods and services if we are to meet the economic challenges coming from countries like China and India. So, the interests of the economy and social justice converge — as a nation we simply must ensure that we provide high-quality schools for the most challenged and challenging of our young people.

A major champion of academies has been Andrew Adonis, the schools minister responsible, until October 2008, for the academy programme. I worked closely with him when he was Prime Minister Tony Blair's adviser on education from 1998 until 2005, and when he was made a life peer and appointed minister for schools from 2005. Speaking to an audience of educators in 2008, Lord Adonis said:

> My vision is for academies to be in the vanguard of meritocracy for the next generation of children in the way grammar schools were for a proportion of the postwar generation — providing a ladder of opportunity, in particular for less advantaged children, to get on and to gain the very best education and qualifications, irrespective of wealth and family background, but without unfair selection at the age of 11.[4]

What is the record of the first thirty-six academies to open and which had GCSE-age cohorts in 2008?

Despite academies having only been open for two or three years, the thirty-six academies converted from low-attaining schools still averaged 53 per cent 5+ A★–C good grades at GCSE in 2008. This compares with only 22 per cent for their predecessor schools, an

---

[4] 'Academies and Social Mobility', speech by Lord Adonis to the Academies conference in London, 7 February 2008. Available at www.dcsf.gov.uk/speeches/search_dctail.cfm?ID = 749.

increase of thirty-one percentage points. Data for the last year of the predecessor school including maths and English is not available. However, since 2004, when the data became available, the proportion of pupils in academies achieving 5+ A*–C grades including maths and English has improved from 15 per cent to 29 per cent – a far faster increase of 14 per cent than the national average increase, which is only eight percentage points.[5]

Perhaps even more significant is the popularity of academies with parents. Every single one is now oversubscribed, whereas there were few first-choice applications for their predecessor schools. The typical academies have three applicants for every place, with some having as many as ten applicants for each place. Academies have an average free school meals eligibility of 34 per cent. This compares to only 13 per cent for all maintained secondary schools – more than double. This is surely proof that the purpose of academies – to raise standards for the socially disadvantaged, is being realised.

Why do academies perform so well versus their predecessor schools?

The first and most important reason is that they appoint first-rate new head teachers, whilst moving on weak heads of departments and ineffective teachers. Typically, an academy will only retain about 80 per cent of the predecessor school's teachers. Unlike weak state schools, academies can, as Jim Collins recommends, 'get the wrong people off the bus and the right people on the bus and in the right seats'.[6] However, under the TUPE laws,[7] substantial compensation has to be paid to staff asked to leave.

The second reason is a focus on creating the essential ingredients and ethos of a good school, including good attendance. The Knights Academy (see Chapter 6) insists on good attendance. Attendance has improved from 60 per cent to 95 per cent, while GCSE results have also dramatically improved.[8]

Third, there is a focus on literacy. We have seen the statistics in Chapter 4. Not being able to read leads to boredom at school, truancy, and sometimes worse things, especially for boys.

Fourth, most academies operate a longer school day. Often their day starts at 7.30 a.m. with breakfast, and continues until 6 p.m., with a wide range of activities after formal classes end at 3 p.m. Instead of children being dumped on the streets at 3 p.m. – many of them have single parents who work – they engage in fruitful after-school activities.

Fifth, bad behaviour is not tolerated. Good behaviour and academic achievement are, of course, the two foundation stones of a high-performing school.

Sixth, almost all academies have post-16 provision or sixth forms. We have seen how half of state schools in this country have no post-16 provision, leaving the UK with relatively low post-16 participation rates. In contrast, most academy students stay on to take either A-levels, or vocational courses at post-16.

Seventh, and perhaps most importantly of all, academies which are independent non-profit charitable trusts give their head teachers the necessary independence and authority to turn round a failing school, including getting rid of ineffective staff.

[5] www.dcsf.gov.uk/performancetables
[6] Jim Collins, *Good to Great: Why Some Companies Make the Leap … and Others Don't*, New York: HarperCollins, 2001, p. 13.
[7] Transfer of Undertakings (Protection of Employment) legislation dictates what happens when a takeover occurs in a company or other entity.
[8] Personal communication with the executive head of the Haberdashers' Federation, Dr Elizabeth Sidwell.

Eighth, academies have the freedom to innovate. For example, the government is now planning to open a number of academies for students aged 14–19, focusing on key vocational skills such as construction skills, financial services skills and IT. Other academies cater for both primary and secondary pupils. Some, like the West London Academy, sponsored by Alec Reed, the founder of Reed Employment, even have a kindergarten, a special school, a primary school and a secondary school all on the same campus.

Ninth, academies have the support of generous sponsors. Many academy sponsors donate £2 million to set up an endowment fund for their academy (where previously they provided capital support). They are a great source of inspiration and support for their schools. Academy sponsors are generous philanthropists who care passionately about the success of their schools. When I spend time visiting his schools with Lord Harris, I can hear him calling his carpet stores to find their takings for the day and his schools to learn their attendance figures. Woe betide a Harris school with too many truants!

Academy sponsors come from a wide range of backgrounds: they include individual philanthropists, businesses, faith communities, livery companies and educational foundations. Each recognises that its role is to challenge traditional thinking and bring fresh ideas and vision to their school to raise educational standards. The second evaluation report on academies by PricewaterhouseCoopers of the Academies Programme, reported that 82 per cent of academy staff agreed that sponsors' resources and contributions made a positive impact on pupils' learning.[9]

Following an announcement by Ed Balls to Parliament in July 2007, universities and high-performing schools and colleges are no longer required to provide £2 million before they can sponsor an academy. However, the establishment of an endowment fund, to counter the impact of disadvantage, remains an absolute requirement for all academies, and £2 million is considered to be a reasonable target. Under the new arrangements, organisations such as those which already run high-performing schools (Harris, KEVI Foundation, etc.), existing multiple sponsors and religious organisations which sponsor multiple academies will also be exempt from the up-front payment. New philanthropic or business sponsors, for example, will still have to provide £2 million before sponsoring an academy. In all cases, the Office of the Schools Commissioner will decide whether an organisation/education institution will be allowed to be a sponsor of an academy. Typically an academy costs approximately £25 million to build or refurbish, which is funded by the government as part of the Building Schools for the Future (BSF) programme. This funding is not made available at the expense of funding for other schools, since all schools are now eligible for capital grants under the BSF initiative.

The funding agreement also provides for recurrent funding on the same per capita basis as for other maintained schools in that area, typically £6,000 per year per pupil or £6 million for the typical academy with 1,000 pupils. The government's financial contribution provides a considerable leverage on the sponsor's investment.

In terms of governance, sponsors set up new limited liability non-profit trusts limited by guarantee with charitable status. Sponsors appoint a majority of founding trustees who in turn appoint the school governors. The governing body carries the duties of the trust in managing the school, including setting the budget, appointing the principal and senior staff, and setting the strategic direction of the academy.

---

[9] Available at www.standards.dcsf.gov.uk/academies/publications

How to apply to be a sponsor

Potential sponsors interested in supporting the Academies Programme should:

1　Contact the Office of the Schools Commissioner (contact details below) for an *initial informal discussion*. A visit to an academy which is already open can be arranged.
2　Academy sponsors are expected to meet stringent due diligence requirements. These include the ability to demonstrate the financial status commensurate with academy sponsorship and/or their ability to raise the necessary funds as appropriate; transparency of business arrangements; a long-term commitment to the UK education sector and the aims of the Academies Programme; the potential to run a successful school and contribute to raising standards; and the ability to promote community cohesion and enhance the reputation of the Academies Programme.
3　If the sponsorship looks likely to proceed there will be a *brokering period* during which suitable schools, sites and partnerships will be identified. If successful, this will lead to a formal *Expression of Interest* which has to be agreed by the secretary of state.
4　The project will then proceed to a *feasibility* stage, the costs of which are met by the DCFS. The following issues will be examined: an estimate of capital costs; timetable and date of opening; age range and number of pupils; specialist subjects; governance proposals; and admission arrangements. Most academy building projects are now an integral part of the Building Schools for the Future programme, whereby the government aims to rebuild or renew every secondary school in England over a 10–15 year period.
5　Assuming a successful resolution of all the issues, a *funding agreement* will be signed between the sponsor and the secretary of state so the project can move on to the implementation stage.
6　The *implementation stage* will include all building/refurbishment works, linked to Building Schools for the Future, and the appointment of key personnel including the project manager as well as the principal and senior school staff.

Depending on the local circumstances, the expectation is that an academy will be in new or refurbished buildings within three years of opening.

Specialist status

Academies usually adopt a particular academic focus, in addition to teaching a broad curriculum, on one of the ten recognised specialist subjects available to specialist schools in general.[10] These are:

- Technology academies specialise in teaching mathematics, science, design technology, information and communications technology (ICT) and vocational studies;
- Arts academies specialise in teaching the performing arts including music, dance and drama; some also specialise in visual or media arts;
- Sports academies specialise in teaching physical education and sport, and also serve as centres of sporting excellence for neighbouring schools;

[10] See Chapter 9 for a detailed discussion of specialist schools.

- Science academies emphasise the study of physics, chemistry and biology, working with leading university science departments, industry and major UK science bodies to create innovative centres of excellence;
- Language academies specialise in teaching modern foreign languages and promote an international ethos across the whole curriculum;
- Mathematics & Computing academies emphasise these two essential prerequisites for further studies in the sciences and technology and for jobs requiring numerical analysis;
- Business & Enterprise academies specialise in business studies and foster an enterprise culture in schools. They teach business studies, financial literacy, enterprise-related vocational studies and marketing skills;
- Engineering academies focus on mathematics and design technology, providing opportunities to study a wide range of engineering disciplines from civil and electrical engineering to telecoms. Their aim is to increase the number of good applicants for engineering degrees;
- Humanities academies specialise in either English (both language and literature), history or geography and foster an understanding of human values and attitudes;
- Music academies specialise in teaching music but also have a secondary focus on mathematics or ICT.

Academies may also combine two or more of the above specialisms. Academies employ qualified teachers who are registered with the General Teaching Council. Some academies operate as part of a federation, which are formed from partnerships of high-achieving and less successful schools.

Criteria for determining whether a school should be converted to academy status

The general principle is that academies will be established on the sites of existing underperforming schools unless there are strong grounds for creating additional school places in a new school in a particular area, or improving the facilities of a school performing reasonably well in difficult circumstances but with poor facilities. There may also be cases where a good school joins with a low-attaining school to become a single academy, thereby exploiting the strengths of a strong existing senior management team and enabling the efficient transfer of best practice.

The key criteria for deciding whether a project is a potential academy are the educational needs of the school and the community it serves.[11] Examples of the factors used in making that judgement are:

- There is a need for the proposed number of pupil places;
- The current performance of the existing school, as determined by average exam and national test results, is well below the average of other schools in the area;
- There is clear evidence of challenging circumstances in a wide variety of other measures including attendance, the ratio of applications to places, the number of exclusions, incidents of bullying, high turnover of staff and a large number of staff vacancies;

[11] For more information visit www.dcsf.gov.uk/schoolscommissioner

- The school is situated in a socially disadvantaged area, as shown by the high proportion of pupils eligible for free school meals or other indices of deprivation including the level of unemployment, single parent families, crime and poverty;
- Academies should be geographically dispersed so that academies are established in all areas of deprivation, both urban and rural (up to sixty of the initial academies will be in London);
- To assist the decision making on the sites of academies, a target list of communities has been established, similar to the procedures which were used to decide the locations of city technology colleges;
- In certain circumstances, academies may be created in new schools starting with a Year 7 intake or even with entry at age 14, providing there is a clear need for the additional school places in socially disadvantaged areas. There may for example be a particular need for academies catering for the post-16 age group because of the likely growth in the need for places for this age group. There will be some all-age academies.
- A small number of academies are all-through schools, catering for the full 3–19 age range.

The Specialist Schools and Academies Trust (SSAT) is the lead advisory body on the specialist schools and academies initiatives for the Department for Children, Schools and Families, providing advice and support for schools seeking to achieve or maintain specialist school status and to sponsors wishing to support specialist schools and academies. Founded in 1987, the SSAT helped first to establish the original fifteen city technology colleges which are now the leading all-ability schools in the country, and subsequently 2,974 specialist schools which are also performing well.

The trust is a registered educational charity which has 300 staff and is funded by fees from its 5,000 affiliated schools, donations from sponsors and foundations, and grants from the DCSF. The SSAT plays an important support role for academies, led by Lesley King, a distinguished former head teacher.[12] In particular, it:

- Provides a support service for academy sponsors and helps them to resolve problems;
- Helps academies raise standards, including establishing links with leading specialist schools;
- Performs a media and communications role.

Key concerns about the future of the academies initiative

If we are to ensure that this important initiative remains successful, there are two concerns which need to be addressed.

The first is to ensure that the prime purpose of the academy initiative remains focused on replacing the country's 337 low-attaining schools with good schools whose purpose will be to raise academic standards for the most socially disadvantaged children in the country. In all, 300,000 children attend these low-attaining schools.

If we can replace most of the 337 low-attaining secondary schools in the country (see Chapter 6) with academies, we will change for the better the lives of over 300,000 children

[12] See the SSAT website, www.ssatrust.org.uk, for a description of its services to schools.

currently attending poor schools, in addition to those who are already benefiting from open academies.

What must be resisted is the temptation to give into pressure from prospective sponsors and to create academies from schools which are already performing well – with the exception, of course, of the original fifteen city technology colleges which need to be integrated into the academy initiative. They are being converted into academies providing they agree to partner a low-attaining school. It will be a tragedy if in five years' time, 400 academies have been created but we still have a significant number of low-attaining schools.

The second concern, which has been highlighted in a recent report by the CBI, is that academies are now being built under the Building Schools for the Future (BSF) programme, a new system for refurbishing English schools. This ambitious £45 billion programme aims to rebuild or refurbish every secondary school in the country. The first 130 academies were built under the direct supervision of their sponsors who appointed the architects, quantity surveyors and project directors.

While it is true that some of the original academies were expensive and indeed a few were poorly designed, most were built on time, within budget and with superb buildings. For example, the Walsall Academy, designed by architect John Cahill of Barnsley, Hewett and Mallinson, chosen by the sponsors the Mercers, together with the support of Thomas Telford CTC, was built on time and within a very tight budget of £17 million. (See the brochure 'On Time, on Budget and on Target: Walsall Academy', published by the SSAT, ISBN 1-905150-67-9.)

Under the new procedure, academies are part of BSF. Local authorities play a leading part in this programme with schools being refurbished or rebuilt in a series of 'waves' over a 10-year period. Partnerships for Schools (PfS), a quango, provides guidance on procedures to be followed. Many sponsors are complaining that the new procedure produces delays and confusion. A particular problem is that the tendering procedures, which must follow overly prescriptive European Union requirements, often make it difficult for previously successful builders and architects of existing academies, such as Barnsley Hewett and Mallinson, to tender. Some of the initial designs produced by BSF are poor. In its review of the BSF programme, the Commission for Architecture and the Built Environment has raised concerns about some forty school designs. Their criticisms including concerns about potential bullying hot spots, noisy open-plan areas, and dark and stuffy classrooms. Fewer than a fifth of the school designs for BSF were considered to be good or excellent.[13]

Another concern raised by academy sponsors has been the very high cost of some of the plans. It is strongly recommended that the procedures for the Building Schools for the Future programme should be reviewed, with a crucial requirement being the use of good standard designs using some of the very attractive initial academy designs *and* the appointment of project directors answerable to the sponsors who will be responsible for ensuring the academy buildings are ready on time and within budget.

However, despite the above concerns, which have to do with implementation of the programme rather than its purpose, the academy programme presents a unique opportunity to ensure that there will be no more low-attaining schools in the future. Clearly, therefore, academies are a very good thing. We need more of them. The current target

[13] See www.cabe.org.uk/default.aspx?contentitemid = 2643

of 400 should be expanded, particularly by the creation of 'all through' academies which combine primary and secondary schools on the same site and academies for 14–19 year-olds specialising in one or more of the new vocational diplomas.

Suggested further reading

Julian Astle and Conor Ryan (eds) *Academies and the Future of State Education*, London: CentreForum, 2008.

Cyril Taylor, 'Are Academies a Good Thing?', Speech to the Institute of Economic Affairs, London, 11 June 2008.

Lord Adonis, 'Academies and Social Mobility', Speech to the Academies Conference, London, 7 February 2008. Available at www.dcsf.gov.uk/speeches/search_detail.cfm?ID = 749

Chapter 8

Halting the demise of the United Kingdom's science and engineering base

Note: this chapter is largely based on the research conducted by Dr Saskia Murk Jansen for Sir Cyril Taylor when she worked as his policy adviser.

In the nineteenth century, Britain was the world's leading exporter of manufactured goods. We had many of the best inventors in the world, including Isambard Kingdom Brunel, James Watt, George Stephenson, Henry Bessemer, Michael Faraday, and Charles Babbage.

Aside from the competition from lower labour cost countries such as India and China, one of the main reasons for the current decline of Britain's position in manufacturing and engineering has been the decline in the teaching of physics, chemistry, biology and advanced maths in our schools, often because of a lack of specialist teachers in these subjects.

One of the causes of this decline was the introduction in the 1990s of the double-science GCSE award in schools at age 16, which was supposed to give equal attention to the teaching of both physics, chemistry and biology and to encourage greater numbers of pupils to take up science at A-level. Already in the 1994 report to the Engineering Council, Alan Smithers and Pamela Robinson[1] remark: 'The introduction of national curriculum science and the double science GCSE have been a great success in increasing participation in science to age 16 and in improving the gender balance, but the apparent failure to lift A-level entries is a mystery.'

Frequently, double science is taught by teachers with only a biology qualification. The Confederation of British Industry, in its evidence to the House of Lords Science and Technology Committee, said that only 19 per cent of school science teachers are physics specialists, and of those teaching GCSE science, 3 per cent of them do not even have an A-level in the subject.[2] Not surprisingly, ambitious 16 year-olds wanting to get into a good university do not believe that their double-science GCSE course has prepared them sufficiently well in physics and chemistry to get a good grade in those subjects at A-level. Recent research by the Centre for Evaluation and Management at the University of Durham has confirmed that good grades are significantly harder to obtain in science than in other subjects.[3]

[1] Alan Smithers and Pamela Robinson, *The Impact of Double Science*, London: The Engineering Council, 1994, p. 5.

[2] *Science Teaching in Schools: Report with Evidence House of Lords Science and Technology Committee. 10th Report of Session 2005–06*, London: HMSO, p. 143

[3] *Relative Difficulty of Examinations in Different Subjects,* CEM Centre, Durham University (July 2008).

Smithers and Robinson suggest that one reason A-level science courses are not popular options is that three separate science A-levels are required for university entrance to study science. Therefore, pupils must be very confident of their abilities and very certain that this is what they want before they make that commitment. They argue that if the norm was to take five A-levels, pupils would be able to do science without cutting themselves off from other options.[4] This is something that already happens with the International Baccalaureate, where students must do a broad mix of subjects to A-level standard. A number of university admissions tutors hoped that the division of the A-level course into AS- and A-level would encourage students to broaden their offering at A-level, taking science to AS-level as well as arts subjects. However, this has not proved to be the case. It remains to be seen whether the diplomas will have a similar effect.

In the last ten years, the number of 16 year-olds taking A-level physics courses has fallen by 56 per cent, and those taking chemistry by 36 per cent. A further problem is that three quarters of those taking A-level physics are boys, who do not generally wish to take up a career in teaching. Of the 25,133 newly qualified teachers in 2007, only 24 per cent were male.[5]

As Table 8.1 shows, currently less than 10 per cent of state-school educated pupils take separate science courses at GCSE. And the proportion is particularly low in comprehensive and modern schools, where fewer than 5 per cent of pupils take a separate science course. It should also be noted that candidates taking separate science GCSE courses can take single-subject science and do not have to take all three subjects, but those that do are even less likely to do a science A-level than those taking the double-award GCSE.[6] Furthermore, the term 'science' can give an over-optimistic picture of the teaching of physics and chemistry, as it includes other subjects such as astronomy, rural science, applied science and, from 2008, psychology.

According to figures in a recent study,[7] 24 per cent of all 11–16 schools do not have a physics specialist teacher who has studied physics at any level at university, and 31 per cent of current physics specialists are due to retire in the next ten years. The supply of physics teachers qualified in physics is diminishing – in 2004, 39 per cent of those leaving the

Table 8.1 GCSE science exams by type of school

Type of school	Numbers of pupils taking GCSE exams in 2006	Numbers taking separate science GCSE exams in		
	Total Pupils	Physics	Chemistry	Biology
Comprehensive	570,000	27,054	27,351	28,911
Grammar	22,500	7,420	7,420	7,440
Independent	50,000	15,084	15,229	16,167
Total	642,500	49,588	50,000	52,518

[4] Smithers and Robinson, *The Impact of Double Science*, p. 27. This was originally suggested in the Higgenson Report, *Advancing A-Levels*, London: HMSO, 1988.
[5] Source: General Teaching Council. www.gtcs.org.uk/Research_/publishedresearch_/TeacherInduction SchemeResearch/research_teacher_induction_scheme.aspx
[6] Smithers and Robinson, *The Impact of Double Science*, p. 12.
[7] Alan Smithers and Pamela Robinson, 'Physics in Schools and Colleges', Centre for Education and Employment Research, University of Buckingham, 2005. www.buckingham.ac.uk/education/research/ceer/pdfs/diploma.pdf

profession had physics as their main subject but this was true of only 32.8 per cent of newly appointed teachers. In the view of the authors of the study, physics is in danger of disappearing as an identifiable subject from much of state education, through redefinition to general science and teacher shortage. This suggests that the government's targets set out in the paper 'Next Steps'[8] are unlikely to be met without some radical intervention.

A situation has been created whereby there are fewer inspiring specialist physics and chemistry teachers in schools, so fewer pupils are taking physics and chemistry at both GCSE and A-level, and fewer are taking these subjects at university, so that as a consequence there are not enough physics and chemistry graduates going into teaching. And despite some recent improvements as a result of university–school partnerships, we are still producing far too few scientists.

The introduction of the double science award in schools in the 1990s has not encouraged more pupils to study A-level physics and chemistry. It is not possible to be a good engineer without having qualifications in both physics and maths. The decline in pupils taking these A-levels has led to a decline in the numbers of English engineering graduates. The decline in engineering graduates in particular has serious implications for the future of the United Kingdom as a significant manufacturing player in the global economy. Sir John Rose, chairman of Rolls-Royce, has pointed out that the UK has an annual trading deficit in manufactured goods of £60 billion whereas Germany, with its highly regulated economy, has an equivalent surplus. The number of secondary school pupils studying the combinations of maths/physics/chemistry or maths/chemistry/biology at A-level (which are the foundation for a scientific or engineering career) is down to 60 per cent of what it was in 2001. Rolls-Royce (which has the contract to supply the next generation of nuclear submarines as well as being the leading manufacturer of jet engines) is concerned that it may not be able to find sufficient suitably qualified staff to replace its retiring engineers over the next decade, and it may have to move its plants abroad.[9]

While the government is taking specific measures to correct this situation, including vigorous advertising campaigns to attract more science graduates into teaching, more could and should be done. The government's Science and Maths Campaigns aim to encourage an extra 20,000 pupils to study physics, chemistry and maths at A-level by 2014. Close attention needs to be paid to why so many pupils do not choose to extend their science, technology, engineering and mathematics (STEM) education beyond 16.

Some sections of society are under-represented in STEM, and correcting this under-representation would do much to solve the problem. For example, only 14 per cent of engineering undergraduates are women; only 3.24 per cent of those studying science, engineering and technology (SET) are black; and 11.11 per cent of those studying SET are Asian, mostly in medicine. Those forming less advantaged socio-economic backgrounds are under-represented in all sectors of education beyond age 16.[10]

There are a number of initiatives which aim to widen participation from these groups. Computer Clubs for Girls[11] provide a range of tailored e-learning activities for girls aged 10–14 years. STEM Access Grants[12] are provided to schools to engage secondary school

[8] 'Youth Matters: Next Steps', London: Department for Children, Schools and Families, 8 March 2006.
[9] 'Rolls-Royce Boss Despairs at Lack of British Engineering Talent', *Daily Mail*, 27 July 2006.
[10] www.dius.gov.uk/publications/science_society
[11] www.cc4g.net
[12] For more information, visit www.stemnet.org.uk

students from black and ethnic minority backgrounds, especially Afro-Caribbean boys and Bangladeshi and Pakistani girls, to become more involved in science subjects. The London Engineering Project[13] also intends to widen and increase participation in engineering in higher education among minority ethnic students, women and adult learners by engaging with pupils through enrichment projects in schools. These initiatives have, however, not yet succeeded to the extent necessary. More research might reveal that they are not yet addressing the key issues from the pupils' perspective. The research model adopted by Lord Harris' academies in a similar situation proved very effective. When the schools had problems motivating Afro-Caribbean boys, they went on a study tour of the Caribbean to look for best practice there. The schools now have some of the best GCSE results for Afro-Caribbean boys in the country.

We must increase the numbers of qualified STEM teachers to teach them, in parallel to solving the supply-side of pupils wishing to take STEM A-levels. To achieve this, a multi-pronged approach is required, including emergency action to restart the supply chain of good specialist physics and chemistry teachers in schools. They are crucial if we are to inspire more children to study these subjects, to take science at university and to become teachers themselves. Equally important are longer-term initiatives to increase the numbers of graduates going into the teaching profession and to reduce the numbers leaving the profession.

Closer cooperation between the Science Learning centres and the Specialist Schools and Academies Trust (SSAT) is increasing their reach and effectiveness. For example, specialist science, engineering and technology colleges could be used as the delivery mechanism for improved science teaching and the mentoring of science teachers in the same way that the sports colleges are used to increase the quantity and quality of P.E. taught in primary schools. They could be local hubs of excellence providing mentoring and additional support to trainee and recently qualified teachers in their areas. Especially important is the dissemination of good practice concerning the teaching of girls as reflected in the research done by the Institute of Physics and disseminated in a pilot scheme by the Science Learning Centres.

A network of government-funded Science Learning Centres[14] was started in 2004 to improve the scientific skills of primary and secondary school teachers in science subjects. Working together with learned professional societies such as the Royal Society of Chemistry and the Institute of Physics, they have greatly increased the capacity and availability of scientific professional development. Some of these centres also loan expensive equipment to schools so that students can easily carry out the practical work in the classroom, using specialist science schools as outreach links to increase the scheme's geographical access. The National Science Learning Centre runs an extensive programme of residential professional development; for example, it is addressing the significant problem of retention by running summer schools for new teachers. The programme offers masterclasses, mentoring, and time to reflect as well as networking opportunities. Feedback suggests that participants felt re-inspired, reassured and better equipped to continue in their chosen career.

Another possible option would be for groups of specialist schools, encouraged by the specialist science hub school and the regional Science Learning Centre, to adopt a

---

[13] www.thelep.org.uk
[14] www.sciencelearningcentres.org.uk

common timetable and together to employ one or more science technicians who could travel between schools to support the practical work of the specialist teachers. It might also be possible for such a federation jointly to provide supply cover for teachers on subject-specific CPD courses.

The National Science Learning Centre's summer course, mentoring and networking scheme for newly qualified teachers (NQTs) should be actively supported. Working more closely with the SSAT and specialist science schools would further increase the scheme's national coverage.

The specialist science colleges are already centres of excellence for science teaching and are required to offer separate science GCSE courses. They should be encouraged to broker the provision of separate GCSE science courses for all pupils who want to take triple science at GCSE, and to develop post-16 courses in physics, biology and chemistry for pupils from other schools, as well as for their own pupils. As scientific hubs of excellence they could also organise a federation of schools in their area, sharing best practice and sharing the cost of expensive equipment. Several schools, encouraged by the specialist science hub school and the regional Science Learning Centre, could also adopt a common timetable and together to employ qualified science teachers who would travel between schools to provide separate science courses at both GCSE and at A-level. It might also be possible for such a federation jointly to provide supply cover for teachers on subject-specific continuing professional development (CPD) courses.

I strongly believe that the 600 specialist science, engineering, and technology colleges should participate in this or other schemes to increase the numbers of science teachers in schools, as well as offering separate science GCSE courses and A-levels if they have post-16 provision. To retain their specialist status and the additional funding, specialist science schools should demonstrate how they plan to support science teaching in other schools in their area. Subject-specific CPD should be required in specialist colleges, and they should develop their hub status as a way of cascading knowledge and skills to a federation of adjacent schools. The specialist science schools should also become the sixth form of choice for able and qualified pupils in their subject, providing excellent teaching and specialist facilities.

The recent government initiative 'Teach First' is attracting many highly qualified science graduates into the teaching profession, and although half leave after the first few years as the name of the scheme implies, many stay and head teachers speak in glowing terms of the effect they have on the motivation and enthusiasm of pupils and staff. Another such scheme is INSPIRE, organised by Imperial College London.[15] Imperial College and its partners GlaxoSmithKline plc and the Specialist Schools and Academies Trust sought to address these concerns with the INSPIRE (Innovative Scheme for Post-docs in Research and Education) scheme. Launched in 2002, the scheme encourages young research fellows to undertake some teaching as well as research at twelve specialist science schools sponsored by GlaxoSmithKline in the London area. Half of those who take part in the scheme take up teaching as a career and all participating schools report a significant increase in GCSE results. I understand that the new proposed INSPIRE scheme will offer a specially designed 9-month PCGE, incorporating two months of integrated INSPIRE activities such as masterclasses, science clubs, science conferences, university-level training for post-16 students, career advice and student visits to university research

---

[15] www3.imperial.ac.uk/inspire

laboratories. The scheme will be available to current post-doctoral researchers and to Ph.D. graduates in physical sciences and engineering. Each post-doc will be linked to a Principal Investigator (head of research laboratory) at Imperial, to enable them to maintain their research links, to use the laboratory facilities and to prepare INSPIRE activities. The key feature of this new scheme is that it is focused on physics and chemistry and is a 9-month intensive course but still retains the crucial INSPIRE elements.[16] An INSPIRE-type scheme could be extended nationally, using specialist science colleges as hub-schools and linking them all to their local university science departments. The university departments could provide specialist lectures and tours of their facilities for pupils of the schools in the same way as the INSPIRE programme currently provides added value to its affiliated schools.

'Transition to Teaching' is a fast-track programme for graduate career changers to go into the teaching of physics and chemistry. The DCSF together with IBM are working on such a programme. Discussions are also underway with the Ministry of Defence to facilitate service-leavers to make this change as well, with the strong support of Sir Jock Stirrup. Once they achieve qualified teacher status, suitable candidates could apply to join the 'Future Leaders' programme whereby qualified teachers, including those who have left the profession, are encouraged to become head teachers by following a series of intensive leadership training programmes. Those completing this course successfully can expect to reach high salary levels in five rather than ten years.

The following specific measures could increase the supply of qualified science teachers, especially in physics and chemistry, in our schools:

- *Immediate and interim measures* – we need to increase immediately the number of specialist physics and chemistry teachers in schools by recruiting science teachers from abroad, especially Germany, where it is understood there is a surplus of 10,000 science teachers, most of whom speak English well; expanding the Graduate Teacher Programme for mature entrants to train in schools; establishing a fast-track programme to attract suitably qualified career changers into science teaching, and with the support of the Joint Defence Chiefs of Staff, establishing a programme to enable those retiring from the armed forces with the necessary qualifications to become science teachers. This would mirror the successful 'Troops to Teachers' ('3 Ts') initiative in the United States.
- *Incentives to teach* – we need to increase the incentives for graduates to become physics and chemistry teachers (they currently receive golden hellos worth £5,000) and for them to stay in teaching. This might involve repaying undergraduate tuition fees for those who go on to take a teaching qualification and accept a teaching post and writing off the student debt of those who stay in the profession for more than five years. However, such a scheme was tried shortly after fees were introduced, but it proved expensive to operate and not very effective. There is anecdotal evidence that many physics graduates are put off teaching as a career because they think they will have to teach biology as well as physics at GCSE and A-level. Offering the option of physics with maths alongside that of physics with biology could increase the numbers of physics graduates choosing to go into a teaching career and would enable those physics graduates currently training to teach maths to teach physics as well.

[16] Source: Personal communication with Dr Naheed Alizadeh, project director, INSPIRE.

- *A differential salary scheme* for teachers in shortage subjects would help to reduce the lure of highly paid jobs in financial services for science graduates until the increased supply of physicists causes the market to adjust. Schools already have the freedom to offer higher salaries to attract good teachers in priority subjects. However, there would be merit in making it a national provision so that head teachers are not put in a difficult position in relation to other staff and to ensure parity across the country.
- *Retention.* Teaching can be a very challenging role, especially for those entering teaching as career changers and through less traditional routes such as the Graduate Teacher Programme and the Registered Teacher Programme. Two fifths of recently qualified science teachers leave teaching before their fifth year.[17] Evidence suggests that the provision of more intensive mentoring and networking schemes helps retention. The National Science Learning Centre's summer course, mentoring and networking scheme for newly qualified teachers (NQTs) should be actively supported. Working more closely with the SSAT and specialist science schools would further improve the scheme's national coverage. Retention could be further increased by introducing a scheme of sabbatical terms for science teachers to update their subject knowledge and to watch others teach. Experienced teachers say they would love to have the chance to watch others teach to brush-up on their skills. If schools had links with their local university, a further enhancement would be to enable teachers on sabbatical to audit courses at their local university. Some physics graduates decide not to go into teaching because they think they will lose touch with their subject – the prospect of sabbaticals to enable them to stay abreast of developments would address this issue. Together with the regional Science Learning Centres, specialist science schools could help to organise schools into groups so that they could together employ an extra member of staff to provide cover for sabbaticals and CPD, and also assist in practicals.
- Replicate for science the Second Specialism incentive to specialist schools in respect of languages and vocational studies. This scheme encourages high-performing specialist schools to apply for a second specialism in one of these two subjects. If successful, the schools receive an additional £30,000 grant over and above the £60,000 other specialisms attract. This could be in respect of a new STEM specialism, rather than limited to science and would need to carry with it a commitment to supporting the national science agenda and to the numbers taking triple science.
- Require that within a reasonable period of perhaps two years, in addition to specialist science colleges, all specialist technology and engineering colleges should offer separate sciences at GCSE taught by a specialist teacher.
- In every area there should be at least one specialist school offering A-level physics and chemistry with an expanded sixth form to accommodate pupils from other schools in the area. If necessary, new sixth form provision should be created to provide A-levels in science.

The Training and Development Agency (TDA) is supporting the development of a number of different ways into teaching. The Registered Teacher Programme enables those with some experience of higher education (a minimum of 240 units) to take a post as a teacher in a registered school and receive on-the-job training while also completing their degree. In this scheme, the school pays the trainee an unqualified or qualified teacher's

[17] Source: Training and Development Agency.

salary depending on responsibilities, experience and location, and in addition, the TDA provides the school with a grant to cover the cost of training. This scheme could be used as a fast-track to science teaching for non-graduates with appropriate scientific experience, such as retiring military personnel. Discussions should be pursued with appropriate universities and the Ministry of Defence to devise a scheme to enable non-graduates leaving the armed forces or other careers with appropriate experience to qualify as a teacher while topping up their qualifications to degree level.

Other options include the Graduate Teacher Programme[18] (GTP) under which recent graduates work for one year as unqualified teachers while qualifying for QTS (qualified teacher status). Around one in six teachers is trained through GTP. As with the Registered Teacher Programme, the school receives up to £14,000 a year towards the trainee's salary. In practice the trainee will be on the unqualified teacher pay-scale and will receive a bit more than this. The school through its training provider also receives a further £4,920 per year training grant depending on the teaching subject and length of programme. Another scheme is the School Centred Initial Teacher Training scheme (SCITT)[19] which lasts a year during which the graduate student is based at one of a consortium of schools, doing teaching practices at others in the group. This attracts similar grants. Finally there is the option of taking a B.Sc. with QTS degree which enables graduates to obtain their qualified teacher status while studying for their first degree. This attracts no additional funding. All these schemes should be targeted and resourced to prioritise chemistry and physics teaching.

In addition, the following measures are also in operation and should continue to be supported.

- *Up-skilling existing teachers*: Subject-specific INSET courses are already in place to increase the physics knowledge base of existing teachers to A-level that makes them comparable to specialists. However, teachers have little incentive to take these up at present. The TDA is working on ways of making these courses more attractive, such as making the courses, and also subject-specific CPD courses, credits towards an accredited diploma or a master's degree. From 2007, Prince Charles' summer schools for teachers will include science as well as languages and history.
- *Retaining the help of staff past retirement*: Since January 2007 the Teachers' Pension scheme allows retiring or recently retired physics and chemistry teachers to mentor new teachers, provide additional classroom support, and CPD supply cover.
- *Improve careers advice in schools* so that pupils are aware of the substantially higher salaries commanded by science graduates and of the many different career options open to them. The Royal Air Force, for example, offers science and maths days in schools which demonstrate the range of (non-military) work for which an understanding of science and maths is important. Sponsors of specialist science, technology and engineering colleges could be invited to make presentations to pupils at local schools to provide further examples.
- *Improve the image of the study of physics and chemistry* by the use of undergraduate role models. Programmes such as the Science and Engineering Ambassadors, Undergraduate Ambassadors scheme and Researcher in Residence already exist and offer a way

[18] www.tda.gov.uk/Recruit/thetrainingprocess/typesofcourse/employmentbased/gtp.aspx
[19] www.tda.gov.uk/Recruit/thetrainingprocess/typesofcourse/postgraduate/scitt.aspx

forward. Students could opt to do work placement in schools in their second year and receive credit towards their degree. This places young undergraduates directly in schools working with pupils. The TDA has recently announced that it hopes to place up to 8,000 volunteer undergraduates in schools along these lines, and the Royal Society of Chemistry is supporting the scheme in respect of chemistry undergraduates. Specialist colleges should be expected to host Science Ambassadors and to enable them to visit other schools in their locality.

- *Launch an advertising campaign* aimed at young people and using multi-media they are familiar with to inspire them and to inform them of the importance of science for the survival of the planet, including measures to combat global warming. Young people are idealistic, and the campaign should explain how science is our only hope of making the lives of millions of people more tolerable and of finding solutions to the problems that face the planet in the twenty-first century. The TDA should use their advertising campaigns to address this issue.

- *Provide classroom support for practicals*: Scientists enjoy practical work and practical work in the classroom is essential to understand concepts as well as being a powerful motivational tool. There is evidence to suggest that some teachers are put off practicals because of concerns about health and safety. The Practical Physics[20] website supports practical work in physics, but increasing the interest and frequency of practical work in schools would be greatly helped by smaller class sizes or additional teaching/technical staff. As already suggested, this problem might be eased by several groups together employing an extra member of staff or teaching assistant.

- *Improve school laboratories*: 66 per cent of all school laboratories were recently rated by OfSTED as either basic or unsatisfactory/unsafe. Money has been earmarked for this in the BSF initiative.

- *Develop holiday schools for gifted and talented science pupils* to target the students that would benefit, to add excitement to the study of physics and chemistry and to supply aspects of science difficult to deliver in schools. A programme of Easter schools would do a great deal to improve performance at GCSE and A-level.

- *Provide incentives* to pupils to study physics, chemistry and maths A-levels along the lines of Education Maintenance Allowance (EMA) payments (which provide up to £30 a week for disadvantaged youngsters who stay in education and meet attendance criteria). For maximum effect, the incentives should be targeted to reward attendance but with a bonus for grades attained. A scheme of industry-sponsored awards for the Young Scientist of the Year would also help raise the profile of science and encourage aspiration.

The fact that insufficient pupils take science and maths A-levels and continue their science education in university is an urgent national problem. However, there is much that can be done at the local school level. Some of the ideas discussed above can be adopted by local schools independent of any national scheme – the consequent improvement in their science results would soon turn them into beacons of good practice for other schools and the government to emulate.

---

[20] www.practicalphysics.org/

Chapter 9

How information communications technology (ICT) can be used to improve learning

The increased use of information communications technology (ICT) in schools has been one of the major reasons for the recent improvement in school standards in England.

As BECTA, the government agency responsible for promoting the use of ICT in schools and colleges, said in a recent report, particular progress has been made in the past five years with now an estimated 60 per cent of our secondary school teachers having access, competence and the motivation to use the internet and computers in the classroom. This is by far the highest proportion among European countries, with only 19 per cent of French teachers having similar skills.[1] The introduction of the General National Vocational Qualification in ICT in the 1980s, which was given the equivalency of four A–C grades at GCSE, was clearly one of the driving forces in this success.

BECTA defines e-maturity as the capacity of a learning institute to make strategic and effective use of technology to improve educational outcomes. They estimate that in 2007, 27 per cent of all secondary and primary schools had achieved e-maturity.[2] However, there are still a significant number of schools which do not yet have either the right equipment or sufficient teachers trained in the use of technology.

Thomas Telford City Technology College, founded in 1991 and under the outstanding leadership of its principal, Sir Kevin Satchwell, has led the way in the use of ICT in schools, including provision of learning materials for the GNVQ in IT. Its pupils got 98 per cent five good grades at GCSE including maths and English, in 2008. Telford CTC pioneered the GNVQ IT course and provided appropriate online teaching materials. With the fees earned from the programme, the school has sponsored seventy-five specialist schools and three academies.

The following is a checklist for the effective use of ICT in schools. Head teachers may find it useful to do a self-evaluation using this checklist.

Wireless technology. Is your school equipped with wireless technology rather than relying on the need to maintain expensive cable and individual power points to access the internet? The huge advantage of wireless technology is that each classroom will need only one access point (usually in the ceiling) rather than a power point and access for every child in the class.

Laptops. Does every child in your school have a laptop? The cost of laptops has gone down dramatically in recent years. With educational discounts, the typical bulk order is now £250 per battery operated laptop with all the necessary software.

---

[1] BECTA, *Harnessing Technology: Next Generation Learning*, London: BECTA, 2008. Available at www.becta.org.uk

[2] Ibid.

School intranet. This is a crucial tool which serves a number of purposes, including:

- Providing instant access for teachers to sophisticated data on the performance of each child, including the target goals for each child in each subject in every year group. Harris Academy pioneered the usage of this pupil database software.
- Providing children with access to information and research sites including Google, as well as some specialised subject databases.
- Enabling schools to install electronic attendance monitoring. Every child should be given a smart card to register their daily attendance and even to monitor attendance in individual classes. The most advanced schools no longer need the teachers to read out the list of children in their class every morning and manually record if a child is absent. Electronic attendance tools enable schools to track absence rates in a much more effective way. For example, some schools now hold their tutor groups in the afternoon as there is no need to record attendance in the morning, and they can ask a child why they missed a particular class, as well as discuss the events of the day.
- Through the use of the same smart card used to register attendance, pupils are able to pay for their school meals. This not only speeds up the lunch line, but enables those eligible for free school meals to join the same lunch line without having attention drawn to their status as eligible for free school meals (FSM) which sometimes causes pupils eligible for FSM to feel ostracised.
- Thomas Telford School also provides parents and students with access to the whole of their curriculum online. This is a huge resource which outlines what is to be studied in each subject throughout the year with detailed information and links (including video) both to suitable resources created by the staff and to the internet. Students can revisit information, e.g. science experiments, from past sessions as well as access extra tasks to continue their exploration of topics. Parents can check to see what homework their children should be doing.

Interactive whiteboards. Does your school have an interactive whiteboard in every classroom? This is a revolutionary teacher's tool which has made obsolete the old school blackboard and chalk, as well as slide projectors. Whiteboards can have a dramatic effect in raising standards. Not only can they show film clips and slides, and enable the teacher to write electronically instead of using chalk, they are also interactive, with pupils being able to access them through their laptops. A good example in the effective use of whiteboards is Kemnal Technology College, an all-boys school in Bromley, Kent, sponsored by Lord Harris. Its outstanding head teacher, John Atkins, grew frustrated a few years ago with the difficulty in recruiting good maths teachers and the resulting poor performance of his boys in GCSE maths.

His solution was to convert, by knocking down the partition walls, three of his classrooms into one large classroom with up to ninety desks. He then hired a master maths teacher at a high salary, plus three teaching assistants. Every one of his boys was then given a laptop. The large classroom was equipped with two interactive whiteboards.

I sat in on a maths class conducted by the outstanding maths teacher. The boys were enthralled by his teaching skills, received personal help from the three teaching assistants, and were able to benefit from three whiteboards in front of them, including learning to solve maths problems.

As John Atkins says: 'interactive whiteboards means that we can "teach the way the students learn"'.

Despite its incoming 11 year-olds having lower than average ability range, 64 per cent of Kemnal Technology College students soon achieved five good grades at GCSE, compared to its expected results using the Jesson Value Added approach, of only 54 per cent. They achieve 47 per cent including maths and English with a similar value added of 10 per cent, and 63 per cent of their boys now achieve A–C grades in GCSE maths.[3]

But, of course, just having the necessary ICT equipment will not by itself raise standards in a typical school. The teachers themselves must be trained in the use of technology and the use of the requisite software.

Sadly, this is not yet a formal part of teacher training, but should be made so. Possibly schools should pay their teachers a special additional top-up salary when they obtain the advanced IT qualifications.

It is also necessary to teach the pupils how to use their laptops for independent learning. Thomas Telford CT starts this process by requiring each of its incoming 11 year-olds to attend a 2-week orientation programme at the school before the regular school year starts.

Kevin Satchwell, chief executive of the Telford group of schools is convinced that equipping students with appropriate ICT skills has a potent effect on their ability to perform better in the other subjects that they study.

Hannelore Fuller, who had the challenging task of typing the handwritten manuscript of this book, clearly wishes that I had been able to type this manuscript on a computer!

Another major use of ICT in helping learning, is helping school children to access their school's intranet from their homes, so that they can send their homework directly to their teacher, as well as sending and receiving other communications.

This, of course, requires the children's home to have internet access with the necessary broadband. BECTA estimates that 80 per cent of English households now have internet access, but a much lower proportion, perhaps only half, have a broadband connection.[4] This means that the 'digital divide' is increasing for children in those households who do not have broadband access. Schools in socially disadvantaged areas could be given special grants to help pay for this.

Finally, it must be emphasised how important it is that all our children are taught first-rate IT skills, including the use of sophisticated software. The International Data Corporation (IDC) published a study commissioned by Cisco Systems in 2005, on the importance of learning IT skills. The paper estimates that in Europe as a whole, there is now a shortage of 500,000 skilled IT workers, with at least a need for 40,000 more skilled IT workers required in the United Kingdom (see Table 9.1).[5]

This is why I used to push so hard as chairman of the SSAT to open Cisco, Oracle and Microsoft learning academies in English schools. The Cisco Academies were founded ten years ago. In 1998, I was able to arrange a meeting between John Chambers, the chief executive of Cisco Systems and the then prime minister, Tony Blair. At this meeting, Cisco agreed to open 500 Cisco Academies in English schools. Already there are 270 Cisco Academies in English schools. One of the first to take advantage of this offer was

---

[3] Source: John Atkins, head teacher of Kemnal Technology College.

[4] BECTA, *Harnessing Technology*.

[5] Marianne Kolding and Vladimir Kroa, 'Networking Skills in Europe: Will an Increasing Shortage Hamper Competitiveness in the Global Market?' London: IDC, 2005.

Table 9.1 Estimated shortage of people with advanced technology skills, by country in Europe 2008

Country	Estimated total of skilled staff required	Estimated shortage of skilled staff	2008 gap (%)
Austria	12,900	3,229	17.8
Belgium	10,100	2,531	15.9
Denmark	7,700	1,921	14.9
Finland	5,300	1,335	15.9
France	40,300	10,072	11.7
Germany	87,800	21,957	17.5
Ireland	7,500	1,886	18.7
Italy	20,800	5,207	9.8
Netherlands	16,700	4,169	14.6
Norway	5,700	1,435	12.0
Russia	60,000	15,011	24.5
Spain	41,800	10,459	15.7
Sweden	8,000	1,989	12.2
UK	39,500	9,890	9.3

Greensward Technology College in Essex, whose principal David Triggs has been a pioneer in the use of IT in schools. In his school, adults are also able to learn the Cisco qualification in the evening and at the weekends.

There are now 600,000 students in the world studying the Cisco Academy programme in 160 countries, including England.[6] Developed by the University of Arizona, the course is taught partly online and partly in a computer laboratory. The introductory diploma, the Cisco Certified Network Associate, requires 280 hours of instruction and coursework. This typically takes 6 months of classes of up to 3 hours per day. The award is recognised throughout the world. Many English sixth formers now stay on for a 'Year 14' in their gap year to take the Cisco diploma before entering university, so valuable is this skill.

Because of the shortage of skilled IT workers, 18 year-olds with a Cisco Certified Network Associate Diploma can earn as much as £25,000 per year. The curriculum covers the following:

- The ability to install, configure, operate and troubleshoot medium-sized routed and switched networks, including implementation and verification of connections to remote sites in a WAN;
- Basic mitigation of security threats;
- Introduction to wireless networking concepts and terminology and performance-based skills;
- Use of IP, Enhanced Interior Gateway Routing Protocols, Serial Line Interface Protocol, Frame Relay, Routing Information Protocol, VLANS, Ethernet, access control lists.

Duncan Mitchell, Vice President UK and Ireland, Cisco Systems, says:[7]

There is a critical shortage of engineers and technicians to build the internet economy in the UK – this is both a skills and competitiveness issue and we are proud to

[6] www.cisco.com/web/learning/netacad/academy/index.html
[7] Quotation from *By Schools for Schools*, London: Specialist Schools and Academies Trust, 2007.

be working with SSAT to address this. We have established Cisco Academies in 270 Specialist Schools and look forward to extending this to develop the skilled work-force that the UK needs to compete in the global economy.

Both Microsoft and Oracle have similar programmes. The Oracle Academy focuses on business, technology and professional skills. I arranged another meeting in 2003 at 10 Downing Street between Oracle's chief executive officer, Larry Ellison, Prime Minister Blair and the secretary of state for education, Charles Clarke, at which Oracle agreed to establish up to 100 Oracle Academies in English schools. The Cisco and Oracle curricula are complementary since Cisco focuses on internet access skills and Oracle on technology skills training.

The Oracle Internet Academy 'Introduction to Computer Science' option allows students to develop technical, analytical and business skills that support the pursuit of professional careers and advanced study.

The Oracle Academy curriculum teaches students to design and implement a database system that supports various business functions, such as sales, human resources, operations and support. By analysing the detailed data requirements of each operating unit, students learn how large, complex and dynamic organisations operate. This ability to merge business knowledge and technical skills is a key to success in the twenty-first century workplace.

Oracle Academy students develop highly practical skills such as designing strategic applications to solve business scenarios. They may also meet with industry professionals who can speak to them about their curriculum vitae and their experiences in the business world. It is anticipated that, on completion of the Oracle Academy Introduction to Computer Science option, students will possess strong presentation, problem solving and project management skills, as well as gaining early exposure to the business, technology and professional skills that apply to a broad range of technology and business careers, including software development, systems analysis, database administration and management consulting. The programme also contains a key component that promotes professional development for teachers. Participating teachers are lead by Oracle experts through 9 weeks on online training and 6 days of in-class training to prepare to teach the curriculum to their students. Throughout the year, faculty members receive instructional support from Oracle mentor instructors.

The Oracle Academy Introduction to Computer Science option offers two courses: Database Design and Programming with SQL (150 hours) and Database Programming with PL/SQL (150 hours). Both courses allow both students and teachers the option of taking the relevant Oracle Certified Associate exam.

Oracle has successfully sponsored 119 English specialist schools to establish Oracle Academies. Ian Smith, the Regional Senior Vice President UK, Ireland and Israel of the Oracle Corporation, says:[8]

> SSAT performs an important role in helping our students to develop the practical skills they will need to be successful in the 21st century workplace. Oracle is delighted to offer the Oracle Academy curriculum via the SSAT programme, because it is an excellent example of how business and education can work together for the benefit of students.

[8] Ibid.

Whilst accessing the Web, Academy students learn how to manipulate and control this important medium. Academy students develop highly practical skills such as designing strategic applications to solve business scenarios. They also meet with industry professionals who speak to them about their curriculum vitae and their experiences in the business world. In the second year, students study the basics of the Java programming language. Having completed the Internet Academy course, students possess strong presentation, problem solving and project management skills combined with working knowledge of the Java programming language.

A similar arrangement has been made with Microsoft, which has sponsored a large number of specialist schools. Bill Gates, the former chairman and chief software engineer of Microsoft, strongly favoured this support:[9]

> Microsoft is passionate about helping people realise their full potential. So I'm delighted that we're working with specialist schools across the UK to excite, inspire and create opportunities for students – in life, at college and in an increasingly digital workplace.

I believe it is crucial that the new National Diploma in ICT includes the Cisco, Oracle and Microsoft professional diplomas. Many more Cisco, Oracle and Microsoft academies should be opened in both our schools and further education colleges.

Suggested further reading

BECTA Education, the Architect of the Networked Economy, and CISCO Networking Academy, *Harnessing Technology: Next Generation Learning*, Available at www.becta.org.uk

Oracle Internet Academy, *Control the Net*, available at www.trinitypride.k12.pa.us/users/hoffmann/Letter%20to%20parents.pdf

Marianne Kolding and Vladimir Kroa, 'Networking Skills in Europe: Will an Increasing Shortage Hamper Competitiveness in the Global Market?' London: IDC, 2005.

[9] Ibid.

Chapter 10

How specialist schools have helped to raise standards in English secondary schools

The origins of the Specialist Schools movement in England go back to a conference on youth unemployment in January 1986, organised by the author on behalf of the Centre for Policy Studies, the leading Conservative think tank at that time, at the request of the prime minister, Margaret Thatcher. Mrs Thatcher was concerned at the very high level of youth unemployment and wanted to hear from leading industrialists what could be done about this problem. The conference was held at the House of Lords and was attended by sixty heads of major industrial, commercial and financial enterprises, and senior civil servants as well as Lord Young of Graffham, then the secretary of state for employment.

At the time, 3 million British workers were unemployed with almost a third of 16 year-olds being neither in education, training or employment. No speaker suggested that the high level of unemployment could be reduced by the government spending large sums to subsidise the creation of more jobs. For example, Larry Tindale, the chairman of Investors in Industry (3i) said that employment is the outcome of business, not its reason. The conference believed the role of central government was to create the conditions in which free enterprise could flourish, including giving priority to reducing inflation, lowering interest rates and wherever possible, reducing unnecessary government expenditure and regulation.

There was, however, unanimity on one particular need for increased government action – the need to create a more skilled workforce by improving schools with a vocational focus. At that time, 45 per cent of all English schoolchildren left school at age 16 without one or more traditional O-level pass or its equivalent.

The conference recommended that the government establish 100 directly funded technology secondary schools supported by industry, which would focus on both raising overall educational standards and improving the technical skills of school leavers, so that they would be more likely to obtain employment.[1]

Thus was born the City Technology Colleges (CTCs) initiative. At the Conservative Party Conference in October 1986, the new education secretary, Kenneth Baker, announced that the government would provide funding initially for the creation of twenty-five city technology colleges, hopefully with the support of private sector funding.

I was subsequently appointed Kenneth Baker's special adviser on the initiative and vividly remember my first meeting with Baker, at which a senior official, John Hedger,

---

[1] I wrote up the findings at the time in my paper 'Employment Examined: the Right approach to more jobs', published in June 1986 by the Centre for Policy Studies.

who was in charge of the initiative, produced a box full of cheques received from the private sector to support the initiative and wondered what they should do with them. I suggested establishing a non-profit charity, the City Technology Colleges Trust, which would use the cheques to provide sponsorship for particular schools. This was the beginning of the organisation which has subsequently grown under its current name of the Specialist Schools and Academies Trust, to represent 3,000 of England's 3,100 secondary schools, as well as having 2,000 overseas schools affiliated.[2]

As Table 10.1 shows, fifteen city technology colleges were established between 1988 and 1993 with the support of £40 million of sponsorship.

Because of the difficulty in persuading local authorities to provide sites for the CTCs, – which were independent of them – only four of the original 15 CTCs were founded on the sites of existing functioning schools, with the remainder being built on sites acquired by the sponsors – usually of schools which had been closed.

Despite admitting a wide range of ability, with a higher than national average free schools meals eligibility among their pupils, these 15 schools are now among the leading comprehensive schools in the country (Table 10.2).

Christine Walter[3] recalls that the original brief of the fifteen city technology colleges was quite specific:[4]

> They were to be state comprehensive schools. They were to be independent of local authority control and they were to serve inner city areas, which were usually areas of considerable social deprivation.
>
> They were to be rich in information technology and, with the exception of the BRIT School, to have a focus on maths, science and design technology. The BRIT School focused on the Performing Arts. Above all they were required to raise educational standards in the areas they served.
>
> A further requirement that is sometimes overlooked is that they had a research and development brief. Another way of putting this is that they were 'laboratory' schools, experimenting with new ways of teaching and learning, challenging established practices and creating new models from which other schools could learn.

So why have the original CTCs been so successful, and how can mainstream comprehensive schools learn from their experience?

All the CTCs meet our criteria for a good school:

- They have outstanding leadership supported by excellent governing bodies;
- They are able to attract and retain good teachers including training their own;
- They without exception perform well in public examinations (Ks3, GCSE and A–levels);
- Nearly all their pupils are in full-time education (usually at the CTC) or training at age 16 and 17;
- A high proportion of their pupils go on to study at university;

---

[2] An excellent history of the CTCs, *City Technology Colleges: Their Conception and Legacy* (2007), has been written by Christine Walter (writing as Christine Prentice). It is available from the SSAT. ISBN 1-905150-67-9.

[3] Writing as Christine Prentice.

[4] Christine Prentice, *City Technology Colleges: Their Conception and Legacy*.

Table 10.1 City technology colleges established between 1988 and 1993

City technology college	Sponsors
Kingshurst CTC in Birmingham (1988)	Hanson Trust and Lucas Aerospace
Djanogly CTC in Nottingham (1989)	Sir Harry Djanogly
Macmillan CTC in Middlesbrough (1989)	BAT Industries, Sir John Hall
Dixons CTC in Bradford (1990)	Dixons, Haking Wong Enterprises
Leigh CTC in Dartford (1990)	Sir Geoffrey Leigh, Wellcome Trust
Thomas Telford CTC in Telford (1990)	The Worshipful Company of Mercers, Tarmac
Harris CTC in Croydon (1990)	Philip and Pauline Harris Charitable Trust
Emmanuel CTC in Gateshead (1990)	Reg Vardy, Safeway, Laings
Bacon's CTC in Southwark (1991)	Church of England, Philip and Pauline Harris Charitable Trust, London Docklands Corporation
BRIT School in Selhurst, Croydon (1991)	BRIT Trust, donations from six major recording companies and proceeds from the Knebworth concert in 1990 organised by Sir Richard Branson
Haberdashers' CTC in Lewisham (1991)	The Worshipful Company of Haberdashers, Hugh de Capell Brooke
ADT College in Wandsworth (now Ashcroft Technology College) (1991)	ADT
Landau Forte CTC in Derby (1992)	Landau Foundation, Forte plc
John Cabot CTC in Bristol (1993)	Cable & Wireless, Wolfson Foundation

Table 10.2 Provisional self-reported CTC GCSE results as at 5 September 2008

CTC	% 5+ A*–C grades	% 5+ A*–C grades including English and maths
ADT, Wandsworth	88	67
Bacon's, Rotherhithe	77	60
BRIT, Croydon	99	53
Brooke Weston, Corby	100	86
Dixons*, Bradford	99	89
Djanogly**, Nottingham	60	32
Emmanuel, Gateshead	98	83
Haberdashers', Lewisham	96	94
Harris, Crystal Palace	93	80
John Cabot, Bristol	87	62
Kingshurst, Solihull	86	54
Landau Forte, Derby	85	71
Leigh*, Dartford	94	40
Macmillan*, Middlesbrough	92	69
Thomas Telford, Telford	100	98
Average	90%	69%

- They have a high level of attendance (usually 95 per cent) – attendance is usually monitored electronically through the use of smart cards;
- They exclude very few of their pupils despite the wide range of ability of their intakes, many of whom come from socially disadvantaged areas;
- Most CTCs open their doors at 7.30 in the morning and serve breakfast for those pupils needing nourishment. They usually remain open until 6 p.m. or even later offering a wide range of extra curricular activities;
- They have a curriculum focus – except the BRIT school with its music specialism – on technology (including IT), maths and science;
- They focus on the basics such as literacy and numeracy;
- They make extensive use of information community technology, including wireless linked laptops, interactive whiteboards and Web-supported learning;
- Crucially, they have the inspirational support of dedicated sponsors.

By 1993, fifteen city technology colleges had been established, but the economic crisis of 1992 caused the government to suspend the programme, even though there were many more sponsors willing to establish new CTCs. When I was asked by John Patten, the education secretary, and John Major, the prime minister, to recommend a way to create CTC-style schools at substantially less capital costs by converting existing secondary schools to a CTC style of operation, I suggested we should introduce technology colleges, converted from existing schools, which would require considerably less capital outlay and sponsorship.

Specialist schools were thus born in 1994 with the creation of the first fifty technology colleges. Initially, the scheme was limited to voluntary aided and grant maintained schools. There was also an expenditure limit on the number of schools which could be designated specialist in any one year. Schools had to raise £100,000 of sponsorship and submit directly to the secretary of state for education a bid for technology college status which would set targets for improving both their GCSE results in technology-related subjects such as design technology, maths and science, as well as overall results. Crucially, the initiative was voluntary, and the decision of whether or not to bid was made by the school's head teacher and governing body while the bids together with targets for achievement were prepared by their head teachers.

The number of specialist secondary schools has grown rapidly since the first fifty were established in 1994.[5] The Labour government which came to power in 1997 decided not only to keep the programme, but to expand it to cover virtually all secondary schools (see Table 10.3).

By September 2008, a total of 3,104, or 90 per cent of all the mainstream 3,431 maintained English secondary schools (including middle, deemed secondary) were either specialist or an academy. The creation of large numbers of specialist schools has undoubtedly been one of the prime reasons, together with the increase in government funding for schools, for the improvement in educational standards in our schools since the Labour government was first elected in 1997.

Overall, the percentage of 15 year-olds achieving five good GCSE grades in any subject has increased from just 44 per cent in 1996 to 63 per cent in 2008. The

[5] Christine Walter (Prentice) has also written an excellent history of the Specialist Schools movement *A History of the Specialist Schools and Academies Trust: By Schools for Schools*, London: SSAT, 2007. ISBN 1-905150-96-2.

Table 10.3 Number of specialist schools (including academies but excluding special schools)

Year	Number of specialist schools established	Cumulative number	New specialisms and types of school introduced
1994	50	50	Technology colleges
1995	50	100	Language colleges
1996	82	182	Arts and sports colleges; Gillian Shephard opens the specialist schools initiative to all schools, not just grant maintained schools.
1997	63	245	
1998	85	330	Specialist special schools
1999	70	400	
2000	150	550	
2001	250	700	Science, maths and computing, engineering, business and enterprise
2002	292	992	Charles Clarke lifts the cap on the number of newly designated specialist schools in any one year.
2003	452	1,444	Music and humanities
2004	511	1,955	Academies introduced
2005	426	2,381	
2006	426	2,807	
2007	54	2,861	
2008	243	3,104	

Table 10.4 Time series of GCSE and equivalent attempts and achievements

	Number of pupils[3]	Percentage who achieved				
		5+ A*–C grades	5+ A*–C grades incl. English and mathematics GCSEs	5+ A*–G grades	5+ A*–G grades incl. English and mathematics GCSEs	Any passes[4]
15 year olds						
1995/96	594,035	44.5	35.2	86.1	83.4	92.2
1996/97[5]	586,766	45.1	35.6	86.4	83.9	92.3
1997/98	575,210	46.3	37.0	87.5	83.8	93.4
1998/99	580,972	47.9	38.6	88.5	85.8	94.0
1999/00	580,393	49.2	40.0	88.9	86.8	94.4
2000/01	603,318	50.0	40.7	88.9	86.9	94.5
2001/02	606,554	51.6	42.1	88.9	87.1	94.6
2002/03	622,122	52.9	41.9	88.8	86.6	94.8
2003/04[6]	643,560	53.7	42.6	88.8	86.7	95.9
2004/05	636,771	56.3	44.3	89.0	86.9	96.4
2005/06	648,942	58.5	45.3	89.4	86.8	96.7
2006/07	656,432	60.8	46.0	90.0	86.4	97.3
Pupils at end Key stage 4						
2004/05	633,414	57.1	44.9	90.2	88.0	97.4
2005/06	645,931	59.2	45.8	90.5	87.8	97.8
2006/07	649,159	62.0	46.7	91.7	87.9	98.9

Table 10.5 Performance of specialist schools by year of designation

Year designated	Number of schools	% 5+ A*–C grades at GCSE in year prior to designation	% of 5+ A*–C grades at GCSE in 2007	Improvement in % 5+ A*–C grades since designation
1994	45	40	74%	+ 34%
1995	39	44	69%	+ 25%
1996	62	50	67%	+ 17%
1997	72	49	64%	+ 15%
1998	82	45	60%	+ 15%
1999	82	45	60%	+ 15%
2000	68	47	61%	+ 14%
2001	124	47	61%	+ 14%
2002	143	46	57%	+ 11%
2003	288	52	61%	+ 9%
2004	427	52	60%	+ 8%
2005	473	52	57%	+ 5%
2006	390	53	54%	+ 1%

proportion including maths and English has increased from just 35 per cent in 1996 to 48 per cent in 2008. The figure is slightly higher when one includes all those who reach the standard by the end of Key stage 4 (Table 10.4).

Specialist schools have been particularly successful in raising their standards of achievement, with a direct correlation between the length of time these schools have been designated specialist and their improvement in performance. Table 10.5 compares the achievement of the specialist schools in the year before they were designated as specialist, to their results in 2007.

Speaking at the SSAT's national conference in November 2006, the prime minister, Tony Blair, said of the Specialist Schools and Academies Trust and its 3,000 affiliated English secondary schools:[6]

> This is now the largest education conference of the year and the Trust the most dynamic education organisation in Britain. You are the true change-makers in our country today. You are lifting the sights of our young people, teaching them better, educating them more profoundly and to a higher standard than ever before in our country's history. It is an amazing achievement.

There are a number of crucial events which helped to achieve this success.

First, Gillian (now Baroness) Shephard, then the Conservative education secretary, announced in 1997 that all schools, not just those with grant maintained status or foundation schools, would be eligible to apply for specialist school status. This was vitally important because it made the initiative acceptable to the Labour Party.

Second, in 1996, the author helped to convince David Blunkett, then shadow education secretary, that specialist schools were a good thing. By chance, one of David's sons attended Yewlands Technology College in Sheffield, which had become a specialist school in 1996. David was impressed by the improvements that specialist status had brought to Yewlands. He spoke at the specialist schools' national conference in Bradford in 1996 and announced

[6] The speech can be read at www.number10.gov.uk/Page10514

his support for the specialist schools concept. It must be remembered that in 1996 there were only 182 specialist schools, including the fifteen original CTCs. Another happy coincidence was that David Blunkett's number two, Estelle Morris, later to succeed him as education secretary, had taught in a specialist school, Sidney Stringer, in Coventry.

The initiative could have easily been terminated by the new government in 1997. Instead, Prime Minister Blair and David Blunkett, the new education secretary, decided to build on the existing strengths of the initiative by adding new dimensions.

The support of Prime Minister Blair was crucial, as was the support of Andrew Adonis, his education adviser from 1998. I met Tony Blair for the first time in December 1996, when I was invited to travel with him on the train to Darlington from London. Mr Blair had been asked to open the Carmel Roman Catholic Technology College in Darlington, where he knew the chair of governors, Fr John Caden. During the train ride, he asked how the specialist schools initiative worked and whether it would be possible eventually for all schools to benefit from acquiring the status.

Subsequently the Labour governments of 1997–2001 and 2001–2005 made the following important improvements to the initiative (see the Department for Children, Schools and Families website):

- **Community dimension**: The additional funding per head was raised from £100 per child to £129 per pupil, but a third of this – approximately £40,000 a year for the typical school – had to be spent helping to raise standards in other schools in the applicant's area.
- *New specialisms* were announced, including special educational needs; science, maths and computing, engineering, business and enterprise, music, and humanities. By 2003 all the subjects in the national curriculum were included as specialist subjects.
- *Cap lifted*: Crucially, Charles Clarke in 2002 lifted the cap on the number of specialist schools which could be designated in any one year. This doubled the annual number of newly designated schools which increased from 251 in 2001 to 511 in 2004.
- *The sponsorship requirement was lowered* from £100,000 in 1997 to £50,000 and in 2002 a Partnership Fund was established with both the support of the Garfield Weston Foundation who contributed £1 million a year for several years, which was matched by the government to help those schools who found it difficult to raise the full £50,000 of sponsorship themselves.
- *Academies*: David Blunkett first announced plans for academies in 2000, and in 2004 a plan was announced to create 200, which would be very similar to the original CTC model. This has subsequently been increased to 400. See Chapter 7.
- *Trust schools*: The Trust initiative was announced in 2005 with the intention that groups of specialist schools would work together to establish new educational foundations under which a group of specialist schools would collaborate and cooperate to raise standards as well as help low-attaining schools. Universities and FE colleges could also be engaged in trusts.
- *Streamlined redesignation*: The number of years for which a school was designated before being required to apply for redesignation was reduced from four to three years, with a favourable OfSTED report being added to the list of redesignation requirements, including delivery of targets for improvement and the setting of acceptably challenging new targets for the new period of designation.
- *High-performing specialists*: When schools apply for redesignation, they can now also apply for high-performing status, to offer a second specialism or become a training

school or to help an under-performing school, entitling them to an additional grant per pupil per year of £60–90 per pupil. There is currently a limit of 1,000 schools that can be given high-performing status, and this cap should be lifted.

- *Special needs*: A particularly interesting new specialism was added in 1998, that of a specialist special needs school. There are now nearly 200 such schools. One of their goals, besides raising the standards of their own pupils, is to help other schools with improving their education of special needs children

By September 2008, there were 3,104 specialist schools and academies.[7] Here is how they currently operate. All specialist schools and academies are maintained schools funded by the government. They must teach the full national curriculum but give particular attention to their specialist subject, sometimes through an extended school day. All maintained secondary schools are eligible to bid for specialist status. There is no government cap on the number of specialist schools and funding is available for every approved bid.

Each prospective specialist school must obtain sponsorship of £50,000 or more from the private sector. The DCSF partnership fund established with the help of the Garfield Weston Foundation assists schools who find it difficult to raise the full sponsorship. Though sponsorship is a one-off charitable contribution, sponsors are encouraged to become involved with their school, either through joining the governing body or offering pupils and teachers work experience or other encouragement. Sponsors may now give additional sponsorship of up to £25,000 when a school applies for re-designation and that sponsorship is matched by the government.

Schools applying for specialist school status submit a detailed development plan to the DCSF with specific targets for improving the school's overall results and raising achievement in their specialist subject. This plan also shows how one third of the extra funding to be received will be used to help other schools, especially feeder primary schools, in their local community to raise their standards.

Successful applicants initially receive a one-off government capital grant of £100,000 together with an annual top-up recurrent grant of £129 per pupil for 3 years, equivalent to about £129,000 for the average sized school of 1,000 pupils. This is equivalent to about 3 per cent of their normal recurrent funding. Thus an investment of £50,000 in sponsorship attracts an initial government grant over the three years for each school of approximately £500,000, a leverage of 10:1. Donations are tax deductible in both the UK and the USA.

Specialist schools must apply for re-designation every three years. Re-designation is now linked to the regular OfSTED inspection cycle. Schools which receive a grade 1 or 2 from OfSTED are automatically re-designated. Schools receiving a grade of 3 are usually re-designated, subject to a review of their performance by the Department for Education. Schools given a grade 4, which puts a school into Special Measures or under notice to improve, are placed on probation and may ultimately lose their designation, but can reapply for designation once improvements have been achieved.

Schools applying for re-designation as a specialist school may, if they wish, apply for a further capital grant of £25,000 from the education department, providing they raise sponsorship of a similar amount and agree to enter into a partnership with one or more local employers.

---

[7] Source: Department for Children, Schools and Families.

High-performing specialist schools[8] are eligible either to add a second curriculum specialism, the vocational option or special educational needs (SEN) specialism, apply for training school status or help an underperforming school. They receive additional grants of between £60 and £90 per pupil per year.

The mission of specialist schools

The mission of specialist schools is to build a world-class network of innovative, high-performing secondary schools. These schools, working in partnership with business and the wider community, bring choice and diversity to the English maintained secondary school system. This initiative is first and foremost focused on raising standards of overall achievement. Specialist schools have high expectations of their pupils and create an ethos of discipline, order and achievement. They seek to ensure that young people are well educated and technologically skilled, ready and able to progress into employment, further training or higher education according to their individual abilities, aptitudes and ambitions. They add to the richness and variety of secondary school provision, acting as a resource for neighbouring schools and the local community.

The 3,104 specialist schools and academies (excluding 188 specialist special schools) educate over 3 million pupils, 90 per cent of all English secondary school pupils in mainstream maintained schools, to an increasingly high standard.

There are eleven different types of specialist school:[9]

- Technology colleges (currently 565) specialise in teaching mathematics, science, design technology, and information and communications technology (ICT).
- Arts colleges (currently 494) specialise in teaching all the performing arts (including music, dance and drama, visual or media arts).
- Sports colleges (currently 401) specialise in teaching physical education and sport, and also serve as centres of sporting excellence for neighbouring schools.
- Science colleges (currently 322) emphasise the study of physics, chemistry and biology, working with leading university science departments, industry and major UK science bodies to create innovative centres of excellence.
- Mathematics and computing colleges (currently 280) emphasise these two essential prerequisites for further studies in the sciences and technology and for jobs requiring numerical analysis.
- Business and enterprise colleges (currently 255) specialise in business studies and foster an enterprise culture in schools. They teach business studies, financial literacy, enterprise-related vocational studies and marketing skills.
- Language colleges (currently 221) specialise in teaching modern foreign languages and promote an international ethos across the whole curriculum.

[8] For the 2008 HPSS round the key criteria are: (a) an overall grade 1 OfSTED marking with a minimum of 30 per cent 5+ A★–C GCSE including English and maths in the 2007 Ks4 results; or (b) an overall grade 2 OfSTED marking with a grade 1 in 'Achievement and Standards' with a minimum of 30 per cent 5+ A★–C GCSE including English and maths in the 2007 Ks4 results; or (c) an overall grade 2 OfSTED with a grade 2 in Achievement and Standards with 65 per cent or above 5+ A★–C GCSE including English and maths in the 2007 Ks4 results; or (d) an overall grade 2 marking with a grade 2 in Achievement and Standards and in the top 20 per cent CVA national ranking (Ks2–Ks4) and a minimum 35 per cent 5+ A★–C GCSE including English and maths in the 2007 Ks4 results. See www.standards.dcsf.gov.uk/specialistschools/

[9] Source: Department for Children, Schools and Families.

- Humanities colleges (currently 129) specialise in either English (both language and literature) history or geography and foster an understanding of human values and attitudes.
- Engineering colleges (currently 57) focus on mathematics and design technology, providing opportunities to study a wide range of engineering disciplines from civil and electrical engineering to telecoms. Their aim is to increase the number of good applicants for engineering degrees.
- Music colleges (currently 28) specialise in teaching music but also have a secondary focus on mathematics or ICT.
- SEN specialism (currently 111). A total of 188 special schools have so far achieved specialist status, with 77 opting for a specialist subject designation.
- There are 130 schools with combined specialisms. Additionally, schools in rural areas may add a rural dimension in any of the above specialisms.
- The 130 academies currently open specialise in a variety of specialist subjects.

Role of sponsors

Sponsors of specialist schools, either individually, or collectively with other sponsors, provide the following assistance:

- A one-time financial contribution which totals at least £50,000 per school. Donations are deductible against tax in both the UK and the USA and can be given either in cash or in suitable kind but cannot be conditional upon purchase of the sponsors' products. There is no ongoing obligation to provide additional financial assistance.
- They are encouraged (but not required) to enter into long-term support relationships with their school. This may include one or more of the following:
    - Appointing governors to serve on the school's governing body;
    - Encouraging the schools to report annually on their progress;
    - Providing work placements for teachers and students, providing careers advice for students and mentoring of both students and teachers.

Above all, sponsors are invited to help schools develop a businesslike ethos which encourages delivery of a high-quality education and value for money. Some sponsors enter into long-term funding agreements (3 years or more) under which a number of schools are supported over a period of time. For example, HSBC have backed over 100 language schools, many of which now teach Mandarin. Six hundred sponsors over the past twenty years have contributed over £300 million of sponsorship to specialist schools and academies.

Record of specialist schools

As described earlier in this chapter, the record of specialist schools in raising standards is impressive.

- In 2007, 62.3 per cent of the half million students in specialist schools achieved five or more good grades at GCSE in any subject, an increase of more than a third over the past ten years.[10]

---

[10] www.dcsf.gov.uk/performancetables

- They averaged 48.3 per cent including maths and English.
- Research by Professor Jesson shows that specialist schools regularly achieve a higher actual performance than their intakes of ability at age 11 would predict.

The success of the specialist schools programme has led the Confederation of British Industry and the Institute of Directors, as well as many leading firms and distinguished foundations, to endorse the programme:

> The CBI formally endorses the specialist schools programme as a key contributor to raising educational standards and improving the skills base of the UK. It encourages its members to become involved in partnerships with education in whatever way is most appropriate for the business concerned.[11]
>
> The IoD endorses the specialist schools programme as an outstanding example of effective business/school links. We would encourage our members to support specialist schools through sponsorship, appointment of business governors or through the provision of work experience for both teachers and pupils.[12]

A recent evaluation by OfSTED says that specialist schools are performing better and improving faster than other schools. David Bell, writing in 2005 as Her Majesty's Chief Inspector of Schools, said:

> Being a specialist school makes a difference. Working to declare targets, dynamic leadership, a renewed sense of purpose, targeted use of funding and being a contributor to an optimistic network of like-minded schools, all contribute to a climate for improvement and drive forward change.[13]

How English schools acquire specialist status

Applications for specialist school status are made to the Specialist Schools Unit at the DCSF.[14] The application must contain the following:

- Information about the school, including size, legal status and recent examination results;
- A development plan to achieve measurable improvements both in the specialist subjects and overall, to include quantified performance targets to be achieved over the three-year designation period;
- Evidence of how the school will work with other schools and the wider community;
- An outline of the bid for capital grant from the DCFS (grants may be used for the purchase of equipment, furniture and associated building work in order to enhance facilities for the teaching of the specialist subjects);
- An outline of how the recurrent grant would support the development plan;

---

[11] www.cbi.org.uk. See Specialist Schools and Academies Corporate Brochure 2007.
[12] www.iod.com. See Specialist Schools and Academies Corporate Brochure 2007.
[13] OfSTED press release, 16 February 2005.
[14] For detailed guidance, see DCSF generic guidance setting out the criteria for all specialist schools (and combinations) plus separate sections for each of the ten specialisms at www.standards.dsfs.gov.uk/specialistschools

- Details of sponsorship confirmed. The details of the proposed ongoing partnerships with sponsors, including co-option on to the governing body.

There are normally two application rounds for specialist schools each year, in March and October.

Role of the Specialist Schools and Academies Trust and the Youth Sport Trust

The Specialist Schools and Academies Trust[15] is the lead advisory body on the specialist schools initiative for the DCSF, providing advice and support for schools seeking to achieve or maintain specialist school status. Founded in 1987, the trust is a registered educational charity which has 400 staff and is funded by fees from its 5,000 affiliated schools, donations from sponsors and foundations, contracts and grants from the DCSF. Its work includes the promotion and support of specialist schools' and academies' curriculum development and innovation, teacher training in ICT, conference and seminar activities, and a publications programme. The SSAT plays an important role in raising sponsorship and introducing potential sponsors to suitable candidate schools. The Youth Sport Trust[16] supports schools seeking sports college status.

The 2007 corporate brochure of the SSAT, written by the author together with the assistance of the trust's dynamic and outstanding chief executive Liz Reid and her team of programme directors, describes in full the work of the trust. Its overall mission is to provide services by schools for schools, in order to help all English schools, both primary and secondary, to raise their standards.

The trust hopes to achieve this goal by the following:

- Helping the remaining 5 per cent of state-funded English mainstream secondary schools to become either a specialist school or an academy;
- Giving specialist schools and academies the maximum support possible to raise their standards and to retain their specialist status with the additional funding which comes with it;
- Helping all low-attaining schools to raise their standards by linking them with stronger schools;
- Helping to establish 400 academies and to raise their standards of achievement, enabling them to become an active part of a mutually supportive and innovative network of specialist schools;
- Developing expertise in each of the specialist subjects and making each specialist school the local centre of excellence in that subject;
- Raising standards in key strategic subjects such as science, mathematics and languages;
- Focusing on the improvement of standards in literacy and numeracy;
- Improving the teaching of vocational subjects in schools and encouraging more schools to offer distinct choices in vocational education, starting at age 14;
- Developing the community plans of specialist schools by encouraging them to work together and play a significant role in the community. Lead roles can then be played

[15] www.ssatrust.org.uk
[16] www.youthsporttrust.org

by groups of specialist schools in realising the potential of more of the students in their area;

- Encouraging schools to raise educational attainment for children in care;
- Providing support and opportunities for gifted and talented pupils;
- Offering facilities to adults in the evenings and at weekends;
- Improving the education of special needs children;
- Continuing to develop links with overseas schools and businesses through iNet (SSAT's international arm, sponsored by HSBC) engendering a spirit of cooperation and understanding and increasing knowledge of global issues;
- Helping to integrate minority groups better through the development of urban community schools;
- Developing the next generation of school leaders to tackle the substantial gap in supply (as there are currently 600 English primary and secondary schools without a permanent head teacher);
- Building partnerships to develop mutually beneficial relationships between schools and local, national and global businesses;
- Developing the financial independence of the SSAT by reducing its reliance on direct government grants and through charging fees for enhanced provision of support to affiliated schools, as well as tendering for government contracts.

How the SSAT sees its role is shown in Figure 10.1.

In the eight years since she was appointed chief executive, Liz Reid has led an extraordinary expansion in the number of services which the trust supplies to an ever growing number of affiliated schools – now over 3,000 English schools and almost 2,000 schools in other countries. The trust now employs 400 full-time staff and has an estimated annual income of £85 million.

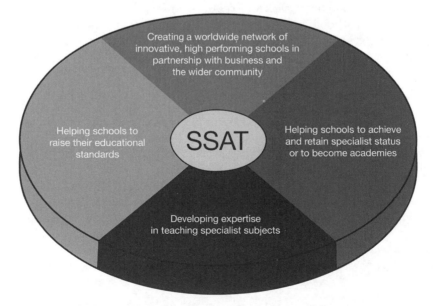

Figure 10.1 The role of the SSAT

One of its key roles since 1987 has been to encourage business and philanthropists to sponsor CTCs, specialist schools and academies. The corporate brochure lists the 600 sponsors who have contributed over £300 million to support the 3,000 specialist schools and academies. Many of the world's leading companies are supporters of specialist schools and academies. Writing in the 2007 SSAT corporate brochure, the sponsors said:

> From our earliest involvement with the specialist schools project, we have just been supporting success. Brooke Weston CTC has become a fantastic school, the 500 specialist schools we have helped sponsor have done well and we look forward to seeing the new Academy we are helping to build thrive as well. It's been a joy to have been involved.
>
> (George Weston, chief executive of Associated British Foods and trustee of the Garfield Weston Foundation)[17]

> Providing a good education for every child is crucially important. That is why we are sponsoring a group of 12 academies and specialist schools in south London which will work closely together to raise standards.
>
> (Lord Harris of Peckham and Dame Pauline Harris DBE, Harris Federation of South London Schools Trust)[18]

> Supporting education is very important to HSBC because we know education enriches people as individuals; we know it enriches our communities and it makes the world a more prosperous place. The aim of the HSBC Global Education Trust is to enhance educational opportunities for young people all over the world, so we are delighted to have been able to support more than 100 UK schools in their bids to seek specialist college status and to provide funding for two academies.
>
> (Stephen Green, group chairman, HSBC Holdings plc)[19]

> The Mercers' Company has been a sponsor of great schools for many generations. In keeping with this tradition, in the 1990s we founded Thomas Telford School, an outstandingly successful CTC, and more recently we have sponsored Walsall Academy and Sandwell Academy. We have an enduring commitment to the success of these independent publicly-funded schools through our representation on their governing bodies.
>
> (Christopher Clayton, master of the Mercers' Company)[20]

> The Specialist Schools programme has improved UK state schools more than any other educational initiative of recent years. It has given them impetus for change and the resources to achieve it. To sponsors the leverage is irresistible but I also think that schools have appreciated our involvement in other ways.
>
> (Sir Peter Ogden, chairman of the Ogden Trust)[21]

---

[17] Quotation from *By Schools for Schools* published by the Specialist Schools and Academies Trust, 2007.
[18] Ibid.
[19] Ibid.
[20] Ibid.
[21] Ibid.

Renaissance Learning is very pleased to be working with the SSAT to improve literacy and numeracy in UK schools. SSAT promotes personalized learning which research shows to be essential to accelerating learning and it's personalized literacy and numeracy learning that our technology supports.

(Terry Paul, CEO, Renaissance Learning)

We really want to support schools that intend to put ICT at the heart of their strategic vision. With the SSAT we hope that we can support these schools in their ambitions and help unlock the considerable benefits that the pupils will reap from achieving specialist status.

(Tim Pearson, chief executive, RM)[22]

High value added manufacturing is crucial to the future prosperity of our nation. That is why Rolls-Royce has sponsored a number of both technology and engineering specialist schools to ensure that school leavers have the skills necessary to work in our industry.

(Sir John Rose, Chairman, Rolls-Royce)[23]

iNet is the SSAT's international arm (principal sponsor HSBC). Its mission is to ensure outstanding outcomes for students in all settings. This is carried out by creating a powerful and innovative network of schools from all over the world that commit to achieving a systematic, significant and sustained change.

International partnerships give students a better insight into global issues and help them develop into active and thoughtful citizens. The development of international partnerships with schools in three continents introduces teacher and pupil exchanges, joint curriculum projects and extended language learning.

There are now SSAT networks operating in Australia, Chile, China, Holland, Mauritius, New Zealand, Northern Ireland, South Africa, Sweden, the United States and Wales. They are led by steering groups whose principals agree the activities of the network.

The development of leadership capacity is a key activity and there are Developing Leaders programmes in Australia and Wales. Chile and Georgia (USA) have held leadership festivals. In October 2006, a G100 summit was sponsored by HSBC Asia when 100 principals from 14 countries met in Beijing to discuss the leadership challenges of the twenty-first century. The 4th iNet Conference was held in Beijing in September 2007 and focused on four of the drivers of transformation identified by the G100 – leadership, personalised learning, curriculum development and well-being. There are now 1,000 international schools affiliated to the SSAT.

Writing in the SSAT 2007 brochure, the prime minister, the Rt. Hon. Gordon Brown MP, said:

The success of Specialist Schools and Academies is testimony not only to the hard work of heads, teachers, staff and pupils, but also the commitment of external sponsors.[24]

---

[22] Ibid.
[23] Ibid.
[24] Extract from letter in *By Schools for Schools* published by the Specialist Schools and Academies Trust, 2007.

So now that nearly all English schools are either specialist schools or academies, what does the future hold for this initiative?

Overall, the government gives specialist schools nearly half a billion pounds of tax-payer revenues including both the recurrent grant and the initial capital grant per school of £100,000. The huge improvement achieved in recent years in raising standards clearly justifies this investment. But as the author was asked recently, if all schools in England become specialist, what will be so special about them?

Clearly the SSAT and its affiliated specialist schools will need to justify this public investment by continuing to improve standards in their schools. A crucial aspect of the initiative is that schools have to rebid to keep their specialist status every three years, and thus to retain the additional £130,000 or so of annual recurrent specialist top-up fund-ing, as well as the possibility of additional capital grants.

The author strongly recommended that the criteria for re-designation remain strin-gent and that those schools who lose their designation as a specialist school − currently about 2 per cent of those applying for re-designation − must face demanding require-ments for regaining their status. The SSAT and its 3,000 English affiliated schools also need to encourage collaboration and cooperation between specialist schools, possibly through the setting up of new trusts which link a number of schools in a partnership under new foundation status.

As explained earlier, such links of schools will achieve significant benefits, including:

- Persuading high-attaining schools to help improve low-attaining schools;
- Providing centres of excellence in each area in particular subjects, especially maths and science, with possible new joint sixth forms being established on a cooperative basis as per the Sleaford model (see Chapter 15);
- Helping to provide support for gifted and talented students through Saturday morn-ing and summer programmes organised on a group basis;
- Helping to improve the education of children in care and those with special educa-tional needs through the appointment of lead schools in these areas;
- Helping to deliver the new National Diploma Programme thus ensuring that all 16 and 17 year-olds receive a good education.

The SSAT itself can, and will play a crucial role in helping to deliver the above objectives.

It must continue to focus on its mission of helping to raise academic standards in its affiliated schools. It will increasingly become a body which depends for the bulk of its income on payment for services to its affiliated schools and government contract work tenders and less on government grants. Already the proportion of its funding received in the form of grants has been reduced to only 20 per cent of its funding for the 2008/9 financial year.

A crucial service provided by the trust is helping to spread best practice through its network of schools. Every group of specialist schools has its own network with a sepa-rate programme of conferencing and publicity. The trust annually publishes over fifty papers. Its publications programme should be a major focus for the future. Providing both the specialist schools themselves and the SSAT continue to focus on their primary mission of raising standards, the future will be bright for both specialist schools and the SSAT. Below is a case study describing how specialist status helped Bartley Green School in Birmingham to improve its standards.

Case study: the impact of specialist status on Bartley Green School, by Christine Walter[25]

Background

Bartley Green School in Birmingham is in an area of significant social and economic disadvantage. It is, in fact, in one of the most deprived wards in the country and it experiences high levels of crime and poor health. Most of the students, around 90 per cent, are of White British origin with the remaining 10 per cent of Black or mixed heritage. The school is smaller than average with just under 900 pupils on roll. There are more boys than girls in the school and the percentage eligible for free school meals is around 40 per cent. As academic selection still exists in Birmingham, fewer academically more able pupils attend Bartley Green School, as these attend the local grammar schools. OfSTED found that attainment on entry at Year 7 (age 11) is broadly average, but literacy and numeracy skills are below average. The number of pupils with statements of special educational needs is among the highest in the country with eighty pupils, some 10 per cent of the school population. The school has a Special Education Unit (SEU) for fifty statemented pupils with speech and language or communication difficulties, including autism and Asperger's syndrome. A further thirty statemented pupils are in mainstream. A significant number of these have social, emotional and behavioural difficulties.

History

When the present head teacher, Chris Owen, was appointed in 1994, attainment at Bartley Green was low. Only 9 per cent of pupils achieved five or more good GCSEs. Between 1994 and 2000 an improvement agenda was followed and progress was clear, especially in the ethos of the school and the attitude of its pupils. However, it was slow to show through in attainment and hard results. The school acquired technology college status in 2000, and this brought both increased resources and a new drive for innovation in the school. Contact, support and networking with other schools increased, expectations rose and improvement gathered pace. Capacity was built among the staff. The school expanded and developed in line with the plan it had set itself in its bid for specialist status. The context in which the school works remain the same – it is very challenging – but the impact of specialist status is very significant. How can it be broken down for analysis?

The specialist dividend

The school anticipated two main benefits from its specialist technology status.

- The first was a rigorous framework for continued school improvement by means of a plan, which covered most subjects, set challenging targets, involved external evaluation and generally developed the ethos of the school.

---

[25] Statistics obtained from information published by OfSTED and the Department for Children, Schools and Families. Information obtained from conversations with the head teacher, Chris Owen. The case study has been approved by the head teacher.

- The second was the provision of additional resources and support through the capital funding and annual grant; help with staff development and curriculum development. There was also access to the SSAT network of interesting ideas and practice and work with primary schools through the community programme.

Bartley Green's head teacher, Chris Owen, believes that the contribution of specialist status has been immense. It has become 'normal' to see incremental year on year improvements and enhancements. All areas of the school have felt the impact. The main areas, which she believes have improved pupils' attainment, are:

- *Teaching and learning*: A huge investment in teaching and learning led the specialist plan. It included: time for curriculum development; visiting other schools and 'pinching' good ideas; appointing three Advanced Skills Teachers[26] internally; developing a new culture where teachers openly observe each other's classes; mini-projects including teaching and learning 'swop shops'; pupils reviewing of teachers online; project-based learning; an extensive programme of visits and enrichment for pupils; professional development in the latest approaches including thinking skills, accelerated learning and multiple intelligences; membership of the Recommending Body (RB – QTS awarding) partnership; and training of GTPs, which aids recruitment.
- *ICT*: A huge investment in ICT included: the use of ICT across the curriculum including staff appointments to ensure this actually happened; department-based access to scanners, printers, digital cameras and subject-based software; technical support, centrally resourced; wireless and hardwire throughout the school; digital projectors in all rooms and interactive whiteboards in targeted areas; laptops for all staff; a move to internal e-mail; accessible data and computer management systems to reduce bureaucracy; home access for staff and pupils; e-learning days for whole year groups. Pupils work at home, in the library, at friends' houses or come into school, to complete online subject-specific tasks
- *Curriculum development*: Increased flexibility and innovation included: early GCSE entries in Years 9 and 10 in French, humanities, statistics, English and Year 8 SATs; a broader curriculum including applied GCSEs/GNVQs in science engineering, manufacturing, health and social care, leisure and tourism, ICT and BTEC sport; a huge amount of personalised mentoring and support for pupils; use of a flexible curriculum, particularly for challenging pupils, work placements and individual timetables; no study leave for Year 11s (schools increasingly fear that this time is misused); intensive support for pupils falling behind with coursework; all statemented pupils expected to get minimum of five GCSEs, some at grade C; an in-house behaviour centre to develop and improve classroom learning skills; close monitoring of individual pupil performance and appropriate intervention.

Bartley Green's remarkable improvement in exam results is shown in Table 10.6.

In terms of value added, in 2007 the school had a CVA from Ks2–4 of 1078.7, putting it in the top percentile. In addition, Professor Jesson's analysis shows a positive score

---

[26] Advanced Skills Teachers are excellent teachers who wish to remain in the classroom and spend the equivalent of one day a week supporting other teachers in developing their skills and experience through the sharing of best practice ideas and approaches.

Table 10.6 Bartley Greens's remarkable improvement in results between 1999 and 2007

	5+ A*–C	5+ A*–G	1+ A*–G	5+ A*– E	1+ A*–C
1999	19%	87%	98%	51%	n/a
2007	77%	97%	99%	91%	96%
	48% including English and maths				

of +20 including English and maths. In other words, based on attainment on entry to the school, he would have expected the percentage of pupils achieving this to be 28 per cent rather than the 48 per cent who did so.

OfSTED 2008

When OfSTED inspected Bartley Green School in 2008, they awarded it a grade 1, 'outstanding'. They quoted a parent, who they felt was representative, saying 'I am very pleased and proud of the work my child is producing and the results he is attaining. I am proud to give this school my support. The head and her staff should be congratulated.' They were also impressed with a pupil who said, in a very well-informed way, 'this school is one of the best schools in the country'. When asked why, he responded correctly that the school's value-added score was 'in the top 1 per cent of schools nationally'.

OfSTED concluded:

> Anyone associated with Bartley Green should be proud, because it is an outstanding school that is extremely well placed to improve further. Very effective leadership at all levels, consistently good or better teaching and a rich and varied curriculum enable pupils to thrive both personally and academically.

On the impact of specialist status they commented:

> Specialist status has had a very positive impact by increasing the breadth of provision and levels of resources. For example, there has been heavy investment in ICT technology which is used very well in other subjects.

Future challenges

So, what are the future challenges for Bartley Green School? Its head teacher, Chris Owen, has the following observations.

> The fragmentation of educational provision has made the educational landscape become even more complex. Two future academies within two miles of the school and a falling roll situation in local primaries will keep us on our toes!
>
> Right now both schools designated to become academies are performing well below our own standards. Of course with greater funding and increased flexibility they have the opportunity to try to catch up. For our part, we became a Foundation School in 2008, have recently been awarded High Performing Specialist School status. We will continue to discuss with Governors, staff and our community our current and future status.

Succession planning has been a formal part of our School Development Plan for some three years now. Developing leadership amongst our teaching and support staff is essential to maintaining our future high performance.

Participation in the Specialist School and Academies Trust RATL (Raising Achievement Transforming Learning) programme as a mentor school has become part of this strategy. By sharing practice with colleagues from other schools, middle leaders themselves develop. Junior Research Scholarships and identified progression routes within the TLR structure for younger staff are examples of the implementation of our strategy. In a fast changing educational climate, quality leadership throughout the school is key to its continuing success and high performance.

Suggested further reading

Cyril Taylor, 'Employment Examined: the Right Approach to More Jobs', London: Centre for Policy Studies, 1986.

—— 'Raising Educational Standards: A Personal Perspective', London: Centre for Policy Studies, 1990.

The Specialist Schools and Academies Trust 'By Schools for Schools' brochure, London: SSAT, 2007.

Christine Walter, *A History of the SSAT*, London: SSAT, 2007.

—— *City Technology Colleges: Conception and Legacy*, London: SSAT, 2007.

Peter Rudd, Sarah Aiston, Deborah Davies, Mark Rickinson and Louise Dartnall, *High-Performing Specialist Schools: What Makes a Difference*, London: Technology Colleges Trust, 2002.

Tony Blair, Cyril Taylor and Elizabeth Reid, *Education, Education, Education, 10 Years On*, London: SSAT, 2007.

Chapter 11

Why our schools should become centres of community life

Back in 1924, Henry Morris, the then secretary of education in Cambridgeshire, published his famous thesis calling for the establishment of village colleges to serve as centres of their community.[1] At that time, rural schools were not of the same standard as their urban counterparts and were mainly isolated primary schools. Morris recommended and established six community colleges in Cambridge in the period until 1954 when he retired. Several other counties followed his lead, as have school districts in the United States.

Morris believed that a community college should offer the following services:

- Both primary and secondary schools, and further education and adult education, on the same site;
- A kindergarten for pre-school children;
- A village hall for use by the community as a whole, including evening musical and dramatic shows, dances, whist drives and public meetings;
- A library available for both the pupils and adults;
- Extensive sports facilities available to both the pupils and the residents of the community;
- Accommodation for community activities such as the Women's Institute, the British Legion, Boy Scouts and Girl Guides, village cricket and football, health clinics and small business start-up units;
- Employment training.

Uniquely, his village colleges had a body of governors responsible both for academic standards and provision of community services, including a representative appointed by the Senate of the University of Cambridge. To quote Morris, his concept of the village college[2]

> would change the whole face of rural education. Instead of the isolated and insulated local school with no organic connection with higher education, the village college would provide for the whole man and woman and abolish the duality of education and ordinary life. It would not only be the training ground for the art of living, but the place in which life was lived. The dismal dispute of vocational and academic education would not arise because education and living would be equated.

[1] Henry Morris, *The Village College: Being a Memorandum on the Provision of Educational and Social Facilities for the Countryside, with Special Reference to Cambridgeshire*. Cambridge: Cambridge University Press, 1924.
[2] Henry Morris, *The Village College*, section XV, para. 2.

Morris's ideas are particularly relevant today. His community colleges still flourish in Cambridgeshire and have been replicated elsewhere. An outstanding example of one of his colleges is Comberton Village College, which under the inspiring leadership of Stephen Munday, is one of the outstanding schools in the entire country. Stephen has developed Henry Morris's ideas and made his school into the centre of communal life in Comberton.

It is a major recommendation of this book that the concept of the village college be replicated in our urban areas, particularly where communities have become segregated along racial or ethnic lines. In the next chapter, we see how Morris's concept could be replicated in urban areas and learn in some detail about the Oldham project which will provide the first systemic group of urban community colleges in the country, one that hopefully will be the precursor of many other such institutions elsewhere.

Even in areas without a high proportion of ethnic minorities, the concept of an urban community school would be extremely valuable. For example, many schools today do not have adequate libraries (see Chapter 3 on literacy). And it is estimated that in London, it costs on the average £10 per book to loan to a member of the public. So why not move public libraries, as has been done in Westminster, into schools, where during the day they would serve the needs of the children and in the evenings could provide a library service to adults?

Despite the recent downturn in the economy, there is still a shortage of 100,000 skilled IT workers in the UK. Why not establish community schools in urban areas equipped with Cisco, Oracle and Microsoft academies, which could teach the children these skills during the day and adults the same skills in the evening and at the weekend? A young person obtaining a Cisco Certified Network Associate Diploma can easily find a high-paying job of £25,000 p.a. or more. This is why so many specialist technology colleges are now offering a Year 14 to students who have obtained their A-level and obtained entry to a good university, but postpone going to university as a sort of gap year (acquiring the Cisco qualification only requires 6 months' training) in order to take the various IT academy courses.

The author arranged for both John Chambers, the chief executive of Cisco Systems, and Larry Ellison, the chief executive of Oracle, to meet Prime Minister Blair. Both chief executives pledged their support to establish a substantial number of Cisco and Oracle academies in English schools (see Chapter 9 for further information). There are now about 500 such academies, but many more are needed. IT academies should be made an important feature of urban community colleges.

Similarly, in many urban areas, there is a desperate need for sporting facilities for young adults, as well as schoolchildren. While the National Lottery has been funding more all-weather pitches, it is a disgrace that so many school playing fields were sold off in the 1980s and 1990s for development. Surely our young adults would be better off enjoying sport and improving their fitness by being able to use the sports facilities of schools. At the very least this will require the provision of an all-weather sports field by most of our secondary schools. Who knows, we might even improve the results of the English national football team by doing this.

If schools are open from 7.30 in the morning until 9.00 in the evening, catering for both children and adults, more staff will be required in the form of caretakers and teachers. There will, however, be no additional capital costs. It is surely unacceptable that so many secondary schools occupying buildings which are worth £30 million, are only open from 9.00 a.m. until 3.00 p.m. for 190 days in the year. Surely from a total education budget of £60 billion a year, we can find funding for the extra staff to do this.

Case study: Comberton Village College, a school in the Henry Morris tradition, by Christine Walter

Comberton Village College, to the west of Cambridge, is an excellent example of a school operating according to the principles set out by Henry Morris. It is a true community school running a range of courses, which include arts and crafts, children's programmes, computing and information technology, employment skills, fitness and health, languages, music and dance, general interest, and a range of GCSEs. A coherent adult education programme has been designed alongside other village colleges at Bassingbourn and Melbourn to give people greater choice. Courses are delivered all day, in the evenings and at weekends, and it is estimated that around 2,000 adults use the college during the course of a year. The age range of those taking courses goes from children to people in their eighties and nineties.

A good example of the range of provision and how this fits in with the school is the area of ICT. Classes offered to adults include the European Computer Driving Licence (ECDL), New CLAIT,[3] Computers for Absolute Beginners and Web Page Design. At the same time the school's website is used to allow parents and students access to the school community, providing both information and a discussion forum. The school's leisure centre contains computers where members of the public can access the internet. The local library is on the school site where locals can also access computers with broadband. 'Parentmail' is used to enable fast communication. So, the uses of ICT by the school and its community effectively link at several points.

Comberton Village College itself is a very successful school. A sports college with additional specialisms in languages and vocational education, it is also a Training School (helping in teacher training) and a Leading Edge School (sharing its expertise with others). The percentage of pupils gaining five good GCSEs including English and maths is regularly in the 70–80 per cent range. It does serve a relatively prosperous rural catchment area, but Professor Jesson's analysis shows a positive value added score of +10, demonstrating that pupils do make very good progress. OfSTED rated the school as grade 1, 'outstanding'. They singled out excellent teaching for praise – the school has fourteen Advanced Skills Teachers and that number is set to increase to eighteen – and commented that 'the climate for learning is excellent and relationships between adults and students are very good'. They also observed that the college has many different partnerships and commented that 'These strong partnerships at local, county, national and even international levels make a very positive contribution to the college's development and the outcomes for students.'

Stephen Munday, principal at Comberton, believes that the community nature of the school has a very positive effect on its ethos and performance. There is a sense of the school being 'ours' and not an alien environment. There is a sense of belonging. He says: 'There is certainly the feeling that "we are all in this together" rather than this is a building that we have to come to at certain times.' Young people at the school will almost certainly have attended for various activities when younger. The fact that they

---

[3] A package provided by the OCR exam board of three IT qualifications which provide a one-stop shop for learners looking to develop, improve or advance their IT skills.

may meet their parents, grandparents or neighbours on the site at any time of the school day certainly has a positive impact on behaviour. One physical manifestation of this is the almost complete absence of any damage to school facilities and the lack of any deliberate vandalism in the school.

The presence of so many adults gives a valuable message about the importance of education. These people are volunteers; they do not have to be there, but they choose to come and learn. The same applies to youngsters out of school hours. This message about the importance of learning has a very positive impact on the school's climate for learning, described by OfSTED as 'excellent'. Stephen says it would be difficult to quantify the impact on results of being a community school because it is clearly one element in the 'pot' along with others, but having worked in non-community schools as well as community schools, he is convinced that the impact of being a community school on overall performance is very positive.

Is it replicable?

Can the village college model of Henry Morris be replicated in other situations? His vision was of the school being part of rural regeneration. Could it also be a part of urban regeneration?

It has to be admitted that when the incoming Labour government introduced the community element of the specialist school programme in 1997 many schools struggled with the concept. However, Stephen Munday believes the principles certainly would work. He says: 'whilst the context might change, the concept of the school at the heart of the community and as a community resource is one that applies in every context. Henry Morris's ideas are remarkably applicable throughout 21st century schooling.'

So, why did so many schools struggle? One problem is the potential danger inherent in an open access site. Comberton has a system for adults to report to reception, with badges for ID, but it is basically an open site. The high wire fences and strict security that exist in some schools, especially in the inner city, do not sit easily with the concept of a community school. There are schools that keep the local community out for safety reasons. While there are probably ways around this for those with legitimate reasons for entering the school, the open site ideal would need some adapting.

A second problem exists for schools with wide catchment areas, which is the case for some urban schools. A school with a clearly defined local catchment area knows its community. For a school in the middle of London admitting pupils from up to seventy primary schools in many different boroughs and situated in a thinly populated area, the concept is rather more difficult. Such a school has to decide whether its community consists of local people living near the school, of which there may not be many, or the parents of its pupils? Or a mix of both? Stephen Munday agrees that these are difficult issues, but he says they are indicative of wider questions about the school system beyond that of introducing a community programme. The model of a local school serving a local community is the ideal one and if you were building a school system from scratch that is how you would do it.

The future

What of the future for Comberton? One positive development is the introduction of a sixth form in 2010. The new specialist facilities that will come with this should give further opportunities for community provision. There is also the possibility of making some sixth form provision available to adults. This is something the school is currently considering. On the negative side, the cloud on the horizon is the change in the priorities of the Learning and Skills Council (LSC). In the past the LSC subsidised some courses, particularly those leading to accreditation. Now they only subsidise courses leading to level 1 and 2 qualifications for unqualified young adults. This is a national issue impacting on adult education everywhere. It means that many courses need to become self-supporting. At Comberton they are conducting a review of their provision and seeing where costs can be cut. They also have to face the question of how much they can raise prices so that all courses cover their costs. It may mean the programme will become narrower.

Comberton Village College is clearly an outstanding school and its community nature is a very important part of that. Other schools may not be able to replicate what it does precisely, but there is much to be learned from its work and adapted to local circumstances.

Suggested further reading

Henry Morris, *The Village College*, Cambridge: Cambridge University Press, 1924.
Department for Education and Skills, *Extended Schooling*, London: DES, 2002.
J. Boyd, *Community Education and Urban Schools*, Harlow: Longman, 1977.
INFED website: www.infed.org/schooling/
Gerald Love, *Raising Achievement of White Pupils*, Birmingham: Birmingham Local Education Authority, June 2006.

Plate 1 Sir Cyril Taylor with Prime Minister Tony Blair at the SSAT conference in 2001. Reproduced by kind permission of the Specialist Schools and Academies Trust.

Plate 2 Sir Cyril Taylor with Sir John Major.
    Reproduced by kind permission of the Brooke Weston Partnership.

Plate 3 Sir Cyril Taylor, Baroness Thatcher and Mrs Elizabeth Reid. Taken at the launch of the book *City Technology Colleges: Conception and Legacy*, at Church House, Westminster, November 2007. Reproduced by kind permission of michaelwheelerphoto.com.

Plate 4 Baroness Thatcher, Lord Baker of Dorking and Lord Adonis. Taken at the launch of the book *City Technology Colleges: Conception and Legacy*, at Church House, Westminster, November 2007. Reproduced by kind permission of michaelwheelerphoto.com.

Plates 5 Music Class at Temple Grove Primary School.
Reproduced by kind permission of Dr. Elizabeth Sidewell. Photo: Laura Mtungwazi

Plate 6 Art class at Haberdashers' Aske's Hatcham College.
Reproduced by kind permission of Dr. Elizabeth Sidewell. Photo: Laura Mtungwazi

Plate 7 IT class at Haberdashers' Aske's Knights Academy.
Reproduced by kind permission of Dr. Elizabeth Sidewell. Photo: Laura Mtungwazi

Plate 8 Pupils of the Haberdashers' Aske's Knights Academy.
Reproduced by kind permission of Dr. Elizabeth Sidwell. Photo: Layton Thompson.

Chapter 12

How can we better integrate our ethnic minorities into their communities?[1]

There has been much discussion recently about the need to build stronger, more cohesive communities in England. A vision of society where people are committed to what we have in common rather than obsessed with those things that make us different, and where opportunities for advancement are available to all, not just a selected few, is a tantalising prospect. A particular problem in some communities is the lack of English spoken at home, especially by mothers and their children.

There is a range of actions already in hand across government to strengthen cohesion, including a new duty on schools to promote community cohesion, use of extended schools, and work with different faith communities. However, a particularly effective way to promote cohesive communities would be to establish a number of *multi-faith community academies*, modelled on Henry Morris's concept of the village community schools described in the previous chapter.

We have seen how schools like the Comberton Village Community School in Cambridgeshire are the centre of community life, providing both a high standard of education for their children, and serving as a centre of community life for adults. The government has recently provided funding for extended schools, to enable schools to stay open and provide a diverse programme of after-school activities for both pupils and the wider community.

This chapter recommends building on the extended schools concept by adding the essential ingredients of Henry Morris's community schools. To help tackle concerns over segregation in some of our urban areas, it also proposes adding a further vital ingredient of seeking the support of all our major faiths for these schools.

Background

According to the 2001 Census,[2] the total population of the UK is approximately 58.7 million, of which 4.6 million have a black or minority-ethnic background. The Census also showed that 72 per cent of the population in the UK was Christian, 16 per cent had indicated no religion and 7 per cent had chosen not to state their religion in the survey. At 3 per cent, Muslims were the next largest religious group within the total UK

---

[1] This chapter is based on my policy recommendation made to the secretaries of state for the Department for Children, Schools and Families, and the Department for Communities and Local Government, in September 2007, when I was chairman of the Specialist Schools and Academies Trust.
[2] www.statistics.gov.uk/census2001/census2001.asp

population, followed by Hindus at 1 per cent. There are 1.8 million British citizens whom the 2001 Census indicated are Muslim. Over half are aged under 25.

The Department of Communities and Local Government's 'Citizenship Surveys' have found in both 2003 and 2005 that 80 per cent of people in England and Wales perceived that people of different backgrounds got on well in their local areas – so there is a positive national picture overall.[3] However, the Commission on Integration and Cohesion's report, *Our Shared Values*, indicates that cohesion perceptions about people can vary significantly from one local area to another.[4] Key factors affecting perceptions include local attitudes, deprivation, discrimination, crime and anti-social behaviour, level of diversity and immigration.

The commission's report also states that improving community cohesion is about addressing these multiple issues at the same time – taking action on a single issue will only make a small difference – so there needs to be both mainstreaming work and targeted policy interventions.

Multi-faith supported academies

This chapter recommends the establishment in England of two exciting new types of academies, both closely associated with and supported by two or more faith communities. The first would be schools without a religious character but supported by all the major faiths. The second would have a religious character and would be designated as such in accordance with two or more faiths – as the sponsors and local community wished.

Sponsorship of an academy normally requires financial support which is tax-deductible of £2 million per school for the first three academies, and £1.5 million for the fourth and succeeding schools, to form a permanent endowment for each school. Sponsors who are universities or schools and other particular categories are exempt from this payment. The DCSF pays for the building costs either for a new school, or conversion of an existing school premises – usually about £25 million per school – and annual running costs at the same per capita funding as other maintained schools in their area. This is usually around £6,000 per pupil, or £6 million for a typical sized school of 1,000 pupils. There is also a grant to help pay for start-up costs of each school.

The proposed new academies would have two significant objectives in addition to the usual goal of academies of raising educational standards in socially disadvantaged areas of the country.

The first would be to create a new type of urban community school modelled on Henry Morris's concept of the village community school, which has been so successful in Cambridgeshire and elsewhere where similar schools have been created. The schools would be open seven days a week throughout the year (except on national holidays) from 7.30 a.m., with activities running as late as 9 p.m. The schools would offer courses, in the evening and at weekends for adults, for example on information technology. Hopefully, each academy would have a Cisco, Microsoft and an Oracle learning facility which would teach courses to the school children during the day and to

---

[3] Available at www.communities.gov.uk/publications/communities/citizenshipsurveyaprmar08

[4] Available at www.integrationandcohesion.org.uk/Our_final_report.aspx

adults in the evenings. The schools would also offer opportunities to learn English to parents who do not speak English, especially mothers of Muslim children. They would allow their sports facilities to be used by local residents, and provide advice on health and personal issues. Community academies would include all the services recommended by the government for their extended school initiative. Currently, many state schools are only open from 9.00 a.m. until 3.00 p.m. for 190 days in the year, despite costing £30 million to build.

A second major goal would be to encourage the integration of local minority-ethnic groups and to build more cohesive local communities.

Over the centuries, Great Britain has benefited greatly from its various waves of immigrants, including the Huguenots, Jews, African Caribbean people, and in more recent times, Asian people. These new arrivals brought with them new skills and enterprise, and have contributed to the general prosperity of the country, and in most cases were rapidly assimilated. However, possibly because of an over-emphasis on multiculturalism, recent immigrants, including Muslims from Pakistan and Bangladesh, have become increasingly segregated, with particular concentrations in twenty-five urban areas, including Birmingham, Blackburn, Bradford, Leeds, Leicester, Oldham, Slough, and several boroughs in Greater London including Tower Hamlets and Brent.

A Home Office report published in 2001[5] following the serious riots in Oldham, Burnley and Bradford, found 'separate education arrangements, community and voluntary bodies, employment, places of worship, language, social and cultural networks producing living arrangements that provide virtually no contact between the native Caucasian population and the Muslim immigrants'. It is estimated that in 348 primary schools out of 695 in Inner London, at least half the pupils do not speak English as their first language, although many of these children will use both English and their first language at home. Many are bilingual learners, but others are still in the process of learning English.

This de facto segregation is deeply worrying. For a start, it can adversely affect standards in schools.

For example, Grange School, a Leading Edge school in Oldham, is an excellent specialist visual arts and languages college with an outstanding head teacher, Graeme Hollinshead, where 99 per cent of the pupils are of Asian origin and 64 per cent are eligible for free school meals. A large number of the pupils' mothers do not speak English and some, because of their cultural beliefs, rarely leave their homes. In the 2008 GCSE or equivalent examinations, 71 per cent of pupils achieved at least a C grade in five subjects, which is admirable. But, if you include maths and English in this calculation, the proportion falls to just 26 per cent, and as a result, the school is unfairly placed on the list of 'failing schools'.[6] Graeme thinks that the lack of contact his pupils have with English speakers of the same age, may well be the reason why his school has a massive literacy problem. He says 'I, and everyone I have spoken to, agrees that it cannot be right for all our Asian pupils to have little, or no experience of mixing with white pupils until they enter post-16 education at Oldham Sixth Form College or Oldham College.'[7]

[5] www.homeoffice.gov.uk/about-us/freedom-of-information/released-information/foi-archive-crime/ 4387-oldham-riots-policing?view = Html
[6] Source: Personal communication with Graeme Hollinshead, August 2008.
[7] Information on Grange School was provided by the head teacher, Graeme Hollinshead.

This sort of segregation can also allow extremist views and ideologies to be propagated, resulting in the radicalisation of individuals and leading to increased racial and religious tensions, criminal and anti-social behaviour, and ultimately a breakdown of cohesion within the community.

What, therefore, can be done to better integrate our ethnic minorities into their communities and to resolve these problems? The most important way is to avoid racial and religious discrimination of all kinds, but a particularly effective way is to better integrate children of school age.

A number of measures have already been successfully introduced into schools up and down the country, which should be replicated by the proposed new multi-faith community academies. Among important examples is the following:

The teaching of English by schools to parents of their children who do not speak English. One of the most serious problems in England is the large proportion of Muslim mothers who do not speak English, particularly those who arrived in this country through arranged marriages and come from remote villages in Pakistan and Bangladesh where English is not spoken. The government has recently proposed that wives or husbands in arranged marriages should be required to speak English in order to obtain an entry visa. This would be a welcome reform.

But it should be accompanied by a major national initiative to teach English to ethnic minority mothers who do not speak English, with classes being given in the mornings at the schools, both primary and secondary, attended by their children. Funding could come either from the government's Aiming High programme targeted at the 686,000 pupils who are recorded as having a mother tongue other than English[8] or from the recently announced £400 million initiative to help low-attaining schools.

Souad Mekhennet has described in the *New York Times* how, during the first four years after a Moroccan woman, called Sara Tahir moved to Germany to marry her husband, she hardly left her home because she could not speak German.[9] Tahir is quoted as saying she did not want to take a single step outside her home without her husband, even to visit her gynaecologist. Her problems are shared by Muslim mothers all over Europe; unable to speak the language, they find it almost impossible to function in their societies.

But now, as a result of an initiative by the German *Land* or state of Hesse, Tahir can speak German. Twice a week, Tahir goes with her daughter Kawtal to the Albert Schweizer primary school in Frankfurt to learn German. A key ingredient of this successful German programme is that the mothers learn the local language, in this case German, at the school attended by their children. It is most unlikely that Sara Tahir would have gone to another institution to learn German.

Sadly, funding for such initiatives has not been available in England. For example, when St Paul's Way School in Tower Hamlets wanted to offer English language classes to the Bangladeshi mothers of its children who did not speak English, the school was told that the Learning and Skills Council would not fund the programme. Kevan Collins, the local Director of Children's Services, says there is a huge demand for English language courses from adult Muslims, especially women in Tower Hamlets, but insufficient funding for such mothers to learn English at the school which their children attend. This surely is a mistaken policy which should be changed immediately.

[8] See www.standards.dfes.gov.uk/ethnicminorities/raising_achievement/763697
[9] 'Classroom Door Gives Immigrants an Entry to Society', *New York Times*, 13 June 2008.

Other initiatives have already been introduced by some specialist secondary schools with great success.

The transformation of the previously low-attaining St Paul's Way School in Tower Hamlets under the outstanding leadership of Martyn Coles, now the principal of the City of London Academy in Southwark, is a good example of best practice. The school has over 90 per cent Bangladeshi students, with a similar proportion of pupils eligible for free school meals. Most of the children come from single parent families where the mothers are non-English-speaking widows of Bangladeshi sailors who had married in their sixties and subsequently died leaving several children. The school was performing poorly, but had an outstanding visual arts department. So, when it became a specialist visual arts college in 1998, Coles introduced the following measures:

(a) Bangladeshi-speaking receptionists were hired to encourage the Bangladeshi mothers to call the school with their problems.

(b) English classes were organised for the mothers which proved to be very popular, though the local authority was unable to supply sufficient funding to meet the demand, so the programme had to be discontinued.

(c) The visual arts department at the school was developed into a centre of excellence to take advantage of the skills of the local Bangladeshi textile designers, producing outstanding results in GCSE art. This in turn led to an improvement in other subjects through the 'locomotive effect' where outstanding results in one subject lead to improvement in other subjects.

Tony Blair, when prime minister, visited the school in 1998. The improvements from the awarding of specialist status led to the school becoming popular locally, so that it started to attract children more widely from other ethnic backgrounds.

Sir Dexter Hutt, chief executive of Ninestiles Federation of three schools in Birmingham, has used similar measures to diversify the intake of the three schools in his federation. For example, he has created all-girls playgrounds, so that Muslim parents were persuaded to enrol their daughters in a mixed school, leading to a more even ethnic balance. The all-girls playgrounds proved very popular with non-Muslim girls too.

Haydn Evans, the head teacher of Sir John Cass Church of England Language College in Tower Hamlets, has a policy of accepting pupils with a wide range of religious backgrounds even though it is a Church of England school. Interestingly, Muslims now account for 50 per cent of the pupils. Relations between the different ethnic groups are extremely good. The school teaches a dozen different languages, including Arabic and Mandarin (subjects both promoted by the SSAT). See the case study on the school in Chapter 13.

But we should do much more, and the proposed new multi-faith academies could play a major role in the better integration of ethnic minorities into our local communities. The first tranche is being established in Oldham. Five schools, including Grange, Kaskenmoor Comprehensive (which is almost exclusively White British), Breeze Hill, Counthill and South Chadderton, will be closed and combined into three new state-of-the-art academies which will be supported by all the local faiths, including Christian, Muslim and Jewish, as well as those of no faith. It is hoped that other such schools will be multi-faith schools; others will be non-sectarian, but all will be supported by all three major faiths. By redrawing catchment areas, it is hoped there will be a more balanced intake of pupils into each school. The schools have agreed to this move – as has the local council, and the local authority has secured the appropriate sponsorship to build the new academies.

It is believed by all concerned, that the pupils in the proposed Oldham academies will welcome better integration. Most commentators underestimate the desire of British ethnic minorities, especially the young, to integrate better with their local communities. For example, most children from the Asian subcontinent think of themselves as British, not as Indian, Pakistani or Bangladeshi. These children may not pass Lord Tebbitt's test of Britishness – which depends on which national cricket team you support – but they are proud to be British.

White British children will also welcome the end of segregation. A 2007 report by Sir Keith Ajegbo said White pupils feel isolated when they attend schools where they are in the minority.[10] At these new multi-faith academies, pupils will learn about all religions, not just their own. Crucially, there will be improved teaching of British history and citizenship and religious studies, hopefully on a multi-faith basis. The academies will include community facilities which can be used after hours by all faiths in the community. For example, Muslim children could be taught to read and understand the Koran at their school after hours instead of being taken to their local mosque.

These measures should encourage better understanding of the different faiths, as well as persuading parents from different faiths to develop closer links with their children's school. I hope that similar academies to those proposed in Oldham will eventually be built in all of the areas in England which have high concentrations of ethnic minorities. Of course, none of this means that the work of the hundreds of excellent schools with a religious character in England – whether they are Muslim, Jewish, Anglican or Catholic should not continue to be highly valued. Quite the reverse. Faith schools have a high standard of discipline, a great community ethos and achieve some of the best results in the country. The Church of England has recently agreed that all of their schools should accept at least 25 per cent of their intakes from other faiths, and it is hoped other faith schools will follow this lead.

Support for the proposal

The proposal to set up multi-faith community academies has the support of the DCSF and the Department for Communities and Local Government (CLG). The Church of England has expressed support, as have Muslim leaders in Oldham and elsewhere. Sir Sigmund Sternberg, Chairman of the Three Faiths Forum, is particularly enthusiastic. Finally, international scholars like Jessica Stern of Harvard University, author of *Terror in the Name of God*,[11] believes this initiative could give a world lead to the challenge of improving relations between people of different faiths.

The encouragement of better relations, understanding and tolerance between the 2 billion Muslims in the world and the other 4.5 billion non-Muslims is of crucial importance for the future of our planet. Britain, with its tradition of tolerance, could lead the way in developing new ways to achieve this. Making our schools strong community centres, supported by all of the major faiths, would not only raise academic

---

[10] *Diversity and Citizenship Curriculum Review*, London: DfES, 2007.
[11] Jessica Stern, *Terror in the Name of God*, New York: HarperCollins, 2004. ISBN: 0060505338.

standards, but help to foster better relations between all our citizens, whatever their ethnic or religious background.

Suggested further reading

Christopher Caldwell, 'After Londonistan', *New York Times Magazine*, 23 July 2006.

Rageh Omaar, *Only Half of Me: Being a Muslim in Britain*, London: Viking, 2006.

Jessica Stern (Professor of the Harvard University Kennedy School of Government), *Terror in the Name of God*, New York: HarperCollins, 2004.

Ed Husain, *The Islamist*, London: Penguin, 2007.

Souad Mekhennet, 'Classroom Door Gives Immigrants an Entry to Society', *New York Times*, 13 June 2008.

Ibrahim, I. A., *A Brief Illustrated Guide to Understanding Islam*, Houston TX: Darussalam Publications, 1997. www.islam-guide.com

Chapter 13

Are schools with a religious character a good thing?

There have been recent criticisms of both the admissions policies and the very existence of schools with a religious character. Most of the criticism is unwarranted and is usually based on misunderstanding of both the numbers of faith schools and how they operate.

David Jesson has produced for this book a special study of these schools. In his view, there has been a fundamental confusion between the total number of 1,150 voluntary aided and foundation schools, which account for 37 per cent of all maintained secondary schools, with the assumption being that most of these schools are schools with a religious character, and the much smaller number of these schools which are actually faith schools who together total only 526 or 17 per cent of all maintained schools

Table 13.1 shows that value added (VA) and foundation schools (with CTCs and academies) comprise around *one third* of all secondary schools. They are their own admissions authorities. However, as Table 13.2 shows, only half of voluntary aided and foundation schools are faith schools.

It is true that both the 526 voluntary aided and foundation schools with a religious character, (including the twenty-one selective schools) together with the 645 non-faith voluntary aided and foundation schools are responsible for their own admissions. But all

Table 13.1 Composition of secondary schools

Governance	Total number	Comprehensive/modern	Selective
Academy/CTC at August 07	56	56	–
Community	1,923	1,886	37
Voluntary controlled	90	78	12
Voluntary aided	518	485	33
Foundation	542	460	82
Total	3129	2965	164

Table 13.2 Religious affiliation of non-selective secondary schools

	Number	Percentage
No religious affiliation	2,547	83
Church of England schools	162	5
Roman Catholic schools	330	11
Other Christian faith schools	21	} 1
Other faiths (Jewish, Muslim, Sikh)	13	
Total	3,073	100

these schools have to follow the National Admissions Code described in Chapter 2. The code forbids interviews of children seeking admission to a particular school. The accusation that faith schools are selecting more able children from wealthy families through interview and other techniques is simply not true.[1]

Amongst non-selective schools, 83 per cent have *no* religious affiliation (Table 13.3). Amongst selective schools 87 per cent have *no* religious affiliation (Table 13.4).

The first providers of mass public education in England were the churches and particularly the Church of England through the work of the National Society in the nineteenth century. This role was increasingly taken over by the state as demand for secondary education increased in the early/middle years of the twentieth century. Other providers, most notably Roman Catholics, now also have a substantial presence in this field – there are 330 Roman Catholic secondary schools and 162 Church of England.[2]

Governance of schools

There are four major 'types' of governance of schools (not including either academies or middle, deemed secondary schools):

- Community schools   1,923 schools
- Voluntary controlled schools   90 schools
- Voluntary aided schools   518 schools
- Foundation schools   542 schools
- Total   3,073 schools.

Of these schools both 'voluntary aided' and 'foundation' schools are responsible for their own admissions arrangements (subject to national guidelines), whereas both

Table 13.3 Governance and religious affiliation for non-selective secondary schools

Governance	Total number	None	C of E	RC	Christian	Other faith	Total faith
Foundation	460	451	8	1	–	–	9
Voluntary aided	485	24	118	322	8	13	461
Voluntary control	78	43	32	–	3	–	35
Community	1886	1886	–	–	–	–	
Totals	2909	2404	158	323	11	13	505

Table 13.4 Governance and religious affiliation for selective secondary schools

Governance	Number	None	C of E	RC	Christian	Other faith	Total faith
Foundation	82	81	–	–	1	–	1
Voluntary aided	33	15	4	7	7	–	18
Voluntary control	12	10	–	–	2	–	2
Community	37	37	–	–	–	–	
Totals	164	143	4	7	10	0	21

[1] The full prohibition of interviews only came with the 2007 code. But even where interviews were permitted but discouraged, few faith schools used them.
[2] Source: David Jesson's paper on faith schools, July 2008.

'community' and 'voluntary controlled' schools have admission frameworks which are organised by the local authorities within which they are based.

The exception to this is that city technology colleges and academies – otherwise similar to community schools – are responsible for their own admissions and have characteristics in this respect similar to 'voluntary aided' and 'foundation' schools. About a third of the new academies are 'Christian' in religious affiliation.

Admissions policy

The second major dimension differentiating schools is whether they are 'selective' or 'non-selective'. The latter category of schools includes both 'genuine' comprehensive schools and also those in areas where 'selection' exists which take all those pupils who have not been selected for grammar school. (These schools are often described as 'modern' schools in official data, but this definition is applied inconsistently by the DCSF, so we simply describe them as 'non-selective' schools.)

While it is true that the proportion of 11 year-olds entering schools with a religious character who are eligible for free school meals is just 12 per cent compared to 14 per cent for non-faith schools, this does not necessarily mean that faith school admissions are biased towards the wealthy. There are many ethnic minority pupils attending these schools, of which a significant proportion do not apply for reasons of pride for free school meals, even though they are eligible to do so.[3]

There is a modest difference in ability between the 11 year-olds admitted to faith schools and those admitted to non-faith schools. The average per pupil Key stage 2 points for faith school 11 year-olds is 27.6 compared with 26.8 for other schools.[4]

The accusation, therefore, that faith secondary schools are highly selective and are biased towards the wealthy is untrue. What is true, however, is that pupils in non-selective faith schools perform better than those in non-faith, non-selective schools.

Comparisons and relative performance of 'faith' and 'non-faith' schools

Using the 'value-added' frameworks, the outcomes of the two 'types' ('faith' and 'non-faith') of schools can be compared.[5]

Table 13.5 shows that while faith schools recruit on average slightly more pupils, their outcomes are substantially higher than those of non-faith schools. The proportion of pupils eligible for free school meals is slightly lower for faith than non-faith schools, but not substantially so.

By itself the information in this table does not provide clear evidence about the relative 'successes' of the two types of school. To explore that more effectively requires a statistical analysis of their relative value added, the results of which are reported below in Table 13.6.

For each comparison, *VA outcomes in schools with a religious character are significantly better than those in non-faith schools* – suggesting that faith schools are more successful

---

[3] Research by David Jesson for paper on faith schools July 2008.
[4] Research by David Jesson for paper on faith schools July 2008.
[5] The comparison only includes non-selective schools.

Table 13.5 Basic characteristics and performances in faith and non-faith schools

School type	Ks2 pts	% FSM	5+ A–C at GCSE	5+ A–C at GCSE incl. English and maths	3+ A* or A at GCSE
Faith	27.6	12%	67%	52%	23%
Non-faith	26.8	14%	57%	42%	15%

Table 13.6 Value-added characteristics of performances in faith and non-faith schools

School type	5+ A–C at GCSE	5+ A–C at GCSE incl. English and maths	3+ A*/A passes at GCSE
Faith VA	+2.3%	+1.7%	+1.9%
Non-faith VA	−0.6%	−0.4%	−0.5%
Faith VA advantage	+2.9%	+2.1%	+2.4%

in helping their pupils achieve GCSE success than are the larger number of non-faith schools.

A much higher proportion of primary schools are faith schools, with 4,182 Church of England and 1,040 Roman Catholic schools, compared to 9,542 non-faith maintained schools. Faith schools account for 5,822 or 38 per cent of 15,364 primary maintained schools.[6]

However, as the excellent study of faith schools, *Faith in Education*[7] showed, the performance of faith schools is also good in primary schools as well as in secondary schools (see Table 13.7).

This study also confirms that (based on 2007 data) the performance at secondary level of maintained faith schools is better in faith schools than in non-faith maintained schools (see Table 13.8).

Christine Walter's case study below, using data provided by the head teacher, describes how the Sacred Heart Roman Catholic Secondary School achieves such splendid results. The school is oversubscribed, with 800 applications for 120 places. Examination results are outstanding, with an average of 78 per cent of its pupils achieving five good GCSE grades in 2007 including maths and English, even though only 40 per cent of its pupils, based on their Key stage 2 results, would have been expected to do so.

So, if faith schools are achieving such good results, why do they have so many critics: Here we must ask: are faith schools divisive and do they prevent the integration of our communities?

In 2005, I had extensive discussions with Lord Dearing, the Rt. Reverend Kenneth Stevenson, Bishop of Portsmouth (who was the Anglican bishop for education), and Canon John Hall, now Dean of Westminster, who was the chief education officer of the Church of England, over this issue. We agreed at the time that Church of England schools should be asked to admit at least 25 per cent of children from other faiths. This

[6] Source: David Jesson's paper on faith schools July 2008.
[7] John Burn, John Marks, Peter Pilkington and Penny Thomson, *Faith in Education*, with a foreword by Lord Griffiths, London: Civitas, 2001.

Table 13.7 Key stage 1 scores at age 6 for primary schools

Type of school	Number of schools	Percentage	Reading age	Maths age
Non-faith	9,542	62%	7.29	7.38
Church of England	4,182	27%	7.59	7.59
Roman Catholic	1,640	11%	7.63	7.60
Total	15,364	100%		

Table 13.8 Performance at GCSE

Type of school	Number of schools	% with 5+ A*–C grades at GCSE incl. maths and English	Average points per pupil	Percentage of pupils with no A*–C grades
Non-faith	2,434	43%	36	5%
Church of England	137	51%	40	4%
Roman Catholic	338	49%	40	4%

has now been enshrined in the DCSF document 'Faith in the System'.[8] Indeed, some Anglican schools, such as the Sir John Cass Church of England School in Tower Hamlets, admit as many as 50 per cent of their children from other faiths. Furthermore, the Dearing Committee said:

> In considering additional provision we invite dioceses to have a special commitment to expanding provision in areas of economic and social hardship. Referring to the historic mission in education of the Church of England to serve the poor, we say ... It should be an especial care of the Church today to renew that commitment to those who have least in life.

Church of England schools are invited to subscribe to the following principles first as a commitment by each school, as an institution, and by all staff and students as individuals:

> We will offer goodwill and respect to people of all faiths as our fellow citizens.

Second, a commitment by the school as an institution:

> In that spirit, we will seek and promote activities with schools of other faiths.

Many Catholic schools already have a significant proportion of children from other faiths, and have accepted that any new Catholic schools will allow 25 per cent of places for children of other faiths.

There was also support in the discussions between the Specialist Schools and Academies Trust in 2005 and the working party of the Church of England, for establishing more multi-faith schools. Chapter 12 gives details of such an initiative in Oldham, where it is hoped to establish three community academies with the support of all the major faiths.

[8] www.dcsf.gov.uk/publications/faithinthesystem/

Moreover, there are many Church of England schools which have already adopted a multi-faith ethos. We have already mentioned that the Sir John Cass and Redcoat School now admits more than half of its pupils from other faiths, mainly Muslim. A recent paper by Cristina Odone on faith schools published by the Centre for Policy Studies (CPS),[9] described in detail how the Sir John Cass School functions on a multi-faith basis and what remarkable results it is achieving.

Review of the Sir John Cass and Redcoat Church of England schools in Tower Hamlets, by Cristina Odone[10]

Among the high-rise blocks and council flats of Stepney, in Tower Hamlets, the red-brick buildings of Sir John Cass and Redcoat Church of England Secondary School are immediately noticeable behind their towering gates.

In contrast to the graffiti that covers the neighbouring buildings, and the litter on the streets and pavements, the Sir John Cass complex is impressively tidy and clean. Youngsters (the school is co-ed) in navy blue uniforms walk briskly but quietly in the corridors, greeting teachers with 'Hello Sir' or 'Hello Miss.' When they spot the head, Haydn Evans, they fall silent to attention. It is easy to understand their awe: when one boy arrives with his tie askew, Evans, eyebrow raised, picks him up on it: 'Where's your uniform?'

As Evans guides his visitor round the school he stoops to pick up a small paper wrapper from the corridor, and then drops it into one of several yellow litter bins that dot the walls. Attention to every detail, it is clear, is fundamental to his approach to education.

Although this is a Church of England foundation school, and Evans leads the prayer in assembly, 60 per cent of the 1,400 students are Muslim and, reflecting the local community, mainly from Bangladesh.

'We all share in faith, not one faith' Evans explains. As I look over the students sitting in assembly, I see Sikhs and Anglicans and Roman Catholics. In the build-up to the prayer and during the prayer itself, you can hear a pin drop. There is total engagement and respect.

Evans has presided over the extraordinary turn-around of Sir John Cass. When he joined the school in 1996, the number of pupils gaining five or more good GCSE grades had been 8 per cent. By 2002, there were 71 per cent and the school was rated as the most improved school in the country (as it was again in 2003 and 2004). Last year, Sir John Cass was the only school that raised achievement from the lower quarter on entry to the top 10 per cent on exit. This, with a student body that has a 75 per cent take up of free school meals, and for who, in 66 per cent of the cases, English is a second language.

Nor is Evans's achievement exclusively academic. The school offers an extended day (from 7 a.m. to 9 p.m.) for families where both parents work. It also opens its doors to the local community, offering English as a foreign language course, vocational programmes for second language learners and qualifications for business studies. Students are not allowed out during the lunch hour, but an extensive programme of extra curricular activities is provided during this period.

Haydn Evans knows what lies behind his school's success: 'a clear sense of values' shared by the head, the 180 staff (100 of them teachers) the six governors (four of them

---

[9] Cristina Odone, 'In Bad Faith', London: Centre for Policy Studies, 2008.
[10] Reproduced with the approval of Cristina Odone and the Centre for Policy Studies.

Bengali parents) and pupils. Those values, he explains, are faith, discipline, charity and respect for one another. They are incorporated into every aspect of school life, from testing (doing well is important, but doing your best more so), to mutual support (when, recently, a teacher's daughter died, the school behaved like an extended family).

This is the elusive ethos that even secular authorities claim they want.

Sir John Cass is exceptional; but a snapshot of faith schools in this country reveals that the majority share many of the features and achievements that mark the Tower Hamlets School.

The review of the Church of England schools chaired by Lord Dearing in 2001, *The Way Ahead*,[11] rightly called for the establishment of more Church of England schools, especially at the secondary school level, concluding that the Church's mission could only be discharged through more church schools where there was not a sufficient number of these schools to meet demand.

The Dearing Report also gave strong support for Church of England schools to be ecumenical in their approach and suggested that they should cooperate with other faiths. The Dearing Report quotes the words of the late Lord Runcie (who was the moral tutor of the author of this book at Trinity Hall, Cambridge, between 1956 and 1959) when he was the Archbishop of Canterbury, that the mission of church schools should be to:

- Nourish those of the Faith;
- Encourage those of other faiths;
- Challenge those who have no faith.

Clearly, schools with a religious character are of great value to our communities, not only because they achieve good results, but because they teach their children the difference between right and wrong behaviour. It is to be welcomed that so many of the new academies are being sponsored by the Church of England and other Christian sponsors.

But what of other religions? Should the government fund more Muslim schools? Currently there are only four state-funded Muslim primary schools and five Muslim secondary schools. This is a very difficult issue. If taxpayer money can be used to fund Christian and Jewish schools, why can't it be used to fund new Muslim schools?

Chapter 12 argues strongly for the creation of more multi-faith schools such as the Oldham project. This is surely the way to proceed, and the example of the Sir John Cass School shows how successful a multi-faith approach can be in an area such as Tower Hamlets where there is a predominance of Muslim children.

I am sceptical whether non-Muslim pupils would apply to be admitted to a purely Muslim school. There are also issues concerning whether the national curriculum would be taught, and the education for girls and appropriate accountability and inspection measures for Muslim schools. Therefore, the creation of more purely Muslim maintained schools would in all likelihood lead to an even greater segregation of our Muslim ethnic minorities than already exists, and it is therefore not recommended. However, that does

[11] Dearing, Ronald, *The Way Ahead: Church of England Schools in the New Millennium*, report of committee chaired by Lord Dearing, London: Church House Publishing, June 2001. www.natsoc.org.uk/schools/the_way_ahead/report.html

not preclude other forms of assistance to be given by the government to Muslim independent schools.

In conclusion therefore, the statistical evidence quoted in this chapter clearly shows that schools with a religious character are indeed a good thing and their status should be protected.

Case study: Sacred Heart Roman Catholic Secondary School – a school with the 'X' factor,[12] by Christine Walter

Sacred Heart Roman Catholic Secondary School in the London Borough of Southwark serves a disadvantaged catchment area including Peckham and Brixton. A high percentage of pupils speak English as an additional language and attainment on entry to the school is below average. The school is on a cramped site, in an old building which is due to be replaced. Professor David Jesson, in his work for the Specialist Schools and Academies Trust, estimated that in 2007, 40 per cent of pupils would have been expected to achieve five good GCSEs including English and maths. In fact an amazing 78 per cent achieved this, giving a positive value added score of 38, the second highest in the country.

In 2007 OfSTED inspected the school and gave it a grade 1, 'outstanding' rating, something that is celebrated in large letters above the school's entrance. They concluded 'There is no single reason for the school's success. It does have an X factor.' This case study attempts to define what elements go to make up that X factor. It focuses on three: ethos, the size of the school, and 'rank order'.

Ethos

In attempting to sum up the school's ethos, head teacher Serge Cefai, who has been at the school for eighteen years and became head in 2008, talks about 'treating children like children'. Pupils in the school know they are cared for, not in a 'soft' way, but in a disciplined environment which has both traditional values and high expectations. There are clear boundaries for their behaviour. They are expected to show good manners, which was very evident to the author as James Dennis, a Year 9 pupil, showed her around the school. They must respect each other and the adults around them. Female teachers are referred to as 'Madam', not 'Miss'. Pupils open doors for each other and for teachers. There is a strict uniform policy. The pupils look very smart in their grey blazers with the girls in tartan skirts. Punctuality is expected and there are very low rates of unauthorised absence. Mobile phones are not allowed in school. It is explained to pupils that it is important to give a good impression of themselves and that this will stand them in good stead when they enter the jobs market.

Mr Cefai believes that many people underestimate children and try to operate at what they believe is their level, trying to be more like 'hip' friends than adults. In fact children know they need discipline, know when someone really cares, know how to differentiate between a good and a bad teacher and basically want a proper adult relationship.

[12] Statistics obtained from information published by OfSTED and the Department for Children, Schools and Families. Information obtained from personal communication with the head teacher, Serge Cefai. The case study has been approved by the head teacher.

A strong bond with parents underpins the discipline and strong caring ethos of the school. The school knows its pupils and their home circumstances. There is an open door policy for parents, many of whom head a single parent family. The school will even punish children, with parental consent, for misbehaviour at home. This might include a Saturday morning detention or confiscation of a computer game. When children know the school and their parents are working together they cannot play one off against the other. This is very important, as the head teacher believes that one of the things that confuses children and causes problems is when they receive different and conflicting messages from adults about how they are expected to behave.

The school also has strong links with the local police, which can be very helpful when incidents do occur. The school does not turn a blind eye to problems. This is an area with a great many social challenges. There have been incidents and there is great concern for the safety of the pupils. This is the reason they are not allowed out at lunchtime.

The school's community links reinforce its caring ethos. The school works with an orphanage in Thailand, with pupils visiting every two years and raising over £25,000 for this work. They entertain 120 older people from the neighbourhood each Christmas and provide hampers in the area. The school has developed strong links with its feeder primary schools, helped by its language college status and now by its second specialism in maths and ICT.

How important is the Catholic faith of the school to its ethos? The head teacher thinks the 'spiritual side' of school life is crucial. It is used in a positive way and gives pupils and the whole school community something in common. It is far more than the 'National Curriculum plus Mass', to quote the school's website. However, Mr Cefai also believes that it is perfectly possible to reproduce a similar spirituality or ethos in other schools, either of other faiths or no faith at all.

It is also true that, within their shared Catholic faith, the school celebrates the differences among its pupils, for example their different languages and national traditions. Many take early-entry GCSEs in their mother tongue.

School size

Sacred Heart School has around 670 pupils on roll, smaller than most comprehensive schools. It is four-form entry, although these four forms are divided into five sets, as will be explained later. Serge Cefai believes the school's small size is crucial to its success and that no inner-city comprehensive should have more than a five-form entry. The pupils are well known to teachers as individuals, including their home circumstances. If there are problems leading to dips in performance these can be picked up early to prevent pupils falling through the net. The school employs a full-time counsellor and a part-time chaplain. Allowances are made for pupils experiencing difficulties at home, although these are never allowed to become long-term excuses for poor work or behaviour.

No distinction is made between the academic and pastoral side of school life, but the system for what is sometimes called 'pastoral care' is interesting. Heads of year and form tutors will, as far as possible, stay with pupils throughout their time in the school. So, they know them extremely well as individuals and can track their progress. The school has an appropriately named 'track and act' system.

This ethos of individual care is carried through to the 'pathfinder' sixth form where around 12–14 pupils, who are not ready for the more impersonal atmosphere of a sixth form college, stay on part-time at Sacred Heart to continue their education with a mix of school and college courses.

The issue of staff stability is also very important at the school. Sacred Heart likes to keep its staff and to promote internally when possible, rather than recruit externally. For example, the current head of maths, a department highly praised by OfSTED, started as a student teacher, became an NQT and was eventually promoted up to head of department. Recruitment can be difficult, not because of the school's reputation which is excellent, but because of the reputation of the area.

'Rank order'

It would be wrong to separate the ethos of Sacred Heart, with its traditional values and high expectations, from high academic achievement. Mr Cefai says that it was always a friendly, happy school, but that the introduction of 'league tables' and 'rank order' about ten years ago was a 'godsend' which led to a new focus on academic performance.

At this time the school abolished mixed ability teaching. This abolition is something the head believes made the job of his teachers much easier. On entry to the school the four forms of entry are now divided into five sets based on ability. This is done by conducting CATs tests and the school's own literacy and numeracy tests while the pupils are in their last term at primary school. So, they know before they join Sacred Heart what form they will be in and they meet their form tutors. On their first day of the new school year, only Year 7 will be present, but they will be having normal lessons by the afternoon. When their Key stage 2 test results are received by the school (too late to inform the setting arrangements) they are used to set targets for the pupils.

The bottom of the five sets will only have around sixteen pupils, allowing for more individual attention. The idea is to 'push up' from the bottom. Children, who are subsequently tested twice a year, are given challenging targets. They have a 'rank order' in every subject and an overall 'rank order' which gives double weighting to English, maths and science. They are placed in both overall ability sets and are also set for each subject, where possible. (It may not be possible where there are smaller numbers taking particular subjects.)

All this ranking information is open, put on the notice boards and given to parents, who really appreciate knowing how their children are progressing. Success and progress are celebrated, for the least able as well as the most able. For example, progress from level 3 to level 5 for the less able is as important as level 5 to level 7 for the more able. The system seems to work at all levels as the school does very well in terms of A* and A grades, as well as with pupils with special needs. OfSTED concluded that there were no underachieving groups.

Excellent teaching is key, and the school monitors standards all the time. Expert teachers observe the less experienced and pass on good practice. OfSTED found 90 per cent of lessons to be good or better. Accountability and total openness and honesty are the keys for both pupils and staff.

The X factor

Sacred Heart's performance speaks for itself. The school is oversubscribed, with 800 applications for 120 places. Examination results are outstanding. OfSTED talked of 'excellent teaching, a well-designed curriculum and very good leadership' as well as outstanding care, guidance and support. Through a combination of ethos, individual care and a focus on achievement this school seems to have found the 'X factor'.

Suggested further reading

Analysis of value added of faith schools by Professor David Jesson of York University prepared for this book.

John Burn, John Marks, Peter Pilkington and Penny Thomson, *Faith in Education*, with a foreword by Lord Griffiths, London: CIVITAS, 2001.

Department for Children, Schools and Families, 'Faith in the System', London: DfES, 2007.

Cristina Odone, 'In Bad Faith', London: Centre for Policy Studies, 2008.

Ronald Dearing, *The Way Ahead: Church of England Schools in the New Millennium*, London: Church House Publishing, 2001.

Chapter 14

Who will champion our vulnerable children?

There are currently 61,000 looked-after children and a further 323,000 children in need of care in England, who are supported in their families or independently by local authorities. The combined total of 384,000 is equivalent to 5 per cent of all English children. A further 5,000 children are permanently excluded from mainstream schools and are housed in residential special referral units. This data was supplied by government officials to the author for his paper 'Who Will Champion our Vulnerable Children?'[1]

Sadly, the academic performance of most children in care is poor, with only 12.6 per cent of children in care for a year or more obtaining five good GCSEs in any subject in 2007, compared to close to 62 per cent for all children.[2]

The government's 2007 White Paper, 'Care Matters: Time for Change', recommended a number of positive steps to improve the education of children in care.[3] However, even bolder steps are needed to ensure that children in care receive the education they deserve. This chapter is based on my response to the government's paper.[4]

What is the current situation?

As well as the 61,000 permanently looked-after children in England at any one time, a further 25,000 children spend at least some time being looked after during the year. Government figures reveal that the total annual cost of looking after them is £2.4 billion, or approximately £40,000 per child.

Some 41,700 of these children are placed with foster carers, 5,700 are living in children's homes, and a further 7,000 are placed with relatives. The Fostering Network estimates there is a shortage of at least 8,000 foster families. The total annual cost of a child in foster care is close to £20,000 per child, with some independent fostering agencies charging up to £50,000 per child. The foster carer, however, typically receives only £200 per week or £10,000 per year of this amount. The balance of the £40,000 is used for administrative costs.[5]

---

[1] Cyril Taylor, 'Who Will Champion our Vulnerable Children?' London: Specialist Schools and Academies Trust, 2006. Available at: www.hm-treasury.gov.uk/d/cypreview2006_ssatrust2.pdf

[2] DCSF Statistical First Release SFR 08/2008, April 2008.

[3] The report is available at www.everychildmatters.gov.uk

[4] This chapter is based on a paper written by the author and published by the Specialist Schools and Academies Trust in 2006, as a response to the government's Green Paper on children in care published in 2007 prior to the publication of the White Paper in 2007, using data provided by government officials.

[5] See above.

The average annual cost of residential care in children's homes is £114,000 per child, a total of £650 million for the 5,700 children living in hostels.

Despite this huge investment of resources, the outcomes are distressingly inadequate:

- Only 12.6 per cent of children in care for a year or more obtain five or more good grades at GCSE compared to 62 per cent for all children. Despite improvements, the gap is widening.
- According to one study, between a quarter and a third of people sleeping rough had been in care when they were children. Discussions with the Centrepoint charity which looks after young homeless people confirm this figure.
- Although the figure is improving, the proportion of children looked after for at least 12 months aged 11 who obtain level 4 in Key stage 2 English and mathematics is barely half of that for all children.[6]
- Nearly 10 per cent of looked-after children aged ten or over are cautioned or convicted for an offence each year – over twice the rate for all children of this age.[7] Sadly, many of those cautioned will become serial offenders who will be in and out of prison most of their lives. Indeed, one study showed that a quarter of all adults in prison had been in care for at least part of their childhood.
- At age 16, only 66 per cent of looked-after children remain in full-time education or training, compared to 80 per cent for all children aged 16.[8]

This is pretty dismal data. Not only is it costing the taxpayer large sums of money to care for children who are unable to live with their parents (£2.4 billion per annum) but, despite modest recent improvements, the outcomes are simply unacceptable. Moreover the real cost of failing to look after our vulnerable children is much greater than the £2.4 billion of direct costs.

A study published recently by the London School of Economics shows that the overall costs in any one year are close to £10 billion if the following 'knock on' costs are added:

- The cost of apprehending and incarcerating the young offenders who were in care;
- The cost of welfare and unemployment benefit for the large proportion of children in care who did not gain the skills necessary to obtain a job;
- The higher than average health costs of children in care and those who were in care.

A 2006 study by Barnardo's, 'Failed by the System', confirmed these findings, and provided worrying indicators of how far the government was from reaching its targets.[9] Research has also shown that educational level correlates directly with health (mental as well as physical) and social problems such as teenage pregnancy. Raising the educational level is a significant cure as well as a preventative factor.

Why are the outcomes for such substantial expenditure so poor?

---

[6] DCSF Statistical First Release SFR 08/2008, April 2008.
[7] Ibid.
[8] Ibid.
[9] See Barnardo's press release of 23 August 2006.

Children in care frequently change both their home and their school. Shockingly, 13 per cent of children in care experience three or more foster parent placements a year, with serious negative effects in terms of their emotional and behavioural difficulties.

How can any child flourish when they move home three times a year?

A report by the government's Social Exclusion Unit in 2003[10] suggested there were four related key reasons why children in care underachieve:

(a)   Young people in care spend too much time out of school on unauthorised absence;
(b)   Children do not have sufficient help with their education when they get behind;
(c)   Carers are not trained to provide sufficient support and encouragement at home for learning and development;
(d)   Children in care need more help with their emotional, mental and/or physical health and well-being.

Children in need of care

There are 313,000 children in need of care who live with their families or are supported independently by local authorities and a further 10,000 children in respite care. It is from this wider cohort that tomorrow's looked-after children will primarily be drawn.[11]

We need more data about these children.

Effective action at an early stage could prevent these children having to be taken into care at a later stage. Perhaps some of these families with children in need could be given more effective counselling. Prevention is always better than cure. It is strongly recommended that early action be taken to improve looking after children in need of care, as well as those actually in care.

Specific recommendations to improve the care of looked-after children

Sharing responsibility for looked-after children between local authority children's social services and schools

A key to improving provision for vulnerable children must be to provide greater stability. The setting up of children's trusts by local government will hopefully produce a more integrated approach between local authority children's services and schools, which should ensure that schools and children's services work more closely together. Improvements are also being made in the adoption procedures, but much more needs to be done. Local networks of specialist schools could also provide support, but a more radical solution is required to ensure that the aims of the Every Child Matters programme are delivered.

Peter Crook, former principal of the Peckham Academy, South London, believes that care for looked-after children could be improved by more involvement of schools. This could include, on a voluntary basis, responsibility for helping to find and for supervising

---

[10] 'A Better Education for Children in Care', published by the Office of the Deputy Prime Minister and The Social Exclusion Unit 2003. www.cabinetoffice.gov.uk
[11] Cyril Taylor, 'Who Will Champion our Vulnerable Children?'

foster parents. Legal responsibility for the assignment of care status to children would still remain with the local authority social services department. But more of the day-to-day responsibility, including mentoring, could be performed by the school, perhaps through the provision of social services staff in schools. This would include the counselling of pupils and liaising with foster parents.

During his time at the Peckham Academy, Peter Crook had about fifteen looked-after children and a further 100 children in need of care. In one instance, he noticed a looked-after child was absent from school. When he contacted the foster family he was told the child had been moved to another family but he was not told which family. If the school received even a proportion of the funds currently spent on looked-after children by the social services, it is his opinion that the school could employ the qualified staff, such as social workers themselves or trained counsellors, necessary to do a better job of keeping the education as well as the welfare of looked-after children on track. He emphasises that this would need to be done in collaboration with the social services and not in order to replace them.

If responsibility for pupils was given to schools on a joint basis with social services, local networks of specialist schools could collaborate by employing specialist counsellors. Alternatively, particular foster parents could receive specialist counsellor training and act as supervisors for other foster parents and receive additional payment.

The Sydney Russell specialist school in Barking has appointed one of its teachers, Anne-Marie McNamee, to supervise, on a part-time basis, and with the agreement of the local social services department, both their ten children in care and their foster parents. This is working very well and the academic performance of the children in care has improved significantly.

Ms McNamee quotes the former education secretary Alan Johnson, someone who had experience of a tough childhood:

> We must not write off some children as unfit for the world of education. It is our responsibility to make the education system fit the needs of all children. If we are to raise every child's educational attainment, we need to take a more personalised approach to teaching for each and every child.[12]

Some specialist schools use minibuses to bring children in care to school and this, at least, helps to avoid such children having to change schools when they change foster parents.

The guidelines for high-performing specialist schools should also be changed so that a proportion of the additional funding received by a high-performing specialist school (approximately £90,000 per year) could be used to fund the carrying out of a lead role locally in looking after vulnerable children. This could involve recruiting foster parents on a group basis in their area, as well as the provision of specialist counselling support. Perhaps a proportion of community budgets for specialist schools could be used for this purpose. The legal process for placing children in care, however, as well as the administrative costs of payment for foster families, should remain the responsibility of the local authorities. Furthermore, it is not suggested that schools be required to take on additional responsibilities for supporting children in care, but that they should be offered incentives to do so on a voluntary basis.

[12] From a speech at www.fabians.org.uk/events/speeches/schools-for-the-future

Role of special schools

Some looked-after children, with emotional, behavioural and social difficulties, are enrolled in special schools, including some special boarding schools run by organisations such as the Priory Group.

More special schools should play a leading role in looking after children in care. They have particular expertise which could be shared with mainstream schools. The problems of children with behavioural difficulties could also be substantially alleviated by enrolling them in a special boarding school rather than placing them in mainstream schools.

Mentors

One key issue is that many looked-after children do not develop an effective relationship with the social services person assigned to look after them. The reasons are manifold, including the high turnover of social services staff and the large number of looked-after children – as many as thirty assigned to a particular social services official. A particular problem is that in some local authorities, social services assign responsibility for looked-after children on a group 'territorial' basis, rather than giving responsibility for a particular child to a specific social worker.

Charles Parker, Clerk of the Mercers' Company, believes that many of the 24,000 City of London liverymen and women would be willing to act as volunteer mentors for a particular looked-after child. His wife Victoria, who is a magistrate in Winchester, believes that many of the 30,000 magistrates of the courts would also be willing to serve in this role.[13] Churches and religious groups could be an excellent source of mentors – the Tabernacle School in Notting Hill Gate is doing a remarkable job teaching boys excluded from other schools.

Mentors would need training as well as screening, and an acceptable framework would be needed. A possible framework could be as follows:

(a)   The looked-after children would be given a special mobile phone number for the mentor and not their home telephone number or address;
(b)   Mentors would meet the child they are mentoring up to once a month at the foster family's home or at the school to monitor progress;
(c)   Mentors would also be encouraged to meet the child's head teacher;
(d)   Social services would be required to discuss changes of foster parents or schools with mentors before any changes were implemented.

HSBC generously provided a grant of £1 million to trial a mentoring scheme. There should be minimal bureaucratic procedures. The relationship between mentors and their assigned child should be primarily routed through the head teacher of the school and not through social services.

Better training for foster parents

Many foster families are dedicated caring families who wish to provide the very best possible care for the children assigned to them. Many looked-after children, however,

---

[13] Taylor, 'Who Will Champion our Vulnerable Children?', p. 9.

have behavioural difficulties which require specialist expertise and considerable dedication. It is therefore recommended that better training be offered to foster parents. Other sources of providing foster parents, such as religious groups, should also be sought. Foster parents should also be encouraged to take advantage of the Letterbox Club,[14] which supplies children's books free of charge to foster parents of children in care.

Better data

One issue is the current difficulty in obtaining data both on looked-after children and children in need. The data below should be made available more readily by local authorities on a regular basis:

- The ages both of children in care *and* children in need of care;
- The proportion of girls and boys;
- The concentration of looked-after children in particular areas;
- The number of looked-after children in permanent care, e.g. for longer than a year;
- The number of children who change their foster family more than once a year;
- The proportion of looked-after children from ethnic minorities;
- The proportion of looked-after children with special educational needs statements.

Provision of boarding school places for looked-after children

It is acknowledged that boarding schools would only be able to accept a small proportion of the total number of children in care. Nevertheless, even a 5 per cent target, or 3,000 places, would be a great step forward. We currently have thirty-four state boarding schools with some 4,000 boarders, with the average annual boarding charge being £7,000 per year, plus a tuition fee of £6,000 paid by the local authority. This is much less than the cost of a foster family placement and dramatically less than the cost of residential care, although additional arrangements would need to be made for school holidays. Charities, such as the Royal Wanstead Children's Foundation, Christ's Hospital and JET, arrange for hundreds of vulnerable children to attend independent boarding schools.[15]

The Royal Wanstead Children's Foundation has recently published a research study on how boarding schools can transform the lives of vulnerable children.[16]

HRH the Princess Royal, who is patron of the foundation, in the foreword to the study, says the study shows how boarding a child in care at the right boarding school with the right support can make an immense difference to the child's development.

The research was conducted by interviewing nearly 100 vulnerable children placed in six boarding schools through support from the Royal Wanstead Children's Foundation. Below are the major findings of the research.

[14] www.booktrust.org.uk/National-programmes/Letterbox-Club
[15] 'Breaking Through: How Boarding Schools Can Transform the Lives of Vulnerable Children'. Copies can be obtained from the Royal Wanstead Children's Foundation at www.royalwanstead.org.uk/
[16] Ibid.

Children 'at risk' in disrupted and deprived families

- Before they were admitted to boarding school, almost 50 per cent of the children were in the care of a single parent with mental (38 per cent) or physical (11 per cent) illness.
- Thirty per cent of the children had been exposed to violence, abuse or threatening behaviour in the family or home environment.
- Thirteen per cent of these children were themselves believed to be 'carers' of parents or siblings.
- Most (71 per cent) of the children were in the care of mothers, with 53 per cent of them having had no recent contact with the father.

With the structure, security and stimulation of boarding school, once-troubled children can climb to the top of the class:

- Thirty-nine per cent of those who had been assisted boarders for at least 3 years (3+) became 'star performers' in their schools on a range of social emotional and academic criteria within that time – almost three times the number of assisted boarders predicted to achieve that at the time of admission.
- Fifty-seven per cent of these 3+ children achieved or exceeded the average of their peers within three years.
- Of the 73 per cent of the 3+ children assessed on admission to boarding school as being 'at risk' of failing, almost half were rated as on or above their peer group average within three years.
- Eighty-five per cent of the ninety-seven vulnerable children were assessed as being at or above the average of their peers within three years of going to boarding school.

The vital role of boarding schools in a society of fractured families: more children can 'break the cycle of family disadvantage'

- Boarding school is proven to be highly effective in helping the 'recovery' of the vulnerable children in this study. Boarding school helped most of these children achieve the social skills, self-esteem, coping ability and academic performance of their peer group within two to three years.
- The fact that 39 per cent of these vulnerable children from deprived backgrounds became 'star pupils' within three years proves the anecdotal evidence which has indicated that many of these needy children grasp their opportunity with a determination that helps make them above-average achievers in all respects.
- The boarding schools involved in this research have high levels of pastoral care and individual attention, and unparalleled experience in assisted boarding with Royal Wanstead Children's Foundation for the past 36 years. Royal Wanstead believes this proven work could be expanded substantially at a time of rising numbers of 'fractured' families and (it is believed) vulnerable, troubled children.

Some of the new academies, particularly former CTCs converting to academy status, could also provide boarding provision. Many specialist schools have indicated a willingness to establish boarding units. It costs about £25,000 per bed to build a dormitory, or £2.5 million for 100 beds. Even with the annual recurrent boarding costs of £7,000 per year per child, the cost of boarding school provision would be dramatically less than for a council to run a children's home or a special referral unit, and with much better outcomes.

A modest but demanding goal could be set to place at least 5 per cent of all children in care in a boarding school within five years. This would require the funding of at least 3,000 boarding places for looked-after children per year. The record of boarding schools for both independent schools such as Christ's Hospital and state maintained boarding schools, such as the the Royal Alexandra and Albert School in Reigate, in looking after children in care is excellent. If the political will is there, it should not be so difficult to find 3,000 boarding school places for children in care.

Additional boarding places could be provided by:

Expanding existing provision   Many of the existing thirty-four state boarding schools have expressed an interest in expanding their boarding provision. Already the Department for Children, Schools and Families has agreed to expand the number of boarding places at Wymondham by 125 beds. If all the state boarding schools agreed to expand their provision of beds by just 100 places and agreed to reserve 20 per cent of their total provision (including existing beds) for looked-after children, we would have nearly 1,500 boarding places available for looked-after children. The extra provision works out as follows:

Existing provision	4,000
100 extra beds per 34 schools	3,400
Total	7,400

Twenty per cent of beds for looked-after children would total 1,480.[17]

The capital costs would be £85 million. If we assumed 6 per cent interest costs for the capital costs through a Private Finance Initiative (PFI), this would total £5,100,000 per year plus a further £10,150,000 for boarding costs (£7,000 per year per child). The cost of boarding for 80 per cent of the additional places not earmarked for looked-after children would be borne by parents as for the existing places.

Combined, the annual cost would be £15,250,000 or just £10,517 per child – less than the current cost of £20,000 per looked-after child in a foster home. The taxpayer would save £7.5 million a year versus current costs.

It is of course accepted that vulnerable children should only be placed in a boarding school with the consent of the school, the child and the family or guardian. Clearly, children in care with severe behavioural problems cannot be placed in a regular boarding school since they would disrupt the education of the other pupils. Such children belong in residential special schools such as the Priory special needs boarding school. Already placed in residential special schools are 1,100 looked-after children, some on a 52 week per year basis.

Adding boarding in some academies   It is recommend that at least some of the proposed 400 academies (possibly 5 per cent), should add a boarding unit of 100 beds or so.

The same cost calculations used above for the thirty-four state boarding schools would produce annual cost savings to the taxpayer of £1 million. It would also give a

---

[17] Ibid.

boost to the entire academy movement. Dr Anthony Seldon and Wellington College are already sponsoring an academy which will have boarding provision.[18]

More day schools should be encouraged to add a boarding unit   The DCSF is setting up a number of pilot schemes in nine local authority areas to test the feasibility of greater use by local authorities of boarding school provision for vulnerable children. This is a welcome step, but many day schools, such as Sharnbrook School in Bedfordshire, would also welcome the opportunity to add a boarding unit.

Bearing in mind the dramatically better record that boarding schools have in looking after children in care at a much lower cost, we need to be bolder in persuading and funding more state day schools to add a boarding unit. However, we would need to test the potential demand for parents of children not in care, willing to pay the average boarding cost of £7,000 per year, since no boarding school should have more than 20 per cent of its boarders in care.

If we assume that only 20 per cent of boarding places in a particular school can be reserved for children in care (in order to avoid the schools becoming de facto orphanages), we would need to know whether there would be sufficient demand from regular parents to fill the balance of places – possibly 4,000 – if fifty additional state day schools added a boarding unit of 100 beds. Currently there is a waiting list for places in state boarding schools, so I am confident that the demand is there. Adding boarding units in fifty day schools would make 1,000 places available for looked-after children, with savings to the taxpayer of £5 million, but would require a demand for the balance of 4,000 places from parents willing to pay the £7,000 per child annual fee.

Placements in existing independent schools   Finally and perhaps most importantly, the generous offer of independent boarding schools, such as Wellington, both preparatory and secondary, to accept a number of children in care should be accepted. The 600 independent boarding schools, of which 200 are secondary and 400 are preparatory schools, have agreed in principle to accept five children each a year for a total of 3,000 places. The Boarding Schools' Association[19] has indicated that for a fee of £13,000 per child (a tuition allowance similar to state day schools of £6,000 plus the average cost of boarding in a state boarding school of £7,000) many of their member schools would be willing to take up to five looked-after children each. This would save the taxpayer £39 million a year versus the cost of providing accommodation in a foster family while attending a local school.

The general secretary of the Incorporated Association of Preparatory Schools, John Morris, has given formal support for the proposal. This would provide places for younger children aged 5–13. By agreeing to do this the independent schools would not only be doing good, but could also safeguard their charitable status as well as widening the diversity of their student intake. The boarding schools say, however, that it would be better to start boarding children in care in prep schools rather than placing them directly into secondary boarding schools which only accept pupils aged 13.

---

[18] For a longer piece on Wellington's plans see Anthony Seldon's essay in 'Academies and the Future of State Education' (edited by Julian Astle and Conor Ryan, London: Centreforum, 2008).

[19] Personal communications with Hilary Moriarty, national director of the Boarding Schools Association. www.boarding.org.uk/

Target for boarding places

Existing state boarding schools	1,480
20 academies providing 20 places each	400
50 new state day schools providing 20 places each	1,000
600 independent schools accepting 5 looked-after children each	3,000
Total	5,880

If all of these proposals came to fruition, they would produce nearly 6,000 additional boarding schools places and save the taxpayer more than £64 million a year. Surely even a modest goal of just 3,000 places is attainable, saving the taxpayer £32 million.

Of course there are particular issues which would need resolution; for example, where would the children be housed during the holiday periods?

A housemaster at Wellington College, Berkshire, says it is likely that the parents of his existing boys would provide hospitality. Alternatively, holiday foster parents could be found or the school could keep a small boarding unit open during the holiday period. The holidays should also be used whenever possible to maintain the children's natural support networks such as their extended family and previous care givers.

The trauma of abuse and neglect experienced by many looked-after children prior to entering care must, of course, be acknowledged. These children need emotional support to overcome their previous abuse and mistreatment. We would therefore have to ensure that the boarding schools taking in looked-after children have specialist staff trained to care for these children.

Charter of rights for children in care

The problems outlined above are so serious that it is recommended a special charter of rights for children in care be enacted which would provide the following:

- The right of every child to be assigned an adult mentor who must be consulted on issues affecting a particular child, such as change of foster family or school. Children would only be able to contact their mentor by mobile phone number and would not be given the home telephone or address of their mentor.
- Better monitoring of children in care.
- Each authority should be required to publish annual data on the children in their care to include information on how many children had changed either foster parents or schools, their examination results, and statistics on those staying in full-time education.
- Where possible, children in care should be given the possibility of being placed in a boarding school.

For an improvement in the care given to looked-after children, it will be necessary to achieve fundamental changes of attitude in the way local authority social services departments handle vulnerable children. Their educational progress and not just their physical welfare must be made the priority. We must continue to press for better integration between educational and social care services.

Legislative regulations about the problems of looked-after children as well as reviewing adoption procedures must be addressed. Bureaucratic barriers which prevent use of boarding schools for vulnerable children should also be removed.

If local authorities' confidence in the greater use of boarding schools is to be achieved, the boarding school sector must demonstrate how it can engage with the families, carers and communities of the children placed in care, in order to minimise the potential negative impact of separation of vulnerable children from their families and of distance from home. They must also train their teachers even more than they do already in the skills necessary to look after vulnerable children. Many boarding schools already have very high standards of care for looked-after children. But the need to increase the number of boarding schools with carers trained to look after vulnerable children is paramount.

It is rare in government that there is the opportunity simultaneously to do good and to save the taxpayer substantial funds. It is hoped that the proposals in this chapter will be supported by government, and that greater efforts will be made to implement the recommendations of the White Paper.

Suggested further reading

Cyril Taylor, 'Who Will Champion our Vulnerable Children?' London: SSAT, 2006.

Royal Wanstead Children's Foundation, 'Breaking Through: How Boarding Schools Can Transform the Lives of Vulnerable Children', London: Royal Wanstead Children's Foundation, 2008.

Department for Education and Skills, White Paper, 'Care Matters: Time for Change', White Paper, London: DES, 2007.

Audit Commission, 'Misspent Youth', London: Audit Commission, 1996.

Barnado's, 'Failed by the System', London: Barnardos, 2006.

Department for Children, Schools and Families, 'Back on Track', London: DCSF, 2008.

Cyril Taylor (then High Sheriff of Greater London), 'Tough on the Causes of Crime', *Shevrialty News*, June 1997.

Chapter 15

Why and how our gifted and talented children should be nurtured

One of the unintended outcomes of the comprehensive school movement, which replaced most grammar and secondary modern schools in the 1960s and 1970s with all-ability schools, was the assumption that all children should be taught in mixed ability classes. The view that one size fits all became prevalent. The idea that gifted and talented children should receive special nurturing became anathema, possibly because of the false assumption that in order to be gifted and talented you had to come from a rich family.

That has denied many very able English children from socially disadvantaged families the chance to realise their potential. Only in the late 1990s was there a concerted drive to introduce a Gifted and Talented programme into comprehensive schools. Yet even today, a significant minority of schools lacks any additional recognition of the needs of their ablest pupils.

In 2003, Lord Quirk of Bloomsbury asked a series of parliamentary questions on A-level performance by type of school.[1] The replies to the questions show that in 2002, only 21,390 of the 258,226 A-level candidates achieved three or more A grades at A-level – this is just 8 per cent of the total number of candidates and only 3.4 per cent of the total age cohort. Though the figure has risen a little since, to 10 per cent in 2008, it is hardly evidence of grade inflation. Moreover, of these 21,390 students, 7,656 attended independent schools and 3,394 attended grammar schools. On a combined basis, this is 54 per cent of the total, even though grammar and independent schools only accounted for 20 per cent of the total candidates. Particularly worrying is the proportion of pupils by type of school achieving three or more A grades at A-level, with only 5 per cent of comprehensive school A-level candidates doing so versus 23 per cent for independent and 19 per cent for grammar schools (see Table 15.1).

Clearly, a large proportion of able children attending comprehensive schools are not realising their potential – the results for more recent years are unlikely to be much different from the above.

A particular problem is that half of English schools only offer courses for 11–16 year-olds, and children attending these schools who wish to take A-levels must apply to another school at age 16. Frequently, the gifted and talented children attending these schools do not even remain in full-time education to take A-levels or are not encouraged by their schools to take the challenging A-levels necessary to gain admittance to a distinguished university.

Recent research by Professor Jesson indicates that less than one third of the gifted and talented children aged 11 in 1999 who scored in the top 5 per cent raw marks in Key

[1] House of Lords – Hansard 8 September 2003, Column WA50 and WA51.

Table 15.1   A-level performance by type of school

	Proportion of candidates		Proportion of candidates at each institution gaining 3 As at A-level	
	Total	*%*	*Total*	*%*
Comprehensives and other non-selective schools	110,000	43	5,821	5
Grammar	18,265	7	3,394	19
Independent	32,873	13	7,565	23
Sixth form (FE) per cent other	44,473	17	3,561	6
Other FE	52,493	20	1,049	2
Totals	258,226	100	21,390	8

stage 2 maths and English, achieved the three A grades at A-levels seven years later in 2006 at age 18. Three As at A-level, in appropriate subjects, are usually necessary to get into a leading Russell Group university. The proportion of very able children achieving three A grades who attended schools with no post-16 provision, and who therefore had to transfer to another school, sixth form college or FE college, was even lower, at around 20 per cent. Moreover, only 5 per cent of A-level candidates attending comprehensive schools achieve three A grades at A-level compared to 19 per cent for grammar school pupils and 23 per cent for independent school candidates. This, of course, follows from the obvious fact that the intakes to these institutions are very different. We should pay tribute to the fact that comprehensive schools have massively widened opportunity for pupils to study post-16 and so helped contribute to government targets for recruitment to higher education.

But, of the 30,000 children classified as gifted and talented using raw scores for Key stage 2 maths and English in 1999, less than one third were realising their potential 7 years later at A-level. This is a tragic waste of natural talent, and calls for more focus on the potential that these young people represent. However, it is also the case that substantial numbers of pupils not identified as being in the 'top 5 per cent' also achieved three As. This suggests the importance of regular monitoring of pupils' progress over the years of compulsory education so that those with potential revealing itself at a later stage than age 11 can also be classified as gifted and talented and added to the list of gifted and talented students.

The data are even worse for particular subjects such as science. Sir Richard Sykes, former rector of Imperial College, indicates that of the undergraduates entering Imperial College, more than half are international students; of the remaining half, who are British, nearly all come from either independent schools or grammar schools, with only a small proportion coming from comprehensive schools.[2] There is also the problem of the 'missing 3,000' students identified by the Sutton Trust with three As at A-level who do not gain admission to a leading university.

This chapter recommends a framework for an effective national gifted and talented programme in English schools, as well as giving details of the approach used, with its strengths and weaknesses, in the United States, and the record of the National Association of Gifted and Talented Youth at the University of Warwick, for gifted and talented students which was first introduced in 2002, but was sadly closed down in 2007.

[2] Personal communication with Sir Richard Sykes, January 2007.

Provision in the United States

There is no national talent search for gifted and talented students in the United States. However, four universities – Johns Hopkins, Northwestern, Duke and Denver – organise regional talent searches using tests of their own as well as other recognised ability tests, such as the Preliminary Scholastic Aptitude Test (PSAT) of the college board, given to 11 year-olds.

However, these regional talent searches identify only a small proportion, perhaps 10 per cent, of the estimated 1.5 million gifted and talented children in the United States aged 8–17. There are 3 million children in each age cohort in the US, so there should be 150,000 very able children identified in each age cohort using the 5 per cent eligibility criterion. Assuming the need to identify all the gifted and talented children aged 10–17, this means that the total number of gifted and talented children in the United States should number at least 1,200,000, but only 200,000 have been identified by the four universities. Unfortunately, the universities conducting talent searches do not share their names with other interested parties.

The four universities conduct residential summer schools for the gifted and talented at some thirty or so universities throughout the country for approximately 20,000 children. In addition, private organisations such as the Summer Institute for the Gifted organise programmes at leading universities for perhaps another 5,000 students. However, the total enrolment in such courses is only a small proportion of the total number of gifted and talented children in the United States – perhaps only 2 per cent.

Most American state education authorities employ a gifted and talented coordinator, but only modest funds are made available. The amount of funding available, especially that provided by the federal government, has been reduced by The No Child Left Behind[3] initiative, which focuses attention on the lowest-attaining children, especially in numeracy and literacy.

Some states, such as Connecticut, make outstanding provision for the gifted and talented, but the overall provision, especially for very able children from socially disadvantaged urban and rural schools, is modest. This has three causes:

- Such programmes are considered elitist and do not conform with the traditional egalitarian focus of US education.
- The federal government's role in education is limited and therefore national initiatives are difficult to organise, as education is principally the responsibility of individual states and local school boards.
- The mistaken assumption on the part of many policy makers that most gifted and talented children are members of middle- or upper-class families which can take care of their own children's needs by themselves. In other words, they believe you have to be rich to be gifted and talented.

Nevertheless, many of the most prestigious universities in the United States spend large sums of money encouraging the most able children to apply to their universities, whatever their social background. These universities provide substantial scholarship funds for students unable to pay their very high fees. There is therefore a paradox in American

---

[3] www.ed.gov/nclb/landing.jhtml

education. There is no national initiative to identify gifted and talented children until they reach school leaving age, when the universities spend very large sums of money to identify the most able children.

There are lessons to be learned from the American experience: the importance of having a nationally organised programme as well as the need to counter the false assumption that the majority of gifted and talented children have middle- and upper-class parents and therefore do not need special support.

Provision in England

The 1944 Education Act[4] established a formal statutory framework for English secondary education under which children either went to a highly selective grammar school on the basis of a national test given at age 11, or to secondary modern school with some technical schools available in certain areas. By the early 1960s, approximately one third of 11 year olds who passed the 11+ examination went to the 1,000 or so grammar schools, with the remainder going to secondary modern schools and a small number of technical schools.

The unfairness of this system, with its reliance on the 11+ examination, began to be recognised in the mid-1960s, and gradually the secondary modern and grammar schools were replaced by comprehensive schools so that by the late 1970s, only 254 grammar schools were left.[5]

However, in the 1980s, a growing concern developed that, while the comprehensive system was eminently fairer than the previous secondary modern/grammar schools, the formula of 'one size fits all' was not necessarily the best way to realise every child's potential, and thus setting and streaming was introduced within many schools. In addition, the introduction of the national curriculum, OfSTED inspections and Key stage tests – in addition to published GCSE and A-level results – many of them flowing from the Education Reform Act of 1988,[6] brought in significant accountability to schools and a focus on improving standards. Concurrent with this reform was the introduction of specialist schools, with the idea that each school should have one or more centres of excellence, and each school should set targets to raise standards as well as securing the support of both local and national companies and sponsors.

Despite the creation of many excellent comprehensive schools, there was a growing concern in the 1990s that some very able children, especially those in socially dis-advantaged areas, were not receiving the special care and attention necessary to realise their potential. Scrutiny of the students accepted by the Russell Group of leading universities indicates that independent and grammar schools have a very large proportion of the places at these universities awarded to their students. In 1999, the Excellence in Cities programme established an expectation that secondary schools in the inner cities should make special provision for gifted and talented children through masterclasses and summer schools.

In 2001, William Brady, the president of Johns Hopkins University (one of the leading US universities providing gifted and talented programmes), was invited to Number 10

---

[4] www.opsi.gov.uk/RevisedStatutes/Acts/ukpga/1944/cukpga_19440031_en_1
[5] Hansard, 13 December 1991, column 559. By 1997, the number had fallen to 166, although the number of pupils in grammar schools has increased in recent years.
[6] www.opsi.gov.uk/RevisedStatutes/Acts/ukpga/1944/cukpga_19440031_en_1

to discuss gifted and talented programmes with Tony Blair. I organised a follow up meeting with Lord Adonis, then Blair's adviser on education, with leading educators including Dr Geoff Parks, director of admissions at Cambridge University, Stephen Schwartz, vice chancellor of Brunel University and Anthony McClaran, director of UCAS. As a result, the National Association for Gifted and Talented Youth (NAGTY) was established at the University of Warwick. NAGTY was given a budget of some £5 million a year for five years, most of which was spent on organising residential summer schools for some 4,000 very able children on the campuses of leading British universities.

By 2007, NAGTY had some 150,000 very able children registered as members, though one third of secondary schools declined to be involved. NAGTY supported both schools and very able students, as well as serving as a national research centre for gifted and talented education.

In the summer of 2006, the Department for Education and Skills organised, with the help of Professor David Jesson, a national talent search for pupils aged 11–17. This study identified 30,000 very able children in each of the last six year groups starting in 1999 – using raw scores in Key stage 2 tests, given at age 11, in maths and English to identify the top 5 per cent of the most able 11 year-olds in each age cohort. This produced a total of 180,000 names of very able youngsters aged 11–17. Schools were encouraged to add, if they so wished, additional children with talents in other subjects such as music and sport, or late developers. This latter group have been shown to provide substantial additional numbers of those gaining three A grades at A-level in 2006. All the 3,100 national English secondary schools were sent a list of the very able children in their school with a request that each of these children should be given the support necessary to realise their potential, including registering them with NAGTY. It is believed this is the only national talent search in existence throughout the world, and the government, especially Lord Adonis, who later became the schools minister, is to be commended on this initiative.

By 2007, there was therefore in England, uniquely both a national talent search in place and a functioning organisation, NAGTY, in place to support these very able children. However, NAGTY lost the contract to manage the gifted children programme in 2007, and there are still significant weaknesses in provision.

In particular, only 150,000 children were registered with NAGTY before it was closed, of whom about a third were attending independent schools. Therefore, less than half of the 180,000 maintained school children assigned 'very able' status on the basis of their test scores status were registered. Furthermore, one third of English maintained secondary schools had not nominated any children for membership of NAGTY – presumably because of ideological opposition to gifted and talented programmes as elitist, or possibly because they did not believe they had any qualified children.

The budget for NAGTY was only £5 million a year. As a result, it could only afford 4,000 residential summer school places annually, at a cost of about £1,000 per child for a 2-week programme. Although these were excellent programmes together with others, provided without government funding, by such organisations as the Sutton Trust, it meant that only a very small proportion of the 180,000 children identified as very able were enrolled on such programmes. To provide 2-week residential summer schools at a cost of £1,000 per child for 180,000 children would cost £180 million versus the current NAGTY budget of £5 million.

Clearly an increase in the size of the budget of this magnitude was simply not feasible. Even a modest programme for all 180,000 children is likely to require a budget of at least £36 million a year of direct support – £200 per pupil – plus funding from other sources.

Other programmes for gifted and talented children which are less expensive than residential summer schools have been developed. However, even with the provision of less expensive programmes, including Saturday morning classes and day programmes in the summer, it is clear that a very significant increase in the size of the budget for the gifted and talented will be required, possibly funded from other existing areas of the overall schools budget of £50 billion a year. For example, schools with high-performing specialist status could use part of their additional funds to support gifted and talented programmes.

Tragically, in the summer of 2007, possibly because of overly rigid application of European Union tendering rules, a new approach was introduced. An absurdly complicated and confused tendering document invited organisations to bid for the right to organise the supply, but not to provide gifted and talented programmes themselves. The University of Warwick decided not to bid for the contract, since they believed they would be unable to ensure its high quality. NAGTY director Deborah Eyre was not even offered a position by the successful bidder, CfBT. This meant that the crucial five years' experience at NAGTY was lost, as the organisation was shut down and its unique expertise was wasted.

CfBT have introduced a totally new system. Instead of identifying the children achieving the top 5 per cent test scores in Key stage 2, all schools are now invited to classify 10 per cent of their own children whatever their ability, as gifted and talented. Both secondary and primary schools have been invited to do this. Potentially, this means that some 60,000 children in each age group (there are 600,000 English children in maintained schools in each age group) will be classified as gifted and talented. If we take the age range of 5–17, this would mean a total pool of over 700,000. Yet the budget has remained at only £5 million, equivalent to only £7 per gifted and talented child per year. Even worse, there are no accountability measures in place to measure the success of the programme. Clearly this is an unworkable system.

To be fair, schools are still being sent the names of their incoming 11 year-olds who meet David Jesson's criteria of being in the top 5 per cent of ability based on their Key stage 2 maths and English raw scores. They will also be asked to report on the progress of these children.

But with such a broad cohort, I fear that the current programme will not succeed in increasing the proportion of our gifted and talented children who achieve three As at A-level and thus gain admittance to a good university.

In order to compete in the global economy, Great Britain needs to first identify all its gifted and talented children, whatever their social background, and then to ensure that every one of them goes to a good university. Hopefully, many of these able young citizens, whatever their social background, will then become the future inventors, business leaders, researchers, authors, outstanding teachers, and yes, even political leaders of our next generation.

What, therefore, should be the crucial elements of a first-rate gifted and talented programme?

First   Objective criteria should be used to identify gifted and talented children such as the children aged 11, who score in the top 5 per cent in maths and English in Key stage 2 – 30,000 children a year.

Second   Children who show talent at a later age in specific subjects such as maths, science, music or sport, should be added to the list.

Third   Gifted and Talented education should be classified as a form of special education, thus making it a more integral part of an education system and not an elitist programme.

Fourth   If, and only if, support resources are available, and again using objective measures, children younger than age 11 should also be identified as gifted and talented.

Fifth   Most importantly, an adequate budget must be given to the gifted and talented programme. A hypothecated £5 million is absurd, even assuming only 200,000 children in the programme. The programme had a bigger budget when the government provided earmarked grants to schools, but the trend away from hypothecation has seen such money incorporated into general pots. Surely out of a total Department for Children, Schools and Families budget of £60 billion a year, £100 million could be earmarked for gifted and talented provision. This would be only £500 per gifted and talented child, but additional funding could be allocated from other sources such as:

- Access funding for universities from the Opportunity For All programme of the Department for Work and Pensions;
- High-performing specialist school funding;
- Core specialist school funding;
- A modest proportion of regular school funding could be hypothecated for this programme, including possible use of some special educational needs funding.

A very wide variety of different gifted and talented support services should be made available for the 200,000 children identified as being gifted and talented. Such provision should include:

(a)   Both setting in individual subjects or even streaming for whole groups of very able children should be used more widely in secondary schools. Some specialist schools have set up fast track sets which enter pupils for GCSEs as early as 14 years of age and Key stage 3 tests at least a year early.

(b)   Saturday morning classes organised with a nearby university, or if there is not one close by, a high-performing specialist school or a private school. The record of such programmes as the Royal College of Music Junior Department has been outstanding in nurturing talent – a substantial proportion of the Royal College of Music's undergraduate intake comes from its Saturday junior department courses. Dr Martin Stephens, the head teacher of St Paul's Boys School, is now providing a gifted maths programme on Saturday mornings for twenty pupils from nearby specialist comprehensive schools in Hammersmith, with support from the government. It should be possible to provide two hours of Saturday morning classes for 40 weeks for £200 per child per year. Weekly Saturday morning classes should be given equal priority with summer schools.

(c)   Provision of supplementary online courses for very able children, possibly by the Open University or other universities. In the United States, the University of Missouri has made available a very effective online service. Perhaps the Open University would provide a similar service in the UK.

(d)   A much larger provision of both non-residential and residential summer courses should be provided at leading universities with part of the cost being borne by the secondary schools or by parents if they can afford to pay, or possibly by sponsors, although this is likely to be limited. It is also strongly recommended that model curricula be developed for these summer schools. Attached as Appendix 5 is the standard curricula across a wide range of subjects developed by the Summer Institute for the Gifted at such prestigious universities as Princeton, UC–Berkeley, UCLA, Emory and Amherst. It is estimated that a child taking the Summer Institute for the Gifted and Talented science curriculum at Princeton will cover in just 3 weeks the normal science curriculum for an entire year at a typical US secondary school. Summer courses, to be successful, need to be rigorous, challenging and requiring total commitment from the students. It is not surprising that successful completion of summer courses such as those organised by Johns Hopkins or the Summer Institute for the Gifted (SIG) can dramatically raise the academic ambitions of gifted children from socially disadvantaged areas as well as helping these students to gain admission to leading universities.

A particular problem for gifted and talented children from socially disadvantaged areas is that they are regarded as 'weirdos' or 'nerds' by their peer group. It is not cool to be a hardworking gifted and talented child in many schools, especially those in socially disadvantaged areas. Enrolment with 200 similarly gifted and talented children of the same age in a summer school at a prestigious university such as Princeton can change a child's life because they are surrounded by able peers. I vividly remember chatting to a very bright young African-American girl from Harlem attending the SIG campus at Princeton. I asked whether she liked the programme. She said she loved it. When asked why, she replied 'I don't have to pretend to be dumb here to make friends.' Sceptics may wish to access the SIG website www.giftedstudy.com to see her actually saying this.

(e) Each secondary school be required to appoint from its teaching staff a specialist counsellor for very able children to give general advice and support as well as counsel on which A-level courses they should take and, if the school is an 11–16 school, to which post-16 institutions their very able children should transfer. Some very able children do not gain admittance to a good university because their advisers do not understand that successful candidates for entry to leading universities need to take relevant A-level subjects. For example, students seeking to study science at a leading university must study at least two science subjects at A-level as well as maths.

(f) Groups of schools who currently only teach children aged 11–16, should be encouraged to offer joint post-16 provision such as the successful programme in Sleaford, Lincolnshire, described in the attached case study.

(g) Most importantly of all, there should be clear accountability to judge whether or not the National Gifted and Talented programme is a success. Clearly the simplest and cheapest accountability would be: (i) the proportion of those identified as gifted and talented who achieve three As at A-level or its equivalent; and (ii) the proportion of these students who are admitted to a leading university.

Overall conclusion

The nurturing of our very able children is not only in this country's economic self-interest, but is also a matter of social justice to ensure that every child, whatever their social background, achieves the potential of which they are capable. It is not about elitism or even about favouring children from socially disadvantaged backgrounds, but ensuring fair chances for all children.

Case study: Sleaford Joint Sixth Form, by Gordon Kay[7]

This is a sixth form collaboration which began in 1983 with the sharing of minority A-level provision between the three schools in Sleaford: Carre's Grammar School (selective boys), Kesteven and Sleaford High School (selective girls) and St George's College of Technology (co-educational comprehensive). Despite the small size of the venture at that stage a director of studies was appointed whose job it was to teach in each school, and to act as liaison between the school staff. Since then, the sixth form in each of the schools has grown considerably. Currently there are 705 students in the joint sixth form.

The collaboration enables students in each of the schools to mix freely and to choose courses that are offered by each of the schools. Three schools working together means that a wide range of courses can be made available and clashes between subjects can be reduced. Students who already attend one of the schools in the consortium remain based at that school for tutorial and other core studies but provided they meet the course entry requirements, they are free to apply for whatever academic courses they wish in the other schools. Students who wish to join the joint sixth form and who have not previously attended one of the Sleaford schools are based at the most suitable school and can choose courses at any of them.

The collaboration is made easier by the fact that the three secondary schools in Sleaford are 10–15 minutes walk from each other. Sixth form courses are taught in 2-hour blocks to reduce movement, and where necessary suitable breaks are provided to enable students to make the short journey between the schools. A high proportion of the students choose one or more courses outside their base school and most will spend time in another school, for example, for enrichment or extra curricular activities.

The curriculum includes a wide range of level 3 qualifications: A-levels, Applied A-levels, and BTEC Nationals. There is a similar range of level 2 qualifications – BTEC, City and Guilds and CACHE (leading qualification for working in children's services). The new Society Health and Development diploma will be offered in 2008 at levels 1–3 and seven other diplomas in 2009.

Apart from the breadth of the curriculum offer, the benefit of three schools working together is evident in the ability of the joint sixth form to offer several courses in popular areas. For example for 2008 in Year 12 there will be ten English groups (language, literature, and combined language and literature courses), there will be five chemistry groups, five maths groups and five psychology groups. Hence, the possible permutations of subject choice are enormous.

Since 2002, in response to the growing size of the joint sixth form, its activities and procedures have been formalised and a clear management structure has been developed to ensure that the responsibilities of governors and the heads towards the 16–19 phase are discharged.

As part of this process, a protocol document was prepared for the chair of governors of each school to sign. This had the effect of making overt many of the underlying

---

[7] Case study supplied to the author by Gordon Kay, director, Sleaford Joint Sixth Form.

principles and agreements which had become custom and practice, and took them out of the realm of oral tradition, stating the clearly and opening them up to examination. In 2008 the protocol document was thoroughly revised by a subcommittee of governors from each school and the director. It is now a substantial document and consists of a detailed memorandum of understanding and several annexes, containing policies on practical matters such as travel routes between schools and Education Maintenance Allowance (EMA) rules.

The importance of this document can not be underestimated as it is a clear public statement of the determination of the schools to work together in a particular way. It was essential once the sixth form grew beyond a small collaboration that working practices and the reasons for the collaboration were clearly articulated and put in the public arena. The impact of this has been to raise the awareness of staff, parents and students about the collaboration, enabling them to play a part as stakeholders in the enterprise.

The memorandum of understanding is signed not only, by the chair of governors of each school but also by the head teacher of each school, ensuring that those charged with governance and those responsible for the operation of the schools take equal responsibility for working together.

The key figure in the collaboration is the director, who has clearly defined delegated responsibilities for the leadership and management of the collaboration. The director has overall responsibility for the effectiveness of the curriculum as well as for ensuring that financial transfers between the schools are as small as possible.

To facilitate the collaboration, there are cross-school groups at all levels. The director is a member of the Joint Committee of Chairs of Governors, Vice Chairs and Heads. This body meets six times a year and is chaired in rotation by the chair of governors of each school. The director chairs the Heads Steering Group, Curriculum team, Pastoral team, Exam team and Quality Assurance team.

The director is supported by administrative staff who deal with enrolment, attendance, EMA, student progress tracking, reporting and all sixth form examinations. A member of staff of one of the schools has responsibility for managing the assessment, tracking and data analysis for the joint sixth form. The results and other achievement data is dissected to provide information about progress at individual student, teaching set, provider, and base school level as well as for the joint sixth form overall. Examinations and all other assessments are entered through a joint examinations centre number. The joint sixth form therefore is the administrative hub of the collaboration. The administrative staff is supported by the CAPITA School Information Management System.

From a financial point of view, it is in the area of administration that the collaboration can assist in making savings. As the joint sixth form office deals with many of the administrative activities associated with the post-16 phase of education for the three schools, there is no need for the activities mentioned above to take place or staff to be employed to perform them in each school. This leads to savings in secretarial time and general administrative costs.

Duplication in other areas such as the delivery of less popular courses is also avoided by the collaboration, leading to savings in staff and other resources. For example, the delivery of Spanish A-level which regularly recruits only a small number of students is shared between two of the schools. This gives each school a stake in the course, enables staff at both schools to have some A-level teaching, but spreads the burden of delivering an uneconomic course.

The way in which the collaboration is structured enables the schools to pursue their own identities and values their specialisms which contribute to the collaborative effort. This also enables students to hold positions of responsibility within their base schools. There are some particular difficulties associated with a collaboration which includes two selective schools, and a key feature of the director's work is diplomatic activity at all levels. Recent parent and student opinion research has shown that the student body is extremely happy with the collaboration as are parents, but it would be wrong to suggest that all partners are happy all of the time. However, the benefits overall in terms of curriculum choice, ensuring that student mix post-16 and the professional dialogue which takes place between staff at the schools teaching the same subject, are considerable. Collaboration is not easy, however, and is a potentially soft target when it comes to a squeeze on funding. Despite the rhetoric about collaboration, some government policies are a hindrance, notably the Performance Tables, where a student's results are applied to the base school rather than to the delivery site or to the joint sixth form as a whole.

As regards progression, currently about 80 per cent of students obtain places in higher education. There is a good record of the remainder accessing employment or further training.

There is no doubt that the strength of the joint sixth form attracts many students to study in Sleaford. It was also a crucial positive element in the Gateway bids for the new 14–19 diplomas, and it underpins the wider collaboration now taking place pre-16. Many of the teething troubles facing other clusters have already been addressed and systems are in place that need only minor revision to be appropriate for pre-16 learners.

The nearest further education college is some 14 miles away but in 2007, the collaboration was widened, post-16, to include work with a local further education college using their outpost in the town, for the delivery of beauty therapy courses. As the diplomas develop, there will be a further widening of provision post-16 to ensure the 14–19 entitlement is available to all students by 2013.

The joint sixth form contains students of wide ranging abilities and the curriculum reflects the need to provide for them. Discussions are taking place about how to stretch and challenge the brightest students. The Cambridge Pre U, the Assessment and Qualifications Alliance (AQA) Baccalaureate and the new Extended Project are all being considered as vehicles for this. The joint sixth form has been identified by Lincolnshire as the centre for the International Baccalaureate in the county, which gives another option to consider, although government support for this has diminished considerably. Whilst considering these possibilities, the provision at level 2, which already includes several BTEC first diploma course and GCSE re-sits, has been enhanced with the development of a construction centre offering BTEC and City and Guilds qualifications. The CACHE NVQ in Children Care and Learning Development, which has been a highly successful feature of the level 2 offer for some time, is now offered to level 3.

As the 14–19 entitlement is rolled out, the joint sixth form puts the Sleaford 14–19 partnerships in a very advantageous position for delivery. Work-based learning and apprenticeships do not feature as much as they should in the Sleaford area and the facilities for students need to be enhanced, but overall the future is bright and there is enthusiasm to move the joint sixth form forward to ensure it offers what students need. The aim is to fulfil the mission statement for the joint sixth form of 'Excellent Post 16 Education for All'.

At the time of its creation, Sleaford schools were already doing well in retaining students post-16. By 1988 there were 250 students taking A-level courses between the three schools. The joint sixth form even at that early stage in its development was proving popular and successful.

Today there are over 700 students in the joint sixth form and with an anticipated enrolment in September 2008 of 450, it will increase further possibly to a total of 780 students.

In 1988 the students had nineteen A-level courses to choose from which, was a good range at that time and one which could only be achieved by the three schools working together. The choice at that time was the envy of schools throughout the county and beyond.

Students enrolling this year have been able to choose from thirty-three A-level courses, four Applied A-level courses, two BTEC Nationals and one Diploma as well as nine level 2 courses. To deliver these courses there will be almost 200 sixth form classes running across the three schools. This expansion in numbers and courses has not been at the expense of academic success, in fact there has been good progress particularly at level 3. In 2000 for example, the A-level (level 3) pass rate at A and B was 35 per cent and at A–C, 55.5 per cent. By 2007 the pass rate had increased at A and B to 43 per cent and A–C to 70 per cent. These are good figures for what is effectively a comprehensive sixth form. The schools are constantly striving to improve on these results and to enhance the value-added performance of the students.

Taking account of its popularity, curriculum choice and success, it is not surprising that the Sleaford Joint Sixth Form remains the envy of other post-16 providers in the county and beyond.

For any further information, please contact the director, Gordon W. M. Kay, at Gordon.kay@sleafordjsf.co.uk

Suggested further reading

Belle Wallace, *Teaching the Very Able Child*, London: NACE/Fulton, 2000.

Sutton Trust, 'Wasted Talent? Attrition Rates of High-Achieving Pupils Between School and University', London: Sutton Trust, June 2008.

American Institute for Foreign Study, *Summer Institute for the Gifted Catalog 2009*, Stamford CT: American Institute for Foreign Study, 2008. www.giftedstudy.com

What lessons can we learn from other countries which have high standards in their schools?

In recent years it has become possible to compare educational standards across the world through the triennial surveys of the knowledge and skills of 15 year-olds published by the Programme for International Student Assessment (PISA) organised by the Organisation for Economic Co-operation and Development (OECD).[1] More than 400,000 students from fifty-seven countries, making up close to 90 per cent of the world economy, took part in PISA 2006. The focus was on science, but comparative performance of the participating countries in maths and reading was also done. In addition, data are collected on pupils' family and social backgrounds which would explain the differences in performance. For a comparison of selective indicators from the study, see Table 16.1.

In the three comparisons of science, maths and reading, Finland, Korea, Canada or Hong Kong, China usually feature in the top three. See charts at the end of this chapter.

While the United Kingdom surprisingly rates number 10 out of 57 countries in science, despite the recent decline in A-level science entries, it ranks only 22 in maths and 14 in reading. The United States ranks 32 in maths, has no measure for reading and rated 24 in science.

A recent Policy Exchange study draws some important conclusions from the data which supports the general conclusions in Chapter 1 of this book on what makes a good school.[2] Importantly, it emphasises that good systems of education must 'generate both a basic level of equity and excellence'.

The study also agrees that autonomy for schools is important providing there are national clear and consistent accountability measures.

One crucial lesson to be drawn from both the OECD data and the Policy Exchange paper is the importance of national accountability standards. The United States, despite its wealth and economic might, rates poorly in the OECD measures. A particular problem is the almost complete absence of national accountability measures. Instead, they are provided either on a state, or local basis. This is the principal reason for the disappointing results of the recent 'No Child Left Behind' initiative of George W. Bush. Despite generous federal financial support, little progress has been made in raising standards in most urban school board funded US schools. There are many reasons for

---

[1] www.oecd.org/home

[2] Cheryl Lim and Chris Davis, 'Helping Schools to Succeed: Lessons from Abroad', London: Policy Exchange, 2008. Available at www.policyexchange.org.uk. Reproduced by kind permission of the Policy Exchange.

Table 16.1 Comparison of selective indicators – PISA study 2006

Indicator	New Zealand	Canada	Hong Kong	Sweden	United Kingdom	OECD average
Percentage of population aged 15–64 that has attained at least upper secondary level	79%	85%	52%	84%	67%	68%
Percentage population that has achieved a tertiary qualification	27%	46%	24%	30%	30%	26%
Annual expenditure per pupil in dollars	$5,815	$6,482	n/a	$7,744	$6,656	$6,608
Public expenditure on education as a percentage of total public expenditure	15.1%	8.20%	23%	8.30%	8.70%	9.20%

this failure, as Chapter 17 explains, including the power of the teachers' unions to frustrate reform, the micro-management of schools by urban school boards and the heavy concentration of ethnic minorities, many of them recent immigrants in some American cities.

As the Policy Exchange[3] study says 'balancing school autonomy with central oversight enables innovation and independent action at the school level while at the same time maximising economics of such a transferral of best practice'.

The Policy Exchange study analyses four particular countries: New Zealand; Canada (Ontario and Alberta); Hong Kong and Sweden, who did so well in the 2006 PISA comparative evaluation.

The study draws the following general conclusions.

New Zealand

Compulsory education in New Zealand lasts ten years and is divided into primary, intermediate and secondary. Schools are increasingly catering for both the primary and secondary levels. There are regular state schools, and specialist schools for the Maori population which teach in the Maori language. Crucially, there are integrated schools (former private schools now funded by the state) and special educational needs schools as well as designated charter schools which espouse particular religious ethos.

In 1988, New Zealand launched the 'Tomorrow's Schools' reforms which focused on devolving power from the central and regional bureaucracy to each individual school and its communities. Effectively the local education departments were eliminated, with the Ministry of Education providing funding and setting the national accountability framework. Studies of the New Zealand reforms indicate that a key component is the encouragement of competition and choice. However, concern has been raised about the poor performance of the Maori pupils. Interestingly for those who question the Key stages 1, 2 and 3 tests in England, there is a complaint in New Zealand that there is no external system with assessment of students' learning until students at age 15 take the National Certificate of Educational Achievement.

[3] Ibid., p. 7.

Canada

In Canada, education is the responsibility of the ten provinces and three territories. However, many provinces such as Ontario and Alberta have several publicly funded private education authorities including English language public and Catholic schools and French language public and Catholic schools. Interestingly, in Ontario, the school leaving age has recently been extended to 18 years. It is too early to learn whether or not this will raise standards of achievement.

The Policy Exchange study analyses the performance of schools in Alberta and Ontario, both of which perform well in the PISA studies. The two provinces have used similar reform techniques to raise standards:

- Accountability. There is an emphasis on collective accountability.
- Collaboration. There is encouragement for schools to work together.
- Delegating authority to schools.

A particularly interesting finding of studies on the effectiveness of the reforms is the belief that reforms take a number of years to become embedded with any given system. Concerns have been raised in both Alberta and Ontario that the system is not being given enough time to make the new initiatives work.

This is a significant lesson for England, where there is a similar complaint of too many government initiatives and unreasonable expectations of instant improvement in results from newly established academies.

Sweden

Particularly interesting is the Policy Exchange analysis of the success of the Swedish school system, where 85 per cent of the population aged 25–64 has attained at least the upper secondary qualification compared to only 67 per cent in the United Kingdom and 68 per cent average for the fifty-seven OECD countries.

A crucial aspect of Swedish schools has been the move to increase choice and diversity through the introduction of independent schools that are privately administered but publicly funded. However, there have been public fears expressed that, in recent years there has been a decline in the quality of education provided by Swedish schools.

In 2006, after twelve years of Social Democratic rule, the four-party coalition, led by the Moderate Party, regained power in Stockholm. The new government has introduced a number of new initiatives, including:

- More national assessment examinations;
- The use of grades in tests from the age of 7 rather than the previous 15 or 16 age group;
- A shorter inspection cycle;
- A tightening of the national curriculum requirements.

Nevertheless, the key advantages of competition and choice have been retained, with an increasing number of state-funded schools being administered by the private sector with a strict requirement that private schools with state funding may not charge top-up fees. Hence the name for independent schools in Sweden: 'free schools'. Ten per cent of

Swedish children are now educated privately compared to only 1 per cent before the reforms were introduced.

Interestingly for comprehensive school supporters in the UK, Swedish society places more value on communalism than individualism. Observers of Swedish culture call this *lagoon*, which perhaps can be translated as 'not too much, not too little'. But egalitarianism in Sweden is different from the UK, with a high minimum standard being set with a requirement that every child should leave school at 16 with the capacity to continue in full-time education. Eighty-four per cent of the Swedish population has attained at least an upper secondary education level compared with only 67 per cent in the United Kingdom.

Finland

The results of recent PISA[4] surveys place Finland in the top three countries for reading, maths and science. A study by Jens Henrik Haar of the Danish Technological Institute in 2005 found the following reasons for this success:

First,   Schools have been given greater autonomy. Schools now decide their own priorities, with a national framework of assessment and evaluation. This gives support to the major recommendations in the book that head teachers should be given greater autonomy.

Second,   There is a core curriculum which starts in the voluntary year of pre-school education at age 5, now received by 90 per cent of each age cohort of children.

Third,   Finland's assessment system relies heavily on self-assessment by teachers, which puts relatively little emphasis on external tests. Learning progress is monitored on individual student report sheets and regularly discussed with each student. Until the age of 13, this assessment is conducted by class teachers who continue to have charge of their children until specialised secondary school tuition starts.

Fourth,   There is a rigorous selection procedure to enter teacher training in Finland, with clearly the teaching profession being happy and high-status, as only 10 per cent of applicants to be teachers are successful.

The report explains that the success of the Finnish schools cannot be explained by any simple factor, but a combination including heavy emphasis on reading and writing skills, a successful use of comprehensive schools satisfying the needs of children with a wide range of abilities, the very high status of teachers, and lastly, and possibly crucially, the cultural homogeneity of Finnish schools with few or no ethnic minorities.

There is also evidence of a relatively low difference between the levels achieved by the highest-performing pupils and the lower-performing, and that the impact of parents' socio-economic status is low.

The high performance in reading in Finnish schools is of particular interest to English schools which suffer from poor literacy levels, especially in socially disadvantaged areas. The study indicates that Finnish children care more about reading, with Finnish schools displaying the highest level of interest in reading in the fifty-seven OECD countries taking part in the PISA study.[5] As in Germany, Finnish students spend more of their free

---

[4] www.pisa.oecd.org
[5] Ibid.

time reading rather than watching the television or playing on their computers. Finnish students are the most active newspaper readers and borrow books from the library more frequently than children in any other OECD country.

Astonishingly, 41 per cent of Finnish boys say that reading is their favourite hobby, while 60 per cent of the girls say the same.

These findings give support to the recommendations on improving literacy in England described in Chapter 4 of this book.

The status of teachers is another key factor for the Finnish success, with considerable resources being invested in teacher training. All teachers have a master's degree either in education or in their particular subject.

With regard to school autonomy, the PISA 2000 study shows that Finnish head teachers are vested with a considerable degree of decision making authority as regards school policy and management. Governing bodies of schools, local authorities and the central government have much less decision making power than in the other OECD study countries.

Finally, as described above, Finland has the huge advantage of being a small, culturally homogeneous country with non-national students making up only 1 per cent of the population, compared with close to 10 per cent in the UK.

For a copy of the complete report by Jens Henrik Haar, readers should visit www. danishtechnology.dk and access 'Explaining Student Performance, annex 2'.

England compared with France and Germany

It is also useful to compare the English secondary schools system with the French and the German systems. Chapter 5 explains the extraordinary diversity of the German education system with its dual system which results in a workforce with such high skills in engineering. Sixty per cent of German children participate in upper secondary education compared to only 42 per cent in the UK.

As described in the paper by Ute Hippach-Schneider and her colleagues (see the suggested further reading list at the end of this chapter),[6] at age 10, German children have the choice of moving to either a grammar school (*Gymnasien*) with 33 per cent in 2005 taking this option, or an intermediate school (*Realschule*) with approximately 27 per cent taking this option, and the remainder opting for example for a secondary general school (*Hauptschule*). Uniquely, the first two years of the German secondary system are called 'orientation stages' for pupils aged 10–12. Pupils can switch schools at age 12 if they or their teachers recommend this. At age 16, the pupils attending either *Realschulen or Hauptschulen* have a wide choice of different post-16 provision including the dual system (part in-company training and part vocational schooling), vocational extension schools, specialist schools for nursing, midwifery, etc., or full-time vocational schools (*Berufsfachschulen*).

The 27 September 2008 issue of the *Economist*[7] shows that Germany has the highest trade surplus in the world, with an estimated trade surplus in 2008 of $285 billion. This compares to the Chinese surplus of $253 billion, the British deficit of $187 billion, and the American deficit of $845 billion.

---

[6] 'Vocational Education and Training in Germany', CEDEFOP Panorama Series 138, Luxembourg: Office for Official Publications of the European Community, 2007. Copies in English can be accessed at www.cedefop.europa.eu

[7] *Economist*, 27 September 2008, p. 130.

We can also learn from the French system, where while the required education age is the same as in England – sixteen years – nearly 90 per cent of French students transfer at age 15 or 16 to either a *Lycée Enseignement Générale et Technologique* or a *Lycée Professionel* or a *Lycée Technologique* to study for the *Baccalauréate* ('le Bac'). Each type of *Lycée* provides for a different type of baccalaureate, namely general (academic), technique (technology or a specialist field like social care), or basic (vocational, accountancy, secretarial skills and professional.)[8]

Success in any of the three Bacs at age 18 entitles students to enter university, though this is something being reviewed by President Nicolas Sarkozy. It is the goal of the French Ministry of Education that 80 per cent of all French students will pass one of the three baccalaureates. Currently, the proportion passing the Bac is about two thirds.

Should the British schools adopt a similar system of different types of post-16 schools for pupils with particular career goals? The introduction of the National Diploma is clearly an attempt to widen the choice of education available for 16 year-olds, but as explained in Chapter 5, there are significant problems with this initiative, including the fact that only half of English secondary schools offer post-16 provision. As recommended in Chapter 5, the introduction of specialist academies offering particular national diplomas such as engineering and construction skills for the 14–19 age group could provide a solution for some pupils.

If we genuinely wish to increase substantially the proportion of our pupils staying on in full-time education at age 16, we will have to address a number of key issues:

Clearly more schools will need to be funded to offer post-16 provision with different schools offering different post-16 courses. It would be an interesting development of the specialist schools initiative if specialist schools were to offer different post-16 provision including particular National Diplomas, linked to their particular specialism (technology, ICT and engineering, science, maths, arts, sports, business and enterprise, languages, music and performing arts, etc.) as well as the existing A-level courses.

What is not possible is for every school to offer a very wide range of post-16 specialisms. This would be economically unviable. Most individual schools simply do not have nearly enough post-16 students to offer courses in both academic and vocational courses in a wide range of subjects.

Suggested further reading

Cheryl Lim and Chris Davis, 'Helping Schools to Succeed: Lessons from Abroad', London: Policy Exchange, 2008.

OECD, 'Programme for International Student Assessment (PISA)', OECD, 2007. www.oecd.org

Jens Henrik Haar, 'Explaining Student Performance', annexe 2, at www.danishtechnology.dk

Cyril Taylor and Conor Ryan, *Excellence in Education*, London: David Fulton, 2005, ch. 15.

Alan Smithers, 'England's Education: What Can Be Learned by Comparing Countries?', Liverpool: University of Liverpool Centre for Education and Employment Research, 2004.

Ute Hippach-Schneider, Martina Krause and Christian Woll, 'Vocational Training in Germany', CEDEFOP Panorama Series 138, Luxembourg: Office of Official Publications of the European Communities, 2007.

---

[8] For more, see Cyril Taylor and Conor Ryan, *Excellence in Education: The Making of Great Schools*, London: David Fulton, 2004.

Chapter 17

Could British educational reforms be introduced into the United States?

The extraordinary paradox in comparing educational standards in the United Kingdom and the United States is that two of the most important recent English educational reforms – the introduction of specialist schools and academies – both originated in US schools.

In the 1960s and 1970s, Magnet schools, which besides teaching a broad curriculum, were centres of excellence in one or more particular subjects, were an important American schools innovation. For various reasons, including their use by the federal government in an abortive attempt to integrate ethnic minorities into US schools, Magnet schools became less popular. They have, however, recently become popular again. Magnet schools were introduced as Specialist Schools in 1994 in England, where they now account for 90 per cent of all schools. Similarly, the British City Technology Colleges, and their successors, the City Academies, emulate US Charter schools. There are now over 3,500 charter schools in the United States, but they still only account for 3.5 per cent of all US public schools, whereas the goal in England will be to have at least 400 academies equivalent to nearly 15 per cent of the 3,100 secondary schools.

If these two great American reforms have worked so well in the United Kingdom, why have they been less successful in the United States? Could American schools learn from the way that specialist schools and academies have transformed English schools, as well as from other English reforms such as the introduction of the national curriculum and national accountability started in 1988? Before answering this question, it is necessary to review the current state of public school education in the United States.

As described in Chris Whittle's book *Crash Course*,[1] the first issue is the sheer size of the American school population, which makes it very difficult to generalise about US educational standards. The total school population in the United States is approximately 49 million children. Each age cohort is over 3 million children (*note*: the 49 million estimated children include PK-12, a total of 14 'cohorts'. In addition, the number of students in each cohort is not the same. For example, in 2005 there were 3.6 million children in kindergarten and 3.1 million in 12th grade), compared to just 650,000 in England. There are an astounding 14,000 school districts, compared to just 140 local authorities with educational responsibilities in England, with 97,000 schools in the public sector of which 73,000 are primary or middle schools (primary schools for children aged 6–11 and middle schools for children aged 11–14) and 29,500 are senior high schools for children aged 14–17.

---

[1] Chris Whittle, *Crash Course: Imagining a Better Future for Public Education*, New York: Riverhead Books, 2005. ISBN: 1-59448-902-5.

Interestingly, there are 29,000 private and parochial schools in the United States – 23 per cent of all schools. Of these, 12,000 have secondary grades out of a total of 42,000 secondary schools, or 29 per cent. Private schools educate 11 per cent of all US children, compared with 7 per cent in private secondary schools in England.[2]

Chris Whittle, the founder and chief executive of Edison Schools, the largest charter school organisation, in his book *Crash Course*,[3] estimates that American public education enrols 50 million pupils in the United States – plus 5 million teachers and support staff – nearly the population of Great Britain. He estimates the average American household pays 4,000 dollars in taxes each year to support American public schools.

He says that 15 million American children go to schools with poor results. The US Federal Government National Assessment of Education Progress (NAEP) shows that 33 per cent of American public school children in 4th grade do not achieve basic proficiency, the lowest classification in reading skills (there are three classifications: advanced, proficient and basic). He further asks: 'Why does the greatest nation in this history of the world allow 33 per cent of its children to languish in functional illiteracy?' (see Table 17.1).

Whittle attributes the low standards in such a large proportion of American schools to many factors, including the power of the teaching unions to delay reforms, the absence of national accountability standards, the heavy concentration of children from socially disadvantaged families in particular districts, and insufficient funding.

The extraordinary power of the American teaching unions (American Federation of Teachers, National Education Association and the United Federation of Teachers) is clearly a factor. In most school districts, every US teacher and school staff member is a member of one of the unions. Their power, particularly over the Democratic Party, which relies heavily upon their funding and canvassing, is such that it is extremely difficult to introduce radical reforms into many US public schools, especially as so many school districts are small, employing few staff capable of taking on the very large teaching unions. When I have worked with a number of New York City schools, high school principals have told me that it is virtually impossible to terminate a poor teacher's employment, despite Mayor Bloomberg's recent reforms.

Yet the average spending per pupil in the US public schools is now over $9,000 per pupil. In New York City, with just 1 million public school pupils, the total school district expenditures in fiscal year 2006 were $15 billion.[4] This means that the average spending per pupil in New York schools is $15,000, which is 50 per cent more than the average of $10,000 per pupil in English schools. Even more interesting is the comparison

Table 17.1 Fourth graders' reading (age 9)

Progress measured by NAEP: percentage of pupils who do not achieve basic proficiency							
1992	*1994*	*1998*	*2000*	*2002*	*2003*	*2005*	*2007*
38%	40%	38%	41%	37%	36%	36%	33%

[2] US Department of Education, National Center for Education Statistics (2008), *Digest of Education Statistics, 2007* (NCES 2008–22). Washington DC: US Government Printing Office.
[3] Chris Whittle, *Crash Course*.
[4] Source: US Department of Education, National Center for Education Statistics, see http://nces.ed. gov/pubs2008/revexpdist06/table 07.asp

with per capita fees for US parochial schools (religious), whose fees are typically only $6,500 per annum. Why, despite this spending, are standards in so many American urban public schools so poor?

There are many reasons, and it is difficult to generalise. There are many school districts, especially in the White suburban areas where standards are very high. Some states, like Georgia, under Governor Zell Miller, have made substantial improvements to their public schools. However, if my American readers will allow me to comment, there are some fundamental causes for the poor standards in so many American schools. These structural problems would have to be remedied before English-style school reforms could be implemented successfully.

We have already discussed the power of the teaching unions to obstruct reform, but there are other causes, as Chris Whittle points out.

Possibly the single greatest problem is the lack of effective national accountability standards. Despite the recent bold attempt of the 'No Child Left Behind' federal legislation, which requires all US schools to report on progress for grades 3–6 in maths and English in raising the academic standards of their pupils using statistics, there are still no federally supervised tests; in England, every pupil takes nationally supervised tests and examinations at 11, 16 and 18, which provide English parents with statistical measures of whether or not a particular school is a good school.[5] I was told by Bernadine Fong, President Emerita, Foothill College, Los Altos Hills, California, that the chief critics of the No Child Left Behind reforms have been the local school superintendents who complain they have to 'teach to the test' – a series of exit examinations by grade level. Yet many school-board schools whose students cannot pass the exit exams can get 'waivers' to move their students to the next grade level. The notion of local control of its schools is so deeply embedded into American education that it probably remains the untouchable element of any school reform movement.

Time magazine has reported that state test results for schools have very little correlation student achievement as measured by the NAEP.[6] Using data from the US Federal Government National Center for Education Statistics,[7] it published a chart which showed, for example, that while Mississippi claims that 90 per cent of its fourth graders score as proficient or better in reading, using its own state test, only 20 per cent achieve the same result on the NAEP. Using its own test, Mississippi ranks first in the fifty US states, but using the NAEP it ranks last. Pupils in Massachusetts scored the best on the NAEP, with nearly 50 per cent of fourth graders scoring as proficient or better in the federal reading test, only slightly less than the state test result.

Terrence Paul, CEO of Renaissance Learning, has written a very interesting paper discussing accountability and literacy tests, 'Reflections regarding Assessment, and Reading and Maths Instruction in the US and England'.[8]

---

[5] There is also a teacher assessment at age 7 which is nationally prescribed.

[6] Claudia Wallis and Sonja Steptoe, 'How to Fix No Child Left Behind', *Time Magazine*, 4 June 2007.

[7] National Center for Education Statistics: the Education Trust: 'Testing, Learning and Teaching' by Martin West, Brown University. See Martin West, 'Testing, Learning, and Teaching: The Effects of Test-based Accountability on Student Achievement and Instructional Time in Core Academic Subjects', in *Beyond the Basics: Achieving a Liberal Education for All Children*, ed. Chester E. Finn, Jr and Diane Ravitch, Washington, DC: Thomas B. Fordham Institute, 2007.

[8] T. D. Paul, 'Reflections Regarding Assessment, and Reading and Maths Instruction in the US and England', 2008. Available online from http://research.renlearn.com/research/pdfs/328.pdf

Another problem as was mentioned earlier, is the very small size of many US school districts, with many having only minimal staff to supervise their schools, yet they exercise great control over their schools. Even the five largest districts are relatively small, compared to the largest US companies (Table 17.2).

Despite their size, US school districts exercise great power over their schools. Whittle is particularly concerned over the very low expenditures on research and replication of best practice. School boards are often highly politicised; many elect one third of their members every year with the teaching unions doing most of the campaigning for candidates for office. Another issue is the very high turnover of school district superintendents. Their average length in office is only two years. A considerable number have their jobs terminated by the school districts while others seek positions elsewhere. This is why Mayor Bloomberg has led fellow mayors in a bid to take control of schools into their offices, in a bid to lift standards, with significant success so far in New York.

Despite the high per capita spending overall, American school principals and their teachers are paid relatively low salaries. The typical US principal of a school earns between $82,000 and $92,000 a year – between £45,000 and £51,000. Some English academy principals are earning over £100,000 or $180,000. The average US teacher earns about $44,500 dollars or £25,000 whereas an English classroom teacher's pay rises to £34,000 ($63,000) with performance pay (even more in London).[9]

In many school districts another reason for their low salaries is the high proportion of funding retained by school boards and not distributed to schools, and the fact that in most schools, funding is not tied to the number of pupils in the school as in the UK. Under the reforms introduced in England by Margaret Thatcher, schools are funded on a per capita basis on the number of children they enrol and school boards may only retain 10 per cent of the total schools budget. More recently the schools budget, which is largely funded directly by central government grant, has been split into a schools and local authority pot, which means local authorities may only spend around 10 per cent of the total school funding paid by the central government. Until recently there were, for example, three different levels of school board in the New York City schools. Mayor Bloomberg has reduced this to only one. Previously less than half of the $15,000 per pupil (which was increased from $10,000 in 2000) available to spend in New York was actually spent in the schools. In 2000, 55 per cent of spending was in the area of 'Classroom Instruction'. Out of the $11 billion budget in 2000, almost $2.5 billion was spent on special education needs, with little or no accountability to demonstrate the

Table 17.2 Comparison of America's top five commercial companies' revenue with the five largest school districts

Largest companies	Total revenue	Biggest school districts	Total revenue
1 Exxon Mobil	$390 billion	New York City	$17.5 billion
2 Wal-Mart	$375 billion	Los Angeles	$ 8 billion
3 Chevron	$214 billion	City of Chicago	$ 4 billion
4 General Motors	$181 billion	Dade County	$3.5 billion
5 Ford Motors	$173 billion	Clark County	$2.5 billion

[9] Source for US figures: Center for Education Reform. www.edreform.com

value of this expenditure. In 2000, $2.1 billion was spent on full-time special education and $400,000 was spent on part-time special education.

Another major issue in urban schools in the United States is the high mobility rate of pupils. The principal of the Brandeis High School on New York's Upper West Side, Dr Eloise Messineo, who has dramatically improved her school, told me that despite the many improvements to the school and to the levels of student achievement that she has managed, the graduation rate continues to remain unacceptably low.

Clearly, therefore, there will need to be major structural changes in US schools before the techniques outlined in this book that Britain and other countries use to raise standards could be successfully implemented in America.

But this is by no means impossible to achieve. Already many school systems such as those in Philadelphia and Washington DC have converted the majority of their schools to charter schools with resulting improvements in standards.

One particular issue has yet to be resolved. Despite the recent Supreme Court ruling that parochial schools in Cleveland could receive taxpayer funds, the funding of parochial schools by school boards in the United States is still rare, despite the fact that standards in many American parochial schools are high, while per capita spending is often only half that for public schools.

In England, as we saw in Chapter 13, 17 per cent of all secondary schools are schools with a religious character funded by the taxpayer, as are 38 per cent of primary schools for pupils aged 5–11. Generally, standards in English faith schools are higher than in non-faith schools. They do, however, have to teach the national curriculum and are encouraged to admit children of other faiths. Clearly, one way to improve US schools would be to establish more taxpayer-funded parochial schools, but there are, of course, constitutional issues raised by this idea.

Nevertheless, there is increasing acceptance in the United States that the way to improve standards is to increase the autonomy of individual schools and to create partnerships with the private sector such as has been created by the Edison schools. It is therefore not impossible that English educational reforms could be introduced successfully into American schools. Harvard University, for example, is working with fifteen school districts to improve standards using these techniques.

Finally, it is also a paradox that despite the low standards in many urban US schools, generally, higher education in the United States is of a high standard, with a much greater participation rate than other countries, including the United Kingdom. The author has recommended that British higher education institutions adopt the key elements of the successful American higher education system. First there is a wide diversity of provisions, with state-funded two-year community colleges offering a wide range of courses, including high school diploma equivalents, and two-year associate degrees with credits transferable to four-year institutions; state funded four-year colleges and universities, many of which have very high standards, such as the University of California–Los Angeles, University of California–Berkeley, and University of Wisconsin–Madison; private colleges, some of which offer four-year undergraduate degrees, and private universities and colleges, like Harvard and Princeton, which offer both undergraduate and graduate degrees. Second, there is a federally administered system of accreditation, with six regional accreditation bodies, and third, there is a unique system of transfer of credits towards degrees from one institution to another if a student changes institution. Fourth, many sources of federal funding for student support goes to the individual student rather than to the university or college. The net result is a highly effective free market in higher education with a wide diversity of choice and the ability to switch institutions easily. Sadly the same choice is not available to American school children.

Concerns about US school standards are shared by the Koret Task Force for K–12 [Kindergarten to Year 12] Education, who visited English secondary specialist schools and academies in September 2004.[10]

Paul Hill, research professor at the University of Washington School of Public Affairs and director of its Center on Reinventing Public Education, wrote the report on behalf of his colleagues who included such distinguished academics as Terry Moe, John Chubb, Chester Finn, Caroline Hoxby and Diane Ravitch. Hill concluded that, while the US federal government has less leverage than the British Department of Education, US state leaders could, if they so wished, act aggressively to implement school reform. They could set standards which required schools to teach core subjects well. Individual states, for example, could introduce a key British reform under which schools are funded on a per capita basis and school heads are given control of spending. Finally, any state, providing it had a determined governor, could require struggling schools and districts to form partnerships with the private sector. Governors in states that have charter school laws (a majority) can insist that charter school organisations take over failing schools, as has happened in Philadelphia and Washington DC.

The Koret Group found that the most important lesson to be learned from Blair's reforms is the importance of good political leadership. They believe that in the United States it would be especially important to gain the support of the Democratic Party, which considers itself the prime representative of government employees, especially teachers and their unions. In England, a crucial aspect of the success in raising standards has been bipartisan support for major schemes such as specialist schools, academies and accountability for schools.

Suggested further reading

Chris Whittle (founder and CEO, Edison Schools), *Crash Course: Imagining a Better Future for Public Education*, New York: Riverhead Books, 2005.

Chester E. Finn Jr, *Troublemaker: A Personal History of School Reform since Sputnik*, Princeton NJ: Princeton University Press, 2008.

Claudia Wallis and Sonja Steptoe, 'How to Fix No Child Left Behind', *Time Magazine*, 4 June 2007.

Paul Hill, 'Lessons from the Blair School Reforms', *Policy Review*, no. 13, June/July 2004, Stamford CT: Hoover Institution, Stamford University.

Stacey Childress, Richard Elmore and Alan Grossman, 'How to Manage Urban School Districts', *Harvard Business Review*, November 2006, pp. 1–14.

---

[10] Paul T. Hill, 'Lessons from the Blair School Reforms', *Policy Review*, no. 13, June/July 2004, Stamford CT: Hoover Institution, Stamford University. Available at www.hoover.org/publications/policyreview/2932961.html

Appendix 1

Example of a parent/school agreement

 **SOUTH LONDON SCHOOLS**
Harris federation

Harris City Academy Crystal Palace
Maberley Road, London SE19 2JH Tel. 020 8771 2261 Fax. 020 8771 7531

Year 7 200xxx

Acceptance Form and The Academy/Parent/Student Agreement

Please do NOT accept our offer of a place unless you are fully committed to your child starting at Harris City Academy Crystal Palace in September.

Please complete in block capitals and sign the Parent/Student Agreement overleaf and return to:
The Academy Admissions Officer, by xxxxxxxxxxxxxxxxxx

Name of Student	Name/s of Parent/s

Address (only if changed)

Tick as appropriate

I /We accept the offer ☐	OR	I /We refuse the offer ☐

The Academy Agreement

As part of its commitment to being an effective Academy, Harris City Academy Crystal Palace has a responsibility to work in partnership with both parents and students. This commitment is clearly manifested in both policy and practice. At the time of writing there are over forty policy statements which are embraced by this Academy Agreement and cover issues such as Equal Opportunities, Student Reward and Support, Parents' Evenings, etc. Regular communication via the Diary Planner demonstrates all partners' commitment to working in unison.

The Academy will...

- Offer a broad, balanced and differentiated curriculum for all students.
- Provide a high quality education designed to allow all students to develop their individual talents to the full.
- Provide an environment which promotes high quality teaching and learning. This will embrace the need to recruit suitably qualified staff and provide on-going staff training.
- Review and update resources in line with changing Academy priorities and curriculum needs.
- Set work which is challenging, yet suitable for the age and ability of the student.
- Provide a high standard of teaching, student support and individual guidance.
- Respect students as individuals.
- Set homework according to pre-agreed schedules or provide explanation of why homework cannot be set.
- Return marked homework to students within a reasonable time period.
- Regularly mark students' work in accordance with the Academy marking policy.
- Continue to improve, where possible, the learning environment with respect to information and other technologies, quiet areas, field trips etc.
- Enforce reasonable disciplinary measures when behaviour warrants it.
- Provide access for parents to meet with staff given reasonable notice.
- Provide a means of assessing, recording and reporting student achievement which is comprehensive, yet meaningful and accessible to parents.
- Provide information to parents, via the DIARY PLANNER.
- Hold at least one Parents' Evening per year for each year group.
- Give briefings/explanations of changes or developments in the curriculum and assessment arrangements.
- Provide interim progress checks and feedback in response to specific requests or concerns from parents.
- Inform parents of any problems or praiseworthy events within reasonable time.
- Inform or consult parents as appropriate on issues of Academy policy.
- Respond positively to parents' concerns and complaints.
- Promote equal opportunities in all aspects of Academy life.

(Please Turn Over)

Students will...

Complete homework/coursework conscientiously and return it within the deadlines set.

* Contribute fully to the life and work of the Academy community and show a willingness to support and participate in all its activities.
* Play a full part in the growth, development and improvement of the Academy by striving to improve standards of work and behaviour at all times.
* Be confident that striving to improve academic performance is recognised as acceptable and that attempts to undermine or devalue this are not.
* Wear correct uniform and conduct themselves in a sensible and orderly manner.
* Show respect to adults and treat people as individuals in the manner that they would expect to be treated themselves.
* Strive to improve attendance and punctuality by maintaining high personal standards.
* Not take holidays during term time.
* Respect other people's personal space and their belongings.
* Demonstrate care towards the upkeep of the environment and exercise common sense and self control in all aspects relating to the health and safety of others.
* Take a positive stance against litter, graffiti and vandalism.
* Conform to the protocols for security and access required for the ICT network.
* Abide by the procedures to ensure sensible use of the Internet.
* To attend Celebration of Achievement Evening each year.
* Ensure all work submitted is their own work and includes no form of plagiarism.
* Give letters and other information from the Academy to parent(s) and return any reply to the Academy promptly.
* Not bring to the Academy anything which is dangerous, illegal or against Academy rules, including a mobile telephone, knives or any implement which could be used as a weapon.

Student Signature	Date

As parent(s) of the student I/we will...

* Support the Academy in general policy including the maintenance of discipline and ensure that my/our son/daughter abides by the Academy rules.
* Ensure uniform is worn correctly at all times.
* Provide feedback to staff on my/our son's/daughter's completion of homework.
* Attend the Academy activities including Parents' Evenings, Celebration of Achievement Evenings, etc.
* Give positive support to my/our son/daughter and provide, where possible, an environment supportive of study at home.
* Help to motivate my/our son/daughter towards improving academic performance.
* Promote excellent attendance and punctuality and inform the Academy of any reason for absence on the first day of that absence.
* Ensure holidays are not taken during term time.
* Support the completion of homework and coursework and sign the DIARY PLANNER every week.
* Inform the Academy of any difficulties which may affect my/our son's/daughter's learning whilst at the Academy.
* Support my/our son's/daughter's intention to continue in full time education or training up to the age of 18.
* Give permission for the Academy to store data on my/our son/daughter.
* Give permission for the Academy to use photographs and film footage of my/our son/daughter in an Academy context for possible public circulation.
* Inform the Academy in writing if it is decided to exercise the right to request withdrawal from sex education or RE lessons.
* Conform to the protocols for security and access required for the ICT network.
* Ensure all work submitted by my/our son/daughter and particularly coursework submitted for examination units is my/our son's/daughter's own work and includes no form of plagiarism.
* Ensure my/our son/daughter does not bring to the Academy anything which is dangerous, illegal or against Academy rules, including a mobile telephone, knives or any implement which could be used as a weapon.

Parent Signature	Date

Parent Signature	Date

Appendix 2

The admission of students to the Harris City Academy, Crystal Palace

The admission of students to the Harris City Academy, Crystal Palace

1 This document sets out the admission arrangements for the Harris City Academy, Crystal Palace. The document forms an Annex to the Funding Agreement between the Academy and the Secretary of State. Any changes to the arrangements set out in this document must be approved in advance by the Secretary of State. The Academy will come into existence in September 2007 and will operate with the admission policy for the former CTC to admit students at the start of the Academic Year 2007/ 08. This Policy covers the period from September 2007 in terms of casual admissions (see paragraphs 16 to 19 below) and applies from September 2008 for all admissions to the Academy.

2 The Academy will comply with all relevant provisions of the statutory codes of practice (the School Admissions Code of Practice and the School Admission Appeals Code of Practice) as they apply at any given time to maintained schools and with the law on admissions as it applies to maintained schools. Reference in the codes to admission authorities shall be deemed to be references to the governing body of the Academy. In particular, the Academy will take part in the Admissions Forum set up by Croydon LA and have regard to its advice; and will participate in the co-ordinated admission arrangements operated by Croydon LA.

3 Notwithstanding these arrangements, the Secretary of State may direct the Harris City Academy, Crystal Palace to admit a named student to the Academy on application from an LA. Before doing so the Secretary of State will consult the Academy.

I Admission arrangements approved by Secretary of State

4 The admission arrangements for the Harris City Academy, Crystal Palace for the year 2008/2009 and, subject to any changes approved by the Secretary of State, for subsequent years are:

(a) The Harris City Academy, Crystal Palace has an agreed admission number of 180 students. The Academy will accordingly admit at least 180 students in the relevant age group each year if sufficient applications are received;

(b) The Academy may set a higher admission number as its Published Admission Number for any specific year. Before setting an admission number higher than its agreed admission number, the Academy will consult those listed at paragraphs

23–24 below. Students will not be admitted above the Published Admission Number unless exceptional circumstances apply and such circumstances shall be reported to the Secretary of State.

Process of application

5   Applications for places at the Academy will be made in accordance with the LAs co-ordinated admission arrangements, and will be made on the Common Application Form provided and administered by the respective home L.A.s of the applicants. The Academy will also require the submission of its own application form which will be used only to make the administration arrangements for the sitting of the 'banding' tests … The Academy will use the following timetable for applications each year (exact dates within the months may vary from year to year) which, whenever possible, will fit in with the common timetable agreed by the Croydon Admissions Forum or LA:

(a)   September – The Academy will publish in its prospectus information about the arrangements for admission, including oversubscription criteria, for the following September (eg in September 2008 for admission in September 2009). This will include details of open evenings and other opportunities for prospective students and their parents to visit the school. The Academy will also provide information to the LA for inclusion in the composite prospectus, as required;

(b)   September/October – The Academy will provide opportunities for parents to visit the Academy;

(c)   October – Deadline for Academy admissions application form to be submitted;

(d)   November – CAF to be completed and returned to the LA to administer; Academy makes arrangements, and issues invitations for banding tests;

(e)   LA sends applications to Academy;

(f)   Academy sends list of students to be offered places to LA;

(g)   February – LA applies agreed scheme for own schools, informing other LAs of offers to be made to their residents;

(h)   1st March offers made to parents.

Consideration of applications

6   The Harris City Academy, Crystal Palace, will consider all applications for places. Where fewer than 180 applications are received, the Academy will offer places to all those who have applied.

Procedures where the Harris City Academy, Crystal Palace is oversubscribed

7   All applicants will be required to undertake a Non-Verbal Reasoning Test (NVRT) on a date to be published each year. There will be arrangements for late tests for any applicants who are ill on the date of the NVRT test. Applicants will be allocated to an ability band on the basis of their NVRT test score. There will be 9 ability bands with the percentage of places available in each band being determined by the profile of the distribution of ability of the applicants for the Academy. All applicants will also

be required to undertake tests designed to produce an objective ranking of their aptitude for Technology as a subject. Where the number of applications for admission is greater than the published admissions number, applications will be considered against the criteria set out below:

(i) Applications will be considered initially in terms of their aptitude in Technology and 10 per cent of the places each year will be allocated to the applicants who obtain the highest scores in the aptitude tests;

(ii) Applications will then be considered against the ability band in which the applicant is placed by the NVRT test score. The number of places available in each ability band will be determined by matching the percentage of places in each band to the ability profile of the applicants for places that year. Those percentages will be applied to the number of places for the year available after deducting the 10 per cent allocated to those applicants with the highest scores for aptitude in Technology (i.e. 162).

(iii) After the admission of students with statements of Special Educational Needs where the Academy is named on the statement, the criteria will be applied in the order in which they are set out below:

    (a) looked after children;

    (b) admission of students whose siblings currently attend the Academy and who will continue to do so on the date of admission; (for this purpose 'sibling' means a whole, half or step-brother or-sister resident at the same address). Admission of students whose siblings currently attend the Academy and who will continue to do so on the date of admission (that is currently in Years 7 to Year 10);

    (c) remaining places in each ability band will be allocated by the drawing of lots in 2 geographical zones. Zone A will be a zone up to 2 mile radius from the fixed point shown on the attached map; Zone B will be a zone over 2 miles radius from the fixed point shown on the attached map. 90 per cent of the places will be allocated to Zone A and 10 per cent to Zone B;

(iv) If at the end of this process there are unallocated places in any band these will be filled by unallocated applicants from the next nearest band(s) using the same allocation criteria set out at (c) above and continuing the sequence of the allocation of places;

(v) If the number of applications from a single Zone is exhausted then all applicants regardless of geographical Zone shall be included in the draw for the remaining places in that band or adjacent bands. The procedure to be followed in operating the drawing of lots is described in Appendix A.

Operation of waiting lists

8 Subject to any provisions regarding waiting lists in the LAs coordinated admission scheme, the Academy will operate a waiting list. Where in any year the Academy receives more applications for places than there are places available, a waiting list will operate until a month after the admission date. This will be maintained by the Academy and it will be open to any parent to ask for his or her child's name to be placed on the waiting list, following an unsuccessful application.

9 Children's position on the waiting list will be determined solely in accordance with the oversubscription criteria set out in paragraph 7 of this Annex. Where places become vacant they will be allocated to children on the waiting list in accordance with the oversubscription criteria.

Arrangements for appeals panels

10 Parents will have the right of appeal to an Independent Appeal Panel if they are dissatisfied with an admission decision of the Academy. The Appeal Panel will be independent of the Academy. The arrangements for Appeals will be in line with the Code of Practice on School Admission Appeals published by the Department for Education and Skills as it applies to Foundation and Voluntary Aided schools. The determination of the appeal panel will be made in accordance with the Code of Practice on School Admission Appeals and is binding on all parties. The Academy should prepare guidance for parents about haw the appeals process will work and provide parents with a named contact who can answer any enquiries parents may have about the process.

Arrangements for admission to post 16 provision

11 The Harris City Academy, Crystal Palace will admit students into its sixth form and have a published admission number of 30. Applicants will need to satisfy minimum entrance requirements to the courses for which they are applying. Where fewer than 30 applications are received and satisfy any such course entrance requirements, the Academy will offer places to all those who have applied.

12 Where more than 30 applications are received and satisfy any course entrance requirements, priority will be given to applicants on the basis of the availability of courses and the provision of efficient education. Where this does not permit dis-crimination between applicants, the decision to offer the place will be based on the distance of the applicant's home from the Academy with those applicants living closest being given priority.

13 The Harris City Academy, Crystal Palace will publish specific criteria in relation to minimum entrance requirements for the range of courses available based upon GCSE grades or other measures of prior attainment.

14 There will be a right of appeal to an Independent Appeals Panel for unsuccessful applicants.

Arrangements for admitting students to other year groups, including to replace any students who have left the Harris City Academy, Crystal Palace

15 Subject to any provisions in the LAs co-ordinated admission arrangements relating to applications submitted for years other than the normal year of entry, the Academy must consider all such applications and if the year group applied for has a place available, admit the child. If more applications are received than there are places available, the place will be allocated to the applicant who is in the same ability band as the student who has left – applying the criteria set out in Paragraph 7 above. Parents whose application is turned down are entitled to appeal.

Arrangements for admission of students as the Academy builds to its full capacity

16 The Harris City Academy, Crystal Palace will open on 1 September 2007 with a Published Admission Number relating solely to students in Year 7 and Year 12. Students in subsequent Years will have been transferred automatically from the predecessor school, Harris CTC, which will close on 31 August 2007.

17 During the period from 1 September 2007 to the admission of Year 7 in September 2011 to the Academy there will not be a Published Admission Number against which to consider applications for admission to all Year groups. Initially in September 2007 there will be four such Year groups reducing by one in each subsequent academic year.

18 Admission to Year groups without a Published Admission Number will be based upon the size of teaching groups already existing in the Academy and the efficient use of resources.

19 There will be a right of appeal to the Independent Appeal Panel for unsuccessful applicants.

II Annual procedures for determining admission arrangements

Consultation

20 The Harris City Academy, Crystal Palace shall consult each year on its proposed admission arrangements.

21 The Academy will consult by 1 March:

   (a)   all relevant Local Authorities;

   (b)   Any other admission authorities for primary and secondary schools located within the relevant area for consultation set by the LA;

   (c)   Any other governing body for primary and secondary schools (as far as not falling within paragraph (b) located within the relevant area for consultation).

   (d)   The Diocesan Boards.

Determination and publication of admission arrangements

22 Following consultation, the Academy will consider comments made by those consulted. The Academy will then determine its admission arrangements by 15 April of the relevant year and notify those consulted what has been determined.

Publication of admission arrangements

23 The Harris City Academy, Crystal Palace will publish its admission arrangements each year once these have been determined, by:

   (a)   copies being sent to primary and secondary schools in the relevant LAs;

   (b)   copies being sent to the offices of the relevant LAs;

   (c)   copies being made available without charge on request from the Academy;

   (d)   copies being sent to public libraries in the area of LAs for the purposes of being made available at such libraries for reference by parents and other persons.

24 The published arrangements will set out

(a) the name and address of the Academy and contact details;
(b) a summary of the admissions policy, including oversubscription criteria;
(c) a statement of any religious affiliation;
(d) numbers of places and applications for those places in the previous year; and
(e) arrangements for hearing appeals.

Representations about admission arrangements

25 Where any of those bodies that were consulted, or that should have been consulted, make representations to the Academy about its admission arrangements, the Academy will consider such representations before determining the admission arrangements. Where the Academy has determined its admission arrangements and notified all those bodies whom it has consulted and any of those bodies object to the Academy's admission arrangements they can make representations to the Secretary of State. The Secretary of State will consider the representation and in so doing will consult the Academy. Where he judges it appropriate, the Secretary of State may direct the Academy to amend its admission arrangements.

26 Those consulted have the right to ask the Academy to increase its proposed Published Admissions Number for any year. Where such a request is made, but agreement cannot be reached locally, they may ask the Secretary of State to direct the Academy to increase its proposed Published Admissions Number. The Secretary of State will consult the Academy and will then determine the Published Admission Number.

27 In addition to the provisions at paragraphs 25 and 26 above, the Secretary of State may direct changes to the Academy's proposed admission arrangements and, in addition to the provisions above, the Secretary of State may direct changes to the proposed Published Admissions Number.

Proposed changes to admission arrangements by the Academy after arrangements have been published

28 Once the admission arrangements have been determined for a particular year and published, the Academy will propose changes only if there is a major change of circumstances. In such cases, the Academy must notify those consulted under paragraph 23 above of the proposed variation and must then apply to the Secretary of State setting out:

(a) the proposed changes;
(b) reasons for wishing to make such changes;
(c) any comments or objections from those entitled to object.

Need to secure Secretary of State's approval for changes to admission arrangements

29 The Secretary of State will consider applications from the Academy to change its admission arrangements only when the Academy has notified and consulted the proposed changes as outlined at 23 – 24 above.

30 Where the Academy has consulted on proposed changes the Academy must secure the agreement of the Secretary of State before any such changes can be implemented. The Academy must seek the Secretary of State's approval in writing, setting out the reasons for the proposed changes and passing to him any comments or objections from other admission authorities/other persons.

31 The Secretary of State can approve, modify or reject proposals from the Academy to change its admission arrangements.

32 Records of applications and admissions shall be kept by the Academy for a minimum period of ten years and shall be open for inspection by the Secretary of State.

Appendix A

After admission of those selected by aptitude in Technology, those to be admitted because of statement of SEN, looked after children and because of sibling qualification will be allocated to ability bands.

1   The remaining places in each ability band will be allocated by the drawing of lots in two geographical zones. Zone A will be a zone up to two mile radius from the fixed point shown on the attached map; Zone B will be a zone over two miles radius from the fixed point shown on the attached map; the first nine places in each ability band shall be available for applicants drawn by lot from Zone A, the tenth place shall be available for applicants drawn by lot from Zone B, the next nine places shall be available for applicants drawn by lot from Zone A, the next single place shall be available for applicants drawn by lot from Zone B, etc. until all places in that ability band are allocated or until all applicants in that ability band are placed. This will result in a provisional allocation of places to Zone A.

2   If at the end of this process there are unallocated places in any band these will be filled by unallocated applicants from the next nearest band(s) using the same allocation criteria set out at 2). above and continuing the sequence of the allocation of places.

3   If the number of applications from a single Zone is exhausted then all applicants regardless of geographical Zone shall be included in the draw for the remaining places in that band or adjacent bands.

4   Because the intention of the process is to allow 10 per cent of the available places to be allocated to applicants from Zone B and the operation of the procedure above may result in fewer than 10 per cent of the available places being allocated to applicants from Zone B, there will be a second phase to the procedure to ensure that 10 per cent of the places are allocated to those applying from Zone B.

5   In the second phase the number of places to be offered to Zone B applicants in order to achieve 10 per cent will be calculated and compared to the number actually being offered. Where there is a shortfall those bands which have the lowest percentage of places offered to Zone B candidates will have an additional place allocated to Zone B and drawn by lot in accordance with paras 1 – 4 above. There will then be a redraw for the applicants identified for provisional places within that ability band in Zone A so that one applicant is removed from the provisional list. This will be repeated until there is a 90 per cent: 10 per cent split between Zone A and Zone B overall.

Appendix 3

How to calculate the value-added of a secondary school

Professor David Jesson, York University

'Value-added' is the description given to the evaluation of the relative educational progress made by pupils in any school. The procedures developed by the Specialist Schools and Academies Trust are in use in thousands of English secondary schools – and involve comparing the GCSE outcomes of individual schools with that achieved 'on average' by 'similar' schools. Where a school's performance is significantly greater than that achieved by similar schools, that school is described as having 'positive value-added'; conversely for schools where GCSE performance is significantly lower than that of similar schools, performance is described as 'negative value-added'. Schools in neither of these two categories are described as 'doing as well as expected'.

For English schools, the most important measure of progress is that made from entry at age 11 to conclusion of GCSE studies at the end of Key stage 4 (normally, but not exclusively at age 16). Pupils take national curriculum tests at age 11 in English, mathematics and science – providing an indication of their attainments across a broad range of activity. These tests are used as a measure of 'entry attainment' for pupils and are expressed in terms of 'Key stage 2 points scores'. Pupils' points scores range from 9 to 36 for Key stage 2 points with an average around 27.0. A school measure of 'intake' is defined as the average of its pupils' Key stage 2 points scores.

Figure A3.1 shows the national distribution of Ks2 'intake' points in 2003 for all non-selective schools – most of whose pupils took their GCSE examinations in 2008.

Figure A3.1 shows how very different schools are in the attainments of their pupils on entry. The national average is around 27.0 points – some schools have very 'low' attaining cohorts whilst others have 'high' levels. This has a substantial influence on achievement at GCSE 5 years later.

Putting school performance 'in context'

Pupils' GCSE results are summarised in various ways, the most important being whether or not they achieved 5 or more A★–C passes including A★–C passes in English and maths.

School performance is calculated by aggregating these 'successes' into a percentage value for each school's relevant cohort. Clearly this 'outcome measure' can range from 0 to 100 per cent – Figure A3.2 shows the outcomes for all English non-selective schools in 2007.

The chart shows that, in general, schools with 'low' average Ks2 scores achieve relatively low GCSE outcomes and vice versa for schools with 'high' average Ks2 scores. However, there is a lot of 'scatter' on the chart and we have identified two schools A and B which appear to be somewhat different from their peers. The chart also shows (by straight lines) the average outcomes for girls', mixed, and boys' schools for each level of 'intake' attainment.

The central line on this chart shows the 'average' or 'expected' outcomes for 'mixed' schools plotted against their average Ks2 points scores. The upper line shows the outcomes for girls' schools whilst the lower – the average outcomes for boys' schools.

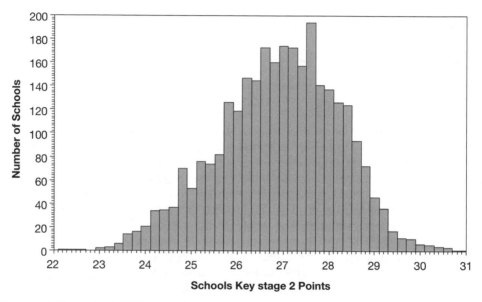

Figure A3.1 How schools 'differ in intake attainment' (Ks2 points)

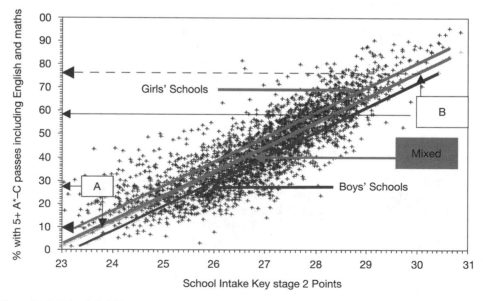

Figure A3.2 School GCSE outcomes versus Ks2 intake

The chart shows that two important factors affect the 'expected' performance of schools:

- The average 'intake' measure (Ks2 points); and
- The gender mix of the school.

This chart indicates that ignoring these characteristics (simply by ranking their outcomes as in school league tables) would seriously misrepresent the 'quality' of schools' performance.

The chart shows that many schools, like School A in Table A3.1, have substantially 'higher than average' outcomes – these are schools with *positive value-added*. There are correspondingly substantial numbers of schools (School B is an example) with **negative value-added**. Most schools' performances, however, place them 'close to' the line indicating their 'average or expected' outcomes – showing that they are doing **as well as expected**.

The frameworks illustrated provide a powerful means of evaluating the quality of any school's performance. It has the great advantage of being simple to apply and provides clear messages for each school represented. We illustrate how to do this in outline – there are underlying statistical considerations which need to be observed but the general principles are indicated in the following example.

Applying 'value-added' measures to two schools

In Table A3.1 School A achieved a performance of just less than 30 per cent of its pupils achieving five or more A★–C passes including English and maths; whilst School B achieved just under 60 per cent. However, these 'raw' figures do no justice to the underlying 'quality' of each school's performance as the following review indicates:

School A has a relatively low average Key stage 2 intake score whilst School B has a relatively high measure. From the table, schools similar to School B achieved on average around 77 per cent on the outcome measure whilst School B itself only achieved 59 per cent – a shortfall of around 18 per cent.

School A, on the other hand, achieved just under 30 per cent whilst similar schools only achieved around 10 per cent on average.

- School A had a 'value-added' of (29 per cent actual minus 10 per cent 'expected') of +19 per cent;
- School B had 'negative value-added' of (59 per cent actual minus 77 per cent 'expected') of −18 per cent.

Translating this into more meaningful terms – if each school had a cohort of 200 pupils, *School A helped 38 MORE of these (19 per cent of 200) gain five or more A★–C passes including English and maths, whilst School B ensured that 36 LESS pupils achieved this level of outcome.*

The contrast could not be more stark – *School A*, with relatively low 'intake' ability, helped its pupils *gain substantial additional success*, whilst *School B managed to depress the outcomes of substantial numbers of its pupils,* even though they had much higher entry ability.

Table A3.1 Applying 'value-added' measures to two schools

School	Cohort	Intake Ks2, points	GCSE, %	'Predicted' GCSE, %	Value added, %
A	203	23.8	29%	10%	+19%
B	196	30.2	59%	77%	−18%

This procedure and its outcomes is summarised in Table A3.1 below:

The 'value-added' measures, shown visually in Figure A3.3 and summarised in Table A3.1 above for our two schools, are calculated *for every school in the nation* and provide an easy to understand indication of whether, and by how much, each school 'adds' or 'subtracts' value for its pupils by giving the predicted 5+ A*–C including maths and English based on the average gross point average of pupils admitted in Year 7. These outcomes are published annually for the SSAT for each specialist school and form an important part of these schools' understanding of how to achieve outstanding and sustained improvement in their examination performance.

Further ways of reviewing and identifying 'good' and 'poor' performance

These summary evaluations are complemented by more in-depth analyses of pupils' performances in major subject areas – the Specialist Schools and Academies Trust has developed a 'Data Enabler' framework[1] helping schools investigate these in considerable detail and identify which pupils and possibly, which teachers, either assist or inhibit pupils' progress. These compare the results for 'similar' pupils grouped into five Key stage 2 based classes – and show what should be 'expected' from each and what actually was achieved. This provides bases for action designed to eliminate 'poor' practice and enhance the 'good'.

Other approaches to calculating 'value-added'

The methods described above are just one way of calculating 'value-added' outcomes for schools, many others have been proposed and used the government's 'official' method (known as 'contextual value-added') uses a highly sophisticated statistical procedure which produces 'official value-added' measures for every school, but which are very difficult to understand and even more difficult to use for what is surely their main role, helping schools improve. A recent report[2] by the Office for Standards in Education (OfSTED) summarises these different methods and states clearly that no single measure can be credited with providing a single 'value-added' measure that overrides all others. The report shows that there are substantial similarities between different methods' results, and that they should be used in a complementary rather than confrontational account of any school's current position.

Most of these other methods of calculating schools' 'value-added' incorporate factors that seek to measure and hence 'account for' the level of 'disadvantage' experienced by

[1] See www.specialistschools.org.uk
[2] OfSTED, 'Using Data: Improving Schools', London: OfSTED, 2008.

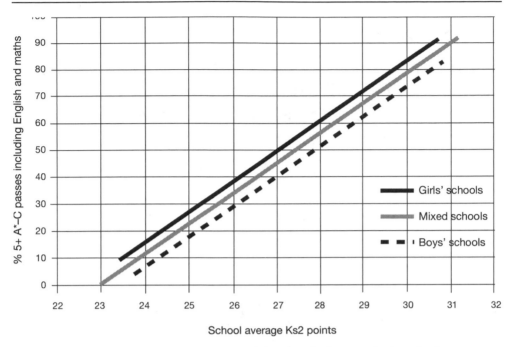

Figure A3.3 Predicted GCSE scores including English and maths for non-selective schools

pupils and their schools. Such matters as 'being eligible for free school meals', 'coming from different ethnic groups', etc., are incorporated in order to reflect more completely their 'characteristics'. Some commentators claim that 'adjustments' made using these factors are 'essential' for a fair evaluation of performance, others suggest that they decrease the 'challenge' that pupils and their schools need to confront in order to achieve high levels of success. A serious question was raised by one school which recruited pupils with high levels of disadvantage:

> our pupils come from disadvantaged backgrounds and pupils like these elsewhere do not do particularly well in GCSE examinations – but why should this set an artificial ceiling to what OUR pupils should achieve?

In the view of the author of this book, the simple and reliable frameworks described here provide a highly motivating and well-regarded system that should be available for all.

Appendix 4

Analysis of a sample group of English schools on the list of 638, who in 2007 did not achieve 5+ A*–C at GCSE including maths and English using the David Jesson Value Added and improvement approach

Sample of 10 schools which did not achieve GCSE results of 30% 5+ A*–C including English and mathematics in 2007 but were on an upward trajectory and had 5 points or over value added; or 5 points or over improvement 2004–2007 on the 5+ A*–C incl. English and mathematics measure. They should NOT therefore be included in any list of 'underperforming schools'. There are 301 such schools on the list of 638 schools published by the government in 2008.

Ranked by this column

	2002 KS2 Avg point score	2007 Subj: English % A*toC	2007 Subj: Maths % A*toC	2004 % 5+A*toC	2007 % 5+A*toC	2004 % 5+ A*toC Eng Ma	2007 % 5+ A*toC Eng Ma	Jesson predicted 2007 % 5A*C Eng Ma	2007 Jesson VA 5AC Eng Ma
1 Cressex Community School Buckinghamshire MOD '11–18 Non specialist Designation yr: Specialism: Aspiring specialist	23.0	50	39	18	38	13	29	2	**27**
2 Carlton Bolling College Bradford COMP '11–18 Specialist Designation yr: 2006 Specialism: Mathematics & Computing	23.1	51	30	19	36	10	24	2	**22**
3 The Academy At Peckham Southwark COMP '11–18 Specialist Designation yr: 2003 Specialism: Academy	23.4	33	45	12	38	10	24	4	**20**
4 Capital City Academy Brent COMP '11–18 Specialist Designation yr: 2003 Specialism: Academy	22.6	46	30	29	52	17	23	3	**20**
5 Walthamstow Academy Waltham Forest COMP '11–18 Specialist Designation yr: 2006 Specialism: Academy	24.0	40	50	27	42	17	28	12	**16**
6 The Bishop David Brown School Surrey COMP '11–16 Specialist Designation yr: 2002 Specialism: Arts	24.2	50	35	23	35	15	30	15	**15**
7 Aston Manor School Birmingham COMP '11–16 Specialist Designation yr: 1999 Specialism: Technology	24.2	44	38	43	56	16	28	13	**15**
8 Islington Arts and Media School Islington COMP '11–16 Specialist Designation yr: 2004 Specialism: Arts	24.3	0	43	47	43	20	27	13	**14**
9 Haberdashers' Aske's Knights Aca Lewisham COMP '11–18 Specialist Designation yr: 2005 Specialism: Academy	23.5	28	29	15	42	6	20	6	**14**
10 City Academy, Bristol Bristol, City of COMP '11–18 Specialist Designation yr: 2003 Specialism: Academy	23.7	46	29	33	49	16	21	8	**13**

Appendix 5

Sample of 10 schools which did not achieve GCSE results of 30% 5+ A*–C including English and mathematics in 2007 and which had under 5 points value added and less than 5 points improvement 2004–2007 on the 5+ A*–C incl. English and mathematics measure. They can therefore fairly be described as low attaining. Based on the 2007 data, there are 337 such schools.

Ranked by this column ⬇

	2002 KS2 Avg point score	2007 Subj: English % A*toC	2007 Subj: Maths % A*toC	2004 % 5+A*toC	2007 % 5+A*toC	2004 % 5+ A*toC Eng Ma	2007 % 5+ A*toC Eng Ma	Jesson predicted 2007 % 5A*C Eng Ma	2007 Jesson VA 5AC Eng Ma
1 School 1 COMP '11–16 Specialist Designation yr: 2005 Specialism: Combined	28.1	57	33	48	40	36	24	57	**-33**
2 School 2 COMP '11–18 Specialist Designation yr: 2003 Specialism: Business & Enterprise	27.1	32	25	27	33	12	14	46	**-32**
3 School 3 COMP '11–18 Specialist Designation yr: 2004 Specialism: Sports	25.7	6	30	23	57	9	3	31	**-28**
4 School 4 MOD '11–16 Specialist Designation yr: 2004 Specialism: Science	26.0	15	27	24	35	11	8	34	**-26**
5 School 5 COMP '11–16 Specialist Designation yr: 2004 Specialism: Sports	26.7	26	29	35	69	18	18	42	**-24**
6 School 6 COMP '11–18 Non specialist Designation yr: 2007 Specialism: Mathematics & Computing	27.2	35	44	41	47	32	24	47	**-23**
7 School 7 MOD '11–16 Non specialist Designation yr: Specialism: Aspiring specialist	26.1	37	28	49	31	31	15	35	**-20**
8 School 8 COMP '11–18 Specialist Designation yr: 2003 Specialism: Mathematics & Computing	27.0	37	38	50	57	31	24	44	**-20**
9 School 9 COMP '11–16 Specialist Designation yr: 2003 Specialism: Arts	27.2	45	36	40	44	23	27	47	**-20**
10 School 10 COMP '11–16 Non specialist Designation yr: Specialism: Aspiring specialist	27.1	27	46	39	30	28	26	46	**-20**

Appendix 6

Standard curriculum used by the Summer Institute for the Gifted in the United States

Curriculum for the non-residential summer schools of the Summer Institute for the Gifted for children aged 6 to 12 years. For details of the curriculum for the residential programmes for children aged 10 to 17, given at the same American universities including Princeton, Berkeley and UCLA, access www.giftedstudy.com Tel. 001 866 3034744

Day program

Student schedules

Each student selects from the listing of courses to create a personal schedule. Students take three courses daily with the option of a 4th class during the recreation period. Students choose courses from the appropriate level as indicated below:

DP10–15   courses for students in Grade K–1
DP20–32:   courses for students in Grades 2 and 3
DP40–53:   courses for students in Grades 4 through 6
DPR   course for students in grades 2–6, offered during the recreation period.

Students attend classes Monday through Friday from 8:45 a.m. until 2:30 p.m. with a break for snack at 10:15 a.m. and lunch at 12:00 noon. Students who do not choose the DPR class have recreational time following the last class from 2:30 p.m. until 4:00 p.m.

Courses by grade level

The following pages list all the courses that are offered at each of the Summer Institute for the Gifted-Day Program sites. Most of these courses will run at each site. However, it is possible that a given course may not run at one of the sites due to under-enrollment for that course.

Courses for students currently in grade K–1

Humanities

The Write Stuff (DP10): Write a postcard from an imaginary place, or a letter in the voice of your favorite cartoon character. Pretend you are a space traveler and write a journal from outer space. Write a diary entry in the voice of a famous person. Use your imagination and love for writing as you create unique stories and illustrations. As a final presentation, you will be able to share your talents with family and friends.

Math and science

New! Mind Math: Game Strategy (DP 11) Opening play, mid-game, end-game–develop these strategies and more as you move across a chessboard or around a cribbage and backgammon board. Improve your memory, concentration, and ability to conceptualize as you engage in these ancient games of kings. Develop your ability to estimate and predict your opponents' moves. Create a personal repertoire of tactics and plays. Create your own game.

Creatures of Habitat (DP12): Become an explorer and a junior zoologist as you research animals and where they live. Find out how animals have adapted to their environments and the role that humans play in protecting those habitats. You'll become familiar with many species of wildlife as you learn about such places as wetlands, drylands, and wood-lands. Create a conservation plan for your favorite animal. Create an advertising campaign to educate others about an endangered species.

The Curious Chemist: Chemistry in Our Daily Lives (DP13). The way materials are put together and the way they act under certain conditions is called the study of chemistry. Chemistry helps us explain the things that happen in nature. Chemists are scientists who use each of their five senses to explore and make sense of life. Experiment with water, acids, bases, and everyday household items to discover the chemical world in which we live. Design a series of experiments to test your predictions about the reactions of substances.

Multi-disciplinary

Aspiring Architects (DP14): Why did the builders of the pyramids choose triangles as their building blocks? Is glass a good material for skyscrapers? Learn about the ways structures are built and understand the concepts of form and function. Test structural principles through simple building projects and experience the creative process of design as you create a structure of your own.

New! Tutankhamun's Treasures: Ancient Egypt Revealed (DP15): From tomb paintings, mummies, and the Great Pyramid, discover the secrets of ancient Egypt. Gain an understanding of the importance of religion to civilization. Decode the messages in hier-oglyphs. Research the Boy King and the guardians of his tomb. Gain an understanding of the relationship between human leadership and the rise or decline of a civilization. Create a presentation that explains how a mummy can be considered a time capsule.

Courses for students currently in grades 2 and 3

Humanities

The Writer's Block (DP20): Where do authors get their ideas? How does a science fiction story differ from historical fiction? What are the elements all stories need? Come have fun and gain writing experience creating new characters and a book of your own. The class will culminate with a reading of original stories to parents at a "Young Authors' Tea."

News Net (DP21): What is news? How would a newspaper be different if it was created from an ant's point of view? What kind of news would dogs like to hear? How do the newspapers of the past differ from today's? You'll have the chance to read, write, edit, report and circulate your idea of the news to the rest of the campus.

New! Character and Citizenship: Laws and Community (DP22) What do rules mean and why do we make them? What is the role of a responsible citizen? How do we decide that a law has been broken? Join us for a course in pre-law that examines the rules of our communities and the greater society. Learn how laws are proposed and accepted. Discover the responsibilities of leaders and followers. Create your own list of rules for citizens to follow.

Math and science

New! Make Charge, Take Charge: An Energy Efficient World (DP23): Explore the environmental impact of five methods of electrical generation: fossil fuels, nuclear, solar, hydroelectric, and wind. Analyze ways to conserve energy in our daily lives. Design energy audits for your class to determine the main consumers of energy and develop plans for less usage. Develop a multi-media presentation to explain each energy source and the ramifications of its use. Create a new idea for energy production.

Be a Pet Vet (DP24): Do pets have personalities? Are they trying to tell us something when they bark, scratch or whinny? If you'd like to know more about the care and understanding of pets, this class is for you. You'll also have the chance to learn more about that special animal that you love the most, whether it's a fish or ferret, hamster or horse! If you think you might want to be a veterinarian someday, this class is for you.

New! Animal Evolution (DP25): Did you know that animals evolved and lived in the sea for 600 million years? Journey back to a time when the land was bathed in lethal levels of UV radiation. Discover how the formation of the ozone layer made it possible for living things to venture onto the land. Investigate the common features humans have with all living organisms. Gain a greater understanding of your own evolutionary history. Predict what the future may hold for the evolution of the animal kingdom.

Rocks, Minerals, and Crystals: Earth's Treasures (DP26): Whether you like to collect rocks or just appreciate the beauty of a colorful gemstone, this class has something for you. You'll learn to analyze and appreciate rocks and minerals by their characteristics, grow crystals, and research related topics that really interest you. Finally you'll determine what makes things like gems valuable to humans.

Sunshine Science (DP 27): What's so hot about the sun? How can a star that is 93 million miles away be the source of all Earth's energy, cause the seasons, affect the weather, and burn your skin? This renewable resource is truly amazing. Come find out more about the benefits and dangers of sunshine and conduct experiments to show how the sun's light can be used to help us in our everyday lives.

Ocean Overview (DP28): How do pearls grow in an oyster? Why do crabs shed their skins? Come explore the world beneath the oceans' waves! The ocean is so huge that it makes the earth appear blue from outer space. You'll discover new information about your favorite ocean creatures and what you can do to help them. (Sarasota and Los Gatos only)

Multi-disciplinary

New! Musical Acoustics: The Math and Physics of Music (DP29): How do the sounds we hear as music actually function? How do our brains and ears work to enable us to hear music? How does a computer analyze melodies? If these questions interest you, join us for a study of how musical instruments work, the parts of the body that help us to sing, and the function of sound waves, air pressure and more. You will develop a deeper appreciation for music and create original music on original instruments.

New! The Detective's Role: Hero of the Street (DP 30) Are you interested in a crime-solving career? Would you like to learn the techniques for interviewing witnesses and interrogating suspects? Have you ever pictured yourself giving evidence in a court room? If so, then join us for a study of the world of the police detective. Learn the procedures of police on patrol and the organization of investigations. Discover the roles detectives play when they go undercover or gain information from an informant. Find out how detectives collect and preserve evidence for court testimony. This course may help you identify your future career choice.

New! Magic Carpet Ride (DP31): Earth is a mosaic of cultural complexity. Discover how culture and experience influence a region's characteristics. Compare and contrast customs in other places to those of the United States. Hypothesize about living with host families in different countries. Create projects, journals, art work, and performances representative of various cultures you research. Gain a greater understanding of the many cultures to better understand your own.

New! Things that Fly! (DP 32): Everyone knows that airplanes and hot air balloons and birds can fly. The ordinary kind of flying is dependent on Bernoulli's scientific principles. But what if we look at flight in a different way to try to determine what it means? Have your thoughts suddenly flown out the window when the teacher calls on you to explain something? Has time ever flown by for you when you are on vacation? Or slowed on a rainy day? Have you ever said the first thing that just flew into your head? Join us for a study of the extraordinary flight of time and thought and other flying things.

Courses for students currently in grades 4, 5 & 6

Humanities

Speaking of Writing (DP40): Creative writing and eloquent speech making join forces in the course. Evaluate and improve your writing skills and then deliver your written word through public speaking practice. Work on precision of language, imagery, figures of speech, and the revision process. Then, learn the skills required for professional speech making. Learn how to move audiences with your written and spoken word.

Going to Court (DP41): "All rise for the honorable judge. ... you!" Through the process of enacting trials, you will experience the justice system of the United States. You'll take on the roles of judge, jury, prosecutor, defender or witness. Through active involvement in the courtroom drama, you will learn to organize facts, develop your speaking and questioning abilities, and understand the concepts of justice through jury deliberation.

Math and science

Anticipating Algebra (DP42): "When will I ever use algebra?" you ask. Here's one way. Introduce yourself to pre-algebra through this class that focuses on applications of algebra in the world. In addition to tackling concepts of linear equations, polynomial functions and factoring, you may also have time for fun with games, tessellations, and probability.

New! Doomsday Scenario: The Lunar Ark (DP43): Did you know that NASA has plans for archiving the records of human accomplishments from the last several thousand years? Did you know that this museum is planned to be housed on the moon? In the event of catastrophe, the genetic information for humans, plants, and animals as well as information for survival techniques such as smelting metal, planting crops, and building houses would all be included in this ark of information. Join us for a study of this plan, including the best location for its construction, how it would be tended and guarded, how it would be powered, and the diversity of species capable of surviving there. Analyze the scientific and ethical implications of such a museum. Create your own plan of what to archive and how it should be done.

Chemistry: The Essential Element (DP44): Welcome to the laboratory that is the world in which you live. Experiment with domestic chemicals, environmental materials, foods, and living organisms to discover the chemical nature of substances, their properties, reactions and uses in daily life. Design a series of experiments to test your hypotheses about the reaction of substances.

Marine Biology (DP45): Oceans cover 71% of the Earth's surface and contain vast resources with 13,000 species of fish and 50,000 species of mollusks. No wonder marine biologists have so much to study! This course will examine the work of these biologists, looking at historical and current research as well as environmental concerns. Find out more about this exciting science and what you can do to protect the ecology of the oceans. (Sarasota and Los Gatos only)

Plants and Insects: A Dynamic Relationship (DP46): Did you know that plants develop defense mechanisms to reduce insect attack? Plants can even change their chemical and physicals characteristics to defend against insects. But insects have developed strategies to overcome these barriers, allowing them to feed, grow, and reproduce on plants. Learn about the amazing interactions between plants and insects and the universal battles being fought in our own gardens and forests. Discover how these interactions affect your own life. (Sarasota and Los Gatos only)

Multi-disciplinary

New! Plastics: Those Popular, Powerful Polymers (DP47): Plastics play a huge part in our everyday lives. They are used in building and construction, electronics, aerospace, packaging, transportation, and the medical field, to name just a few. Emerging science is producing degradable plastics, and plastics play a large role in nanotechnology. Join us for an in depth study of the presence of plastics in our lives. Be better informed about the use of plastics by researching the latest findings from government, academia, and industry. Create a new use for plastic. Research and report on the plastic industry's attempts to go green.

Spying: Secrets, Surveillance, and Science (DP48): Did you know that the newest satellite technology can look into your living room from thousands of miles away in space? Have you ever wondered what it would be like to be a spy and monitor this technology? Did you know that some of the gadgets from James Bond really exist? Come discover how spies keep – or uncover – secrets. Get an inside look at the science behind the spy's tricks of the trade. Create an original spy gadget and persuade your peers of its usefulness.

New! The Way of the Samurai: Japan's Past and Present Social, Political, and Economic Influences (DP49): Discover how a legacy of rigid rules and customs with a class system of very specific roles gave birth to the distinctly unique arts of haiku, kabuki, bunraku, and ukiyoe. Journey with us through Japan's evolution from an agricultural society dependent upon artisans to produce goods in small quantities to the world's leading producer of cameras, watches, motorcycles, and automobiles. Gain personal insights into global culture, trade, and power. Rewrite the Samurai Code as a personal life plan. Assess the value of such a life-plan in today's society.

Move Over Sherlock (DP50): How do real detectives solve mysteries? Come examine how modern crime investigators use cutting-edge scientific discoveries to search for evidence, gather clues, and analyze data. Participate in a simulated mystery where you become the detective as you learn skills in logic, inductive and deductive reasoning, data collection, and analysis. This is a great way to practice using your scientific problem solving skills!

Future City Design (DP51): Explore the challenges of the future! Take on the roles of chemical, mechanical, electrical, aeronautical, and civil engineers as you develop a vision for a future city. Construct a scale model that evidences your ideas for future architectural design, transportation, communication, recreation, environmental concerns, and the health and safety of your future citizens.

Creative and performing arts

Two and Three-D Media: Drawing and Sculpting (DP52): Express yourself in pencil, ink, watercolor, or three dimensions. Develop your techniques in perspective, light, shading, and color theory. Learn the fundamentals of positive and negative space. Create an original, displayable work.

Fitness and recreation

New! Soccer Sense (DP53): Soccer, the world's most popular sport! Learn the principles, positions, and skills of the game everyone loves. Improve your fast-paced footwork and develop your strategies. Dribble, pass, punt, trap and shoot your way to greater success on the field. Dazzle your friends with World Cup knowledge.

Alternative to the recreation period (grades 2–6 only)

New! Experts Present: Student Lead Seminars (DPR): Do you have a subject you are passionate about? Do you like to share you ideas with others? Then this is the class for you. During this class you will research a topic of your choice, determine how you will share your information, and present your new knowledge to the class. Come and discover unique facets of your topic and share your discoveries with others.

Appendix 7

PISA rating of OECD countries by performance in maths, science and reading

PISA ranking of countries/economies on the mathematics scale

	Mean score	S.E.	OECD countries Upper Rank	OECD countries Lower Rank	All countries/economies Upper Rank	All countries/economies Lower Rank
Chinese Taipei	549	(4.1)			1	4
Finland	548	(2.3)	1	2	1	4
Hong Kong-China	547	(2.7)			1	4
Korea	547	(3.8)	1	2	1	4
Netherlands	531	(2.6)	3	5	5	8
Switzerland	530	(3.2)	3	6	5	9
Canada	527	(2.0)	3	6	5	10
Macao-China	525	(1.3)			7	11
Liechtenstein	525	(4.2)			5	13
Japan	523	(3.3)	4	9	6	13
New Zealand	522	(2.4)	5	9	8	13
Belgium	520	(3.0)	6	10	8	14
Australia	520	(2.2)	6	9	10	14
Estonia	515	(2.7)			12	16
Denmark	513	(2.6)	9	11	13	16
Czech Republic	510	(3.6)	10	14	14	20
Iceland	506	(1.8)	11	15	16	21
Austria	505	(3.7)	10	16	15	22
Slovenia	504	(1.0)			17	21
Germany	504	(3.9)	11	17	16	23
Sweden	502	(2.4)	12	17	17	23
Ireland	501	(2.8)	12	17	17	23
France	496	(3.2)	15	22	21	28
United Kingdom	**495**	**(2.1)**	**16**	**21**	**22**	**27**
Poland	495	(2.4)	16	21	22	27
Slovak Republic	492	(2.8)	17	23	23	30
Hungary	491	(2.9)	18	23	24	31
Luxembourg	490	(1.1)	20	23	26	30
Norway	490	(2.6)	19	23	25	31
Lithuania	486	(2.9)			27	32
Latvia	486	(3.0)			27	32

(Table continued on next page)

PISA ranking of countries/economies on the mathematics scale (continued)

	Mean score	S.E.	Mathematics scale			
			Range of rank			
			OECD countries		All countries/economies	
			Upper Rank	Lower Rank	Upper Rank	Lower Rank
Spain	480	(2.3)	24	25	31	34
Azerbaijan	476	(2.3)			32	35
Russian Federation	476	(3.9)			32	36
United States	474	(4.0)	24	26	32	36
Croatia	467	(2.4)			35	38
Portugal	466	(3.1)	25	27	35	38
Italy	462	(2.3)	26	28	37	39
Greece	459	(3.0)	27	28	38	39
Israel	442	(4.3)			40	41
Serbia	435	(3.5)			40	41
Uruguay	427	(2.6)			42	43
Turkey	424	(4.9)	29	29	41	45
Thailand	417	(2.3)			43	46
Romania	415	(4.2)			43	47
Bulgaria	413	(6.1)			43	48
Chile	411	(4.6)			44	48
Mexico	406	(2.9)	30	30	46	48
Montenegro	399	(1.4)			49	50
Indonesia	391	(5.6)			49	52
Jordan	384	(3.3)			50	52
Argentina	381	(6.2)			50	53
Colombia	370	(3.8)			52	55
Brazil	370	(2.9)			53	55
Tunisia	365	(4.0)			53	55
Qatar	318	(1.0)			56	56
Kyrgyzstan	311	(3.4)			57	57

Statistically significantly above the OECD average

Not statistically significantly different from the OECD average

Statistically significantly below the OECD average

Source: OECD PISA 2006 database.

PISA ranking of countries/economies on the reading scale

	Mean score	S.E.	Reading scale			
			Range of rank			
			OECD countries		All countries/economies	
			Upper Rank	Lower Rank	Upper Rank	Lower Rank
Korea	556	(3.8)	1	1	1	1
Finland	547	(2.1)	2	2	2	2
Hong Kong-China	536	(2.4)			3	3
Canada	527	(2.4)	3	4	4	5
New Zealand	521	(3.0)	3	5	4	6
Ireland	517	(3.5)	4	6	5	8
Australia	513	(2.1)	5	7	6	9
Liechtenstein	510	(3.9)			6	11
Poland	508	(2.8)	6	10	7	12
Sweden	507	(3.4)	6	10	7	13
Netherlands	507	(2.9)	6	10	8	13
Belgium	501	(3.0)	8	13	10	17
Estonia	501	(2.9)			10	17
Switzerland	499	(3.1)	9	14	11	19
Japan	498	(3.6)	9	16	11	21
Chinese Taipei	496	(3.4)			12	22
United Kingdom	495	(2.3)	11	16	14	22
Germany	495	(4.4)	10	17	12	23
Denmark	494	(3.2)	11	17	14	23
Slovenia	494	(1.0)			16	21
Macao-China	492	(1.1)			18	22
Austria	490	(4.1)	12	20	15	26
France	488	(4.1)	14	21	18	28
Iceland	484	(1.9)	17	21	23	28
Norway	484	(3.2)	16	22	22	29
Czech Republic	483	(4.2)	16	22	22	30
Hungary	482	(3.3)	17	22	23	30
Latvia	479	(3.7)			24	31
Luxembourg	479	(1.3)	20	22	26	30
Croatia	477	(2.8)			26	31
Portugal	472	(3.6)	22	25	29	34
Lithuania	470	(3.0)			30	34
Italy	469	(2.4)	23	25	31	34
Slovak Republic	466	(3.1)	23	26	31	35
Spain	461	(2.2)	25	27	34	36
Greece	460	(4.0)	25	27	34	36
Turkey	447	(4.2)	28	28	37	39
Chile	442	(5.0)			37	40
Russian Federation	440	(4.3)			37	40
Israel	439	(4.6)			38	40
Thailand	417	(2.6)			41	42
Uruguay	413	(3.4)			41	44
Mexico	410	(3.1)	29	29	41	44
Bulgaria	402	(6.9)			42	50

(Table continued on next page)

PISA ranking of countries/economies on the reading scale (continued)

	Mean score	S.E.	Reading scale			
			Range of rank			
			OECD countries		All countries/economies	
			Upper Rank	Lower Rank	Upper Rank	Lower Rank
Serbia	401	(3.5)			44	48
Jordan	401	(3.3)			44	48
Romania	396	(4.7)			44	50
Indonesia	393	(5.9)			44	51
Brazil	393	(3.7)			46	51
Montenegro	392	(1.2)			47	50
Colombia	385	(5.1)			48	53
Tunisia	380	(4.0)			51	53
Argentina	374	(7.2)			51	53
Azerbaijan	353	(3.1)			54	54
Qatar	312	(1.2)			55	55
Kyrgyzstan	285	(3.5)			56	56

Statistically significantly above the OECD average

Not statistically significantly different from the OECD average

Statistically significantly below the OECD average

Source: OECD PISA 2006 database.

PISA ranking of the countries/economies on the different science scales

	Mean score	S.E.	Science scale			
			Range of rank			
			OECD countries		All countries/economies	
			Upper Rank	Lower Rank	Upper Rank	Lower Rank
Finland	563	(2.0)	1	1	1	1
Hong Kong-China	542	(2.5)			2	2
Canada	534	(2.0)	2	3	3	6
Chinese Taipei	532	(3.6)			3	8
Estonia	531	(2.5)			3	8
Japan	531	(3.4)	2	5	3	9
New Zealand	530	(2.7)	2	5	3	9
Australia	527	(2.3)	4	7	5	10
Netherlands	525	(2.7)	4	7	6	11
Liechtenstein	522	(4.1)			6	14
Korea	522	(3.4)	5	9	7	13
Slovenia	519	(1.1)			10	13
Germany	516	(3.8)	7	13	10	19
United Kingdom	**515**	**(2.3)**	**8**	**12**	**12**	**18**
Czech Republic	513	(3.5)	8	14	12	20
Switzerland	512	(3.2)	8	14	13	20
Macao-China	511	(1.1)			15	20
Austria	511	(3.9)	8	15	12	21
Belgium	510	(2.5)	9	14	14	20
Ireland	508	(3.2)	10	16	15	22
Hungary	504	(2.7)	13	17	19	23
Sweden	503	(2.4)	14	17	20	23
Poland	498	(2.3)	16	19	22	26
Denmark	496	(3.1)	16	21	22	28
France	495	(3.4)	16	21	22	29
Croatia	493	(2.4)			23	30
Iceland	491	(1.6)	19	23	25	31
Latvia	490	(3.0)			25	34
United States	489	(4.2)	18	25	24	35
Slovak Republic	488	(2.6)	20	25	26	34
Spain	488	(2.6)	20	25	26	34
Lithuania	488	(2.8)			26	34
Norway	487	(3.1)	20	25	27	35
Luxembourg	486	(1.1)	22	25	30	34
Russian Federation	479	(3.7)			33	38
Italy	475	(2.0)	26	28	35	38
Portugal	474	(3.0)	26	28	35	38
Greece	473	(3.2)	26	28	35	38
Israel	454	(3.7)			39	39
Chile	438	(4.3)			40	42
Serbia	436	(3.0)			40	42
Bulgaria	434	(6.1)			40	44
Uruguay	428	(2.7)			42	45
Turkey	424	(3.8)	29	29	43	47
Jordan	422	(2.8)			43	47

(Table continued on next page)

PISA ranking of the countries/economies on the different science scales (continued)

	Mean score	S.E.	Science scale			
			Range of rank			
			OECD countries		All countries/economies	
			Upper Rank	Lower Rank	Upper Rank	Lower Rank
Thailand	421	(2.1)			44	47
Romania	418	(4.2)			44	48
Montenegro	412	(1.1)			47	49
Mexico	410	(2.7)	30	30	48	49
Indonesia	393	(5.7)			50	54
Argentina	391	(6.1)			50	55
Brazil	390	(2.8)			50	54
Colombia	388	(3.4)			50	55
Tunisia	386	(3.0)			52	55
Azerbaijan	382	(2.8)			53	55
Qatar	349	(0.9)			56	56
Kyrgyzstan	322	(2.9)			57	57

Statistically significantly above the OECD average

Not statistically significantly different from the OECD average

Statistically significantly below the OECD average

Source: OECD PISA 2006 database.

Bibliography

Adonis, Andrew, 'Academies and Social Mobility,' speech given to the Academies Conference, London, 7 February 2008.

American Institute for Foreign Study, *Summer Institute for the Gifted Catalog 2009*. Stamford CT: American Institute for Foreign Study, 2008.

Astle, Julian and Ryan, Conor, *Academies and the Future of State Education*, CentreForum, July 2008.

Audit Commission, *Misspent Youth: Young People and Crime* (national report) London: Audit Comission, 1996.

Barnardo's, 'Failed by the System', report, 2006. www. barnardos.org.uk

BECTA, *Harnessing Technology: Next Generation Learning*, BECTA 2008. www.becta.org.uk

Blair, Tony, Taylor, Cyril and Reid, Elizabeth, *Education, Education, Education*, London: Specialist Schools and Academies Trust, 2007.

Boyd, J. *Community Education and Urban Schools*, Harlow: Longman, 1977.

Burn, John, Marks, John, Pilkington, Peter, Thomson, Penny, *Faith in Education*, London: CIVITAS, 2001.

Centre for Evaluation and Monitoring, *Relative Difficulty of Examinations in Different Subjects*, Durham University, July 2008.

Christopher Caldwell, *After Londonistan*, New York Times Magazine, 23 July 2006.

Cisco Networking Academy, *Educationg the Architects of the Networked Economy*. Available at: www. cisco.com/web/learning/netacad/career_connection/promoteIT/resourcecenter/docs/News_-Cisco_NetAcadat.pdf

Collins, Jim, *Good to Great: Why Some Companies Make the Leap ... and Others Don't*, New York: HarperCollins, 2001.

Creaser, Claire and Maynard, Sally, *A survey of Library Services to Schools and Children in the UK*, Loughborough: Loughborough University, 2006.

Dearing, Ronald, *The Way Ahead: Church of England Schools in the New Millennium*, London: Church House Publishing, 14 June 2001.

Department for Children, Schools and Families, *Back on Track*, London: DCSF, 2008.

—— *Diversity and Citizenship Curriculum Review*, London: DCSF, 2007.

—— *National Challenge – A Toolkit for Schools and Local Education Authorities*, London: DCSF, 2008.

—— *Promoting Excellence for All*, London: DCSF, 2008.

—— *School Admissions Code*, London: DCSF, 2007. Available at: www.dcsf.gov.uk/sacode

—— *Youth Matters: Next Steps*, London: DCSF, 2006.

——*Care Matters: Time for Change*, Government White Paper, London: DCSF, 2007.

Fox, Jeffrey J., *How to Become a Great Boss: The Rules for Getting and Keeping the Best Employees*, New York: Hyperion, 2002.

Hippach-Schneider, Ute, Krause, Martina and Woll, Christian, 'Vocational Training in Germany', CEDEFOP Panorama Series 138, Luxembourg: Office of Official Publications of the European Communities, 2007.

House of Lords Science and Technology Committee, 10th Report of Session 2005–6.

Husain, Ed, *The Islamist*, London: Penguin, 2007.

Ibrahim, I. A., *A Brief Illustrated Guide to Understanding Islam*, Houston TX: Darussalam Publications, 1997.

Jesson, David and Crossley, David, *Data Driven School Transformation 2007*, London: Specialist Schools and Academies Trust, 2008.

Kolding, Marianne and Kroa, Vladimir, *Networking Skills in Europe: Will an Increasing Shortage Hamper Competitiveness in the Global Market?* London: IDC, 2005.

Lim, Cheryl and Davis, Chris, *Helping Schools to Succeed*, London: Policy Exchange, 2008.

Love, Gerald, *Raising Achievement of White Pupils*, Birmingham: Birmingham Local Education Authority, June 2006.

Morris, Henry, *The Village College: Being a Memorandum of the Provision of Education and Social Facilities for the Countryside*, Cambridge: Cambridge University Press, 1924.

Odone, Cristina, 'In Bad Faith', London: Centre for Policy Studies, 2008.

OfSTED, *Good School Libraries: Making a Difference to Learning*, London: OfSTED, 2006.

—— *The Annual Report of Her Majesty's Chief Inspector 2006/7*, London: OfSTED. 2007.

Omaar, Rageh, *Only Half of Me: Being a Muslim in Britain*, London: Viking, 2006.

Oracle Internet Academy, *Control the Net*. Available at www.trinitypride.k12.pa.us/users/hoffmann/Letter%20to%20parents.pdf

Prentice, Christine, *A History of the Specialist Schools and Academies Trust*, London: Specialist Schools and Academies Trust, 2007.

—— *City Technology Colleges Their Conception and Legacy*, London: Specialist Schools and Academies Trust, 2007.

Rose, Jim, *Independent Review of The Teaching of Early Reading*, final report, March 2006. Available at www.standards.dcsf.gov.uk/phonics/rosercview

Royal Wanstead Children's Foundation, *Breaking Through: How Boarding Schools Can Transform the Lives of Vulnerable Children*, London: Royal Wanstead Children's Foundation, 2008.

Rudd, Peter, *High Performing Schools: What Makes the Difference?* London: Specialist Schools and Academies Trust, 2002.

Smithers, Alan and Robinson, Pamela, *The Impact of Double Science*, London: The Engineering Council, 1994.

Social Exclusion Unit, *A Better Education for Children in Care*, London: Office of the Deputy Prime Minister, 2003.

Specialist Schools and Academies Trust, *By Schools for Schools*, London: SSAT, 2007.

Stern, Jessica, *Terror in the Name of God*, New York: HarperCollins, 2004.

Sutton Trust, 'Wasted Talent? Attrition Rates of High-Achieving Pupils Between School and University', London: Sutton Trust, 2008.

Taylor, Cyril, 'Are Academies a Good Thing?', speech to the Institute of Economic Affairs, London, 11 June 2008.

—— *Employment Examined: The Right Approach to More Jobs*, London: Centre for Policy Studies, 1986.

—— *Raising Educational Standards: A Personal Perspective*, London: Centre for Policy Studies, 1990.

—— *Who Will Champion Our Vulnerable Children*, London: Specialist Schools and Academies Trust, 2006.

Taylor, Cyril and Ryan, Conor, *Excellence in Education*, London: David Fulton, 2005.

Tooley, James and Howes, Andy, *Seven Habits of Highly Effective Schools: Best Practice in Specialist Schools*, London: Technology Colleges Trust, 1999.

Wallace, Belle, *Teaching the Very Able Child*, London: NACE/Fulton, 2000.

Index

eBooks – at www.eBookstore.tandf.co.uk

A library at your fingertips!

eBooks are electronic versions of printed books. You can store them on your PC/laptop or browse them online.

They have advantages for anyone needing rapid access to a wide variety of published, copyright information.

eBooks can help your research by enabling you to bookmark chapters, annotate text and use instant searches to find specific words or phrases. Several eBook files would fit on even a small laptop or PDA.

NEW: Save money by eSubscribing: cheap, online access to any eBook for as long as you need it.

Annual subscription packages

We now offer special low-cost bulk subscriptions to packages of eBooks in certain subject areas. These are available to libraries or to individuals.

For more information please contact webmaster.ebooks@tandf.co.uk

We're continually developing the eBook concept, so keep up to date by visiting the website.

www.eBookstore.tandf.co.uk